Controversies in
Macroeconomics

Controversies in Macroeconomics

third edition

K. Alec Chrystal
National Westminster Bank Professor, City University Business School

Simon Price
Department of Economics, University of Essex

HARVESTER
WHEATSHEAF

New York · London · Toronto · Sydney · Tokyo · Singapore

First published 1994 by
Harvester Wheatsheaf
Campus 400, Maylands Avenue
Hemel Hempstead
Hertfordshire, HP2 7EZ
A division of
Simon & Schuster International Group

Typeset in 10/12 pt Times
by Vision Typesetting, Manchester

Printed and bound in Great Britain by
BPCC Wheatons Ltd, Exeter

British Library Cataloguing in Publication Data

A catalogue record for this book is available from the British Library

ISBN 0-7450-1315-5

---

1 2 3 4 5 98 97 96 95 94

For Alison and Sheila

Contents

Preface to the new edition

This book contains a substantial reworking and extension of the original 1983 edition of the same title. All original chapters, except Chapter 1, have been significantly reworked. There are three new substantial chapters: 'New Keynesians', 'Financial regulation and monetary rules' and 'International macro policy coordination'. The experience of the Thatcher years is central to the events of the past ten years. But the globalisation of finance and developments within the European community are also important. Macroeconomics was always about unemployment and government budgets. The analyses have changed but the central issues remain.

We wish to thank Saira Abbasi and Kathleen Bergin for retyping parts of the new edition. The authors share responsibility for all remaining errors and omissions.

K. Alec Chrystal
Simon Price
London and Colchester
November 1993

PART 1
Background

Introduction

This book is about the academic controversies surrounding macro-economic policy.

Macroeconomics was invented in order to solve the policy problem posed by the recurrence of severe recessions. In the 1950s and the 1960s there were no major recessions and it appeared that the business cycle had been eliminated. Professors of economics gleefully told their students that Keynes had paid all their salaries for the next fifty years. With the fiftieth anniversary of Keynes' death approaching in 1996, economists must pray for a new benefactor . . . and soon.

The promise of an end to the business cycle has not been delivered. The British economy has been through three major recessions in the last two decades – 1974–75, 1980–81 and 1990–93. In the latter two, unemployment rose above three million and yet there was no clear consensus about the causes and the correct policy response. Certainly, the authorities were not persuaded that the solution lay in a fiscal stimulus, as would have been recommended by early Keynesian economics. Indeed, Sir Geoffrey Howe *raised* taxes in 1981, in the depth of the early 1980s recession; 364 economists condemned him for doing so (in a widely reported letter to *The Times*) and yet the economy then grew for the next eight years! However, as Figure I.1 clearly shows, UK real Gross Domestic Product (GDP) has never returned to its 1955–79 trend, even in the boom of 1988 (and after the years of the so-called Thatcher Miracle). At the end of the 1989–93 recession, output is further than ever from this long-run trend.

Evolution of ideas

The 'Big Idea' which came out of early Keynesian macroeconomics was *aggregate demand failure*. Recessions were likely to be associated with a fall

3

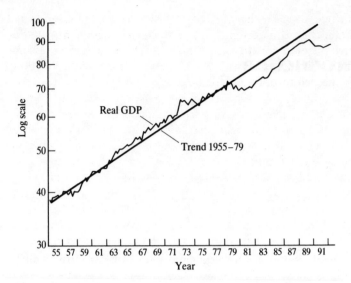

Figure I.1   UK real GDP 1955–93. Source: Datastream.

in exogenous expenditures and the solution would be a policy-induced stimulus, typically through an increase in public spending or a cut in taxes. The research agenda associated with early modelling strategies was focused mainly on categories of aggregate expenditure – predominantly consumption but also investment, imports and exports.

Monetary policy was given relatively little prominence in the United Kingdom. This can be explained partly by the environment created by the 1944 Bretton Woods Agreement. A pegged exchange rate was the monetary target and all else was subjugated by that constraint. However, there was not even a free market monetary system until the 1980s – monetary control was achieved by a mixture of exchange controls, quantitative restrictions and market segmentation plus the traditional 'nods and winks' from the Bank of England.

It is true that there were always dissenters. In particular, groups of economists in the United States who worked with Milton Friedman and Karl Brunner developed a view of the macroeconomy which gave the money stock a central role – particularly as the determinant of inflation, but also as a leading indicator of business cycles. These ideas became more widely accepted for a while in the 1970s under the label of 'Monetarism'.

However, the first major threat to the Keynesian income–expenditure model came from the 'supply side', with the adoption at the end of the 1960s of what is now called the 'natural rate hypothesis'. The original 1957 version of the Phillips curve suggested that there was a stable trade-off between inflation and unemployment. Edmund Phelps and Milton Friedman independently suggested that this was not so. In the long run there was a natural or equilibrium level of unemployment. Only at this level of activity would inflation be stable. At lower levels of unemployment inflation would accelerate. Unemployment levels above the natural rate were needed to bring inflation down.

The acceptance of the natural rate hypothesis might have been a big mistake for Keynesians because it slipped in the assumption that the economy had a real underlying equilibrium to which it would always return and which was unaffected by macroeconomics itself. Subsequently the macroeconomic agenda was restricted to getting the economy back to the natural rate and keeping it there at the lowest inflation rate possible. The modelling of the economy as a supply–demand interaction also created pressure for better 'micro-foundation' of macro models, despite the fact that it was the failure of micro market models to deal with reality that created the need for macroeconomics in the first place.

Macroeconomics abdicated responsibility for shifting the natural rate, claiming that this was a microeconomic phenomenon associated with growth theory or the efficiency of the real economy. Hence, those who wished to stimulate growth turned to 'supply side' policies – such as trade union reform, privatisation and tax reform – while often ignoring the goal of stabilisation. For a while, only the control of inflation was a genuinely macroeconomic issue.

The dynamics of the natural rate model, built as it was around shifting expectations-augmented short-run Phillips curves, put expectations formation at the heart of macroeconomics for the first time (although they were there to some extent in investment functions). This prepared the ground for the 'Rational Expectations Revolution'. This reduced stabilisation ambitions even further by making it seem that only 'surprise' changes in economic policy instruments could have real effects.

The most important long-term effect on macroeconomics of the rational expectations (RE) revolution has been to change the nature of the perceived interaction between policy-makers and the economy. In the Keynesian structure, the policy-maker has superior knowledge and, by pulling certain levers, is able to have a predictable effect on the economy. In the world after RE, actors in the economy are smart and forward-looking. They attempt to forecast what the government is going to do, just as the government tries to forecast what the economy is going to do. Policy-making in this context becomes a complex dynamic 'game' in which credibility and commitment suddenly have great significance. The best long-run inflation–output trade-offs only accrue to credible governments.

Reaction against the nihilism of extreme RE approaches to macro-economics has spawned a 'New Keynesian' agenda. The general purpose of this agenda is to justify an aggregate supply curve which is other than vertical, at least in the short run. The purpose is to show that policy-induced changes in aggregate demand can stimulate output and thereby preserve a role for active stabilisation policy. However, while the original Keynesian focus was on aggregate demand via categories of expenditure, the new focus has been entirely on labour markets. The aim has been to explain why wage and price rigidities may be normal and 'rational', in contrast to the New Classical model which assumes continuous market-clearing. The limited success of the New Keynesians testifies to the level of entrenchment of the market-clearing model in the minds of the economics profession. An apparent trend towards greater policy activism on both sides of the Atlantic owes more to political pragmatism than to intellectual conviction.

Open economies

The 1950s and 1960s were decades of almost universal fixed exchange rates. However, the exchange rate regime was maintained by an array of direct controls, notably exchange controls. Floating exchange rates became normal in the 1970s and 1980s as did the trend towards liberalisation of domestic financial markets and abolition of exchange controls. These trends have heightened the degree of interdependence between economies. So much so that it is common to talk about the globalisation of financial markets. It has also become obvious that no economy can isolate itself entirely from world market forces. Aggregate demand is now world demand rather than local demand.

The business cycles of the last two decades have been worldwide phenomena, suggesting that worldwide solutions might be necessary. International policy coordination has been suggested as a necessity to stabilise the global economy. However, the political obstacles to such coordination are substantial and the potential for gain is controversial.

A second-best solution has been sought by some countries in the attempt to form regional economic units, with some areas (notably the European Community (EC)) planning to introduce a single currency by the end of the 1990s. Again, there remain many political obstacles to progress but if significant structural changes were to occur, macroeconomic policy-making would shift from the nation state level to the currency union. In another decade there may be no such thing as British monetary policy, rather it would be European.

Irrespective of potential structural changes, macroeconomists have had to take on board both floating exchange rates and highly integrated efficient financial markets. Perfect capital mobility now seems like a much more plausible assumption than it did even ten years ago. This has implications for the conduct of macro policy even in the absence of moves towards a single currency. Most importantly, perhaps, models of floating exchange rate economies provide important new insights into the old issue of the transmission mechanism of monetary policy. It is also possible to understand why fiscal policy was a more important instrument under the Bretton Woods fixed exchange rate regime of the 1950s and 1960s while monetary policy entered the centre stage in the 1970s and 1980s.

In the EC context there can be no doubt that debates about the pros and cons of a single currency and the convergence criteria which must be satisfied for membership will dominate the agenda of the next few years.

Tax and spend

If pan-European Monetary Union does become a reality, even in the weaker form of an Exchange Rate Mechanism (ERM) type arrangement, then macroeconomics will come back to where it started – a discussion of the appropriate role of fiscal policy. The existence of automatic stabilisers in the form of rising deficits in recessions seems to be widely accepted, as does the role of fiscal transfers for regional imbalance correction. However, the value of stimulating the economy via discretionary deficit financing seems to be as controversial as ever. A balanced budget 'on average' seems to be a more popular recommendation than it would ever have been in early Keynesian times. Politicians from many backgrounds would support this in principle, though few would achieve it in practice – given the political difficulties involved in raising taxes and cutting spending.

The use of spending as a macro policy tool has always been limited by the difficulties of altering direction in a hurry. The reality of the situation in which virtually all governments find themselves is characterised by growing pressure on public funds to achieve impossible targets. The ageing population alone creates a time bomb for pension provision. This is reinforced by demand for growing health and education standards. The aggregate budget constraint at any feasible tax rates leaves government with virtually no room for manoeuvre on discretionary expenditures.

Accordingly, fiscal policy outcomes seem more likely to be determined by structural public policy concerns than by the needs of short-term macroeconomic policy. Could it be that the business cycle is back and that policy-makers cannot do much about it?

Indeed, the UK experience of the last twenty years has done much to reinforce the view that government policy is likely to exaggerate the business cycle rather than moderate it. Certainly, as Figure I.2 shows, unemployment seems to be cycling about an increasing trend and inflation reached very high levels in the 1970s. In the light of these demonstrable

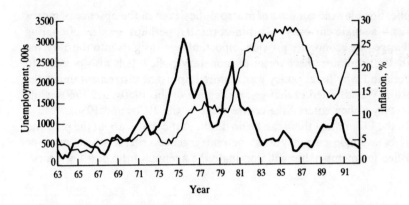

Figure I.2   Unemployment and inflation 1963–92: ———— unemployment, ———— inflation. Source: Datastream.

policy mistakes, the case for constraining policy-makers still further, or handing policy-making discretion to supranational bodies is hard to resist.

Whatever the future holds, it is hard to believe that we have got better at conducting macroeconomic policy than we were over half a century ago when Keynes' General Theory created a new discipline. However many 'Wise Men' are employed by the Treasury, there can be little confidence that policy will be better in the future than it was in the past. Globally diversified pension funds and internationally diversified companies may make local performance less important than it used to be, but high unemployment still threatens lives, so the challenge to comprehend and improve our economic environment is as great as ever. The fact that universal solutions have not been found does not mean that they do not exist. The issues are as important as ever. Macroeconomics is still worth doing . . . and worth doing well.

1

Textbook models

The role of a model is to enable the economist to isolate the principal relationships between economic variables and to explore the logical consequences of changing these relationships. Textbook models start with a small number of simple relationships. Others are added later, in order to increase the realism of the model. How realistic any particular model is is largely a matter of judgement. The major controversies in macroeconomics are exactly about what constitutes a satisfactory model.

Most economists trained in the last twenty years will have been taught at least one of the models outlined below. When asked a question about the working of the economy, they will automatically structure their thought in terms of one of these models. The simple expenditure system and the IS–LM model should be familiar to all economists, though the full model with a supply side may be less so. These models provide a benchmark for the rest of the book. Of central concern throughout are the main channels of causation, rather than the precise form of individual relationships.

Model I: The expenditure system

This is the most familiar of all macro models. It consists of an accounting identity and a number of equations determining various components of national expenditure. For the most part simple linear relationships will be presumed.

$$Y \equiv C + I + G + X - P \tag{1.1}$$

National income, Y, is identically equal to consumption, C, plus investment, I, plus government expenditure, G, plus exports, X, minus imports, P.

$$C = \alpha + \beta(Y - T) \tag{1.2}$$

Consumption expenditure, C, depends upon disposable income (national income, Y, minus taxes, T).

$$P = dY \tag{1.3}$$

Imports, P, are proportional to national income, Y.

$$X = X_0 \tag{1.4}$$

Exports, X, are exogenously determined.

$$G = G_0 \tag{1.5}$$

Government expenditure, G, is exogenously determined.

$$I = I_0 \tag{1.6}$$

Investment, I, is exogenously determined.

If tax revenue is also assumed to be fixed in size, the model is 'solved' by substituting equations (1.2)–(1.6) into (1.1), to yield:

$$Y = \frac{\alpha + I_0 + G_0 + X_0 - \beta T}{(1 - \beta + d)} \tag{1.7}$$

This is the familiar 'multiplier' equation. The multiplier tells us how much national income changes in response to changes in exogenous expenditures. Its value depends upon the size of 'leakages' from the circular flow of income; notably, in this case, the marginal propensity to save, $1 - \beta$, and the marginal (and average) propensity to import, d.

All the action in this model comes from changes in exogenous expenditures. It is presumed that there are unemployed resources so output is entirely demand-determined. Supply factors are passive and do not enter into the determination of national income. Thus the chain of causation in this model leads from exogenous expenditures through the multiplier to national income.

This simple framework is, however, sufficient to explain the essence of the so-called Keynesian revolution. National income could settle at an 'equilibrium' in the presence of unemployed resources. This would happen if exogenous expenditures were insufficient to generate the full employment level of output. The simple solution is that government expenditure should be used, in conjunction with taxes, to stimulate the economy in times of depression and 'deflate' the economy when it is 'overheated'. This, in a nutshell, is the intellectual basis of countercyclical budgetary policy.

Model I is encaptured diagrammatically in Figure 1.1. The 45° line represents the accounting identity, or aggregate supply, since it represents points where domestic expenditure and output are equal.

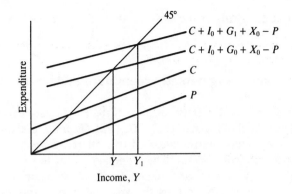

Figure 1.1 The expenditure system.

The C and P lines represent the consumption and import functions respectively. Aggregate domestic demand is given by $C + I_0 + G_0 + X_0 - P$. This determines an equilibrium level of national income (or output), Y. An increase of income and, therefore, of employment can be achieved by increasing government expenditure, G, to G_1. Aggregate demand thereby rises to $C + I_0 + G_1 + X_0 - P$ and income rises to Y_1. Budgetary policy (that is, changes in G and T) can thus be used to regulate the level of activity in the economy.

This is the first model learned by anyone who studies macroeconomics; it is, therefore, unnecessary to dwell upon it. However, a number of points should be made which will be referred to later. The first is that all the variables in the model are in 'real' terms, i.e. they are deflated by an appropriate price index. Thus inflation has no effect, since it does not shift a relationship relative to another. It is common to talk of the existence of an 'inflationary gap' where aggregate expenditure exceeds aggregate output at full employment, but inflation would do nothing in this model to resolve such inconsistency.

Second, the model has nothing to say about the supply side of the economy. It is, in fact, presumed that resources are underemployed so that it is sufficient to look at *aggregate expenditure* in order to explain the determination of national output. National output is demand-determined. Obviously this has some relevance to deep depressions, but it is of questionable value in situations close to full employment. If expenditure exceeds output at 'full employment' the model becomes indeterminate. Finally, it is clear that if the workings of this economy are to be accurately predicted then the major intellectual effort has to go into the correct specification of the various expenditure functions, the consumption function being the most 'important' of these in terms of the proportion of total expenditure involved. It is a matter of some controversy whether the unemployment of the 1980s or the early 1990s could have been cured by Keynesian style reflation.

Model II: The money-augmented expenditure system, IS–LM

Model I was sufficient to explain the essence of the Keynesian revolution, but it was not the model of Keynes' (1936) *General Theory of Employment, Interest and Money.* One interpretation of this offered by Hicks (1937) included a stylised monetary sector. The monetary sector has two assets, money and bonds, the supply and demand for which determine 'the' interest rate, since the interest rate is the yield on bonds. Interest rate changes affect real expenditures through investment behaviour, which is presumed to be interest-sensitive. A reverse link from the expenditure sector to money arises because the demand for money for transactions purposes increases with the level of income. Thus equation (1.6) now becomes:

$$I = \delta - \varepsilon r \tag{1.8}$$

Investment is inversely related to the interest rate.

and in addition we have equations for the demand for and supply of money.

$$M_d = \phi Y - \eta r \tag{1.9}$$

Money demand increases with income and falls with the interest rate.

$$M_s = M_0 \tag{1.10}$$

Money supply is exogenously given.

The interest rate affects the demand for money because it is the opportunity cost of holding money. (Keynes' speculative demand depended on inelastic expectations but the model works in the same way.) There is no need to specify bond market equations because any financial wealth not held in money must be held in bonds. So demand for bonds is just the inverse of the demand for money. This assumption causes difficulty if we want to analyse changes in bond sales. It then becomes necessary to incorporate a wealth constraint explicitly.

The money market can be characterised as in Figure 1.2 where the money demand line is drawn for a given Y. The M_d line traces the relation between r and money demand, or speculative demand. At higher levels of Y the M_d line shifts up because more money is demanded for transactions purposes. Thus for a given money supply higher levels of Y will be associated with higher levels of the interest rate, r. In the expenditure sector higher interest rates produce lower levels of income Y. This is because the

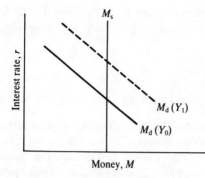

Figure 1.2 The money market.

increased interest rate reduces investment, which through the multiplier process reduces income.

Thus, we cannot solve the monetary sector or the expenditure sector separately since the outcome in each affects the other. The procedure adopted is to trace out two loci of combinations of interest rates and income which are associated with equilibrium in each sector separately. Where these two lines cross, the values of Y and r so determined will be equilibrium values for the model as a whole. In Figure 1.3 the line LM is made up of combinations of Y and r that are associated with equilibrium in the money market (i.e. demand and supply of money are equal) and the line IS is made up of combinations of Y and r associated with equilibrium in the expenditure sector (i.e. injections equal withdrawals). The IS and LM curves are derived algebraically in the appendix to this chapter.

This model still has variables determined in real terms. The money price level does not change, so changes in Y are changes in real output. It is, however, possible to allow changes in the price level but only at the expense

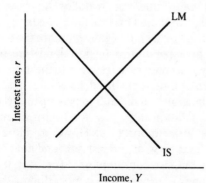

Figure 1.3 Equilibrium aggregate demand.

of fixing real income Y, say at full employment, Y_0. Then Y is no longer a variable and p is introduced in the money demand equation which now becomes:

$$M_d/p = \phi Y_0 - \eta r \qquad (1.11)$$

Real money demand depends upon the interest rate with income fixed.

The change arises because, whereas the money supply is nominal, money is demanded for its real purchasing power. Thus a rise in the price level reduces the *real* money supply. For a given real income the interest rate equating money demand and supply will be higher for a higher price level and for a given *nominal* money supply. To see this, relabel the horizontal axis in Figure 1.2 M/p and shift the M_s line to the left. For a given M_s, M_s/p gets smaller as p rises.

The relevance of this modification to the model will appear below but it does illustrate one case of interest. If, when full-employment real output is fixed, the money supply is increased, the net result will be an increase in the price level proportional to the increase in M. This is the classical quantity theory result and it arises because all the real variables in the system are assumed to be fixed. As a result there can be only one real money stock, in equilibrium. An increase in the nominal money stock will be eroded by a rise in prices until the real money stock of the initial situation has been restored. However, this tells us nothing about the rate of inflation since we have a comparative static model, not a dynamic one. We know that a once-and-for-all rise in the money supply will produce a once-and-for-all rise in the price level, but we cannot say what the time path of this adjustment will be.

Returning to the model where real income is variable and prices are fixed, it is worth noting how monetary factors influence real behaviour. A change in the money supply does not directly influence expenditures. Rather, it leads first of all to a readjustment of portfolios. An excess supply of money is an excess demand for bonds. This leads to a rise in the price of bonds, which is equivalent to a fall in the rate of interest, since the bonds are perpetuities. Only in so far as expenditures (of any kind) are interest-sensitive will there then be any real changes in response to the initial money supply increase. An important point is involved here since researchers working in the 1960s on UK data found it difficult to pick up interest effects in the aggregate investment relationship (save for housing) and thus concluded that money is of little importance. However, more recent research has established clear links between interest rates and not only fixed investment and stockbuilding, but also consumption. Moreover, it is quite possible that the link from money to expenditure is more direct. An excess money supply could be spent, not just on bonds, but also on goods.

If it were the case that an excess supply of money was spent directly on goods this would mean that evidence on the interest sensitivity of investment would not be important for judging the impact of money on the economy. Instead, we should expect to find terms in *excess* money balances appearing in expenditure equations such as the consumption function. It is difficult to incorporate asset stocks in expenditure functions short of specifying a full intertemporal optimisation model in which the time paths of expenditures and assets are simultaneously chosen. The whole attraction of the IS–LM set-up is exactly that the separability of expenditures and asset choices provides for welcome simplicity.

Model III: Aggregate demand and supply

The third commonly used model adds a supply side to the economy. Models I and II are essentially ways of explaining aggregate expenditures. The addition is now made of a productive sector within which the level of employment is determined as well as the level of real output. It is effectively assumed that the capital stock is fixed. There is, therefore, a production function relating output to the input of the variable factor (labour).

Labour is hired up to the point where the value of the marginal product of labour is equal to the wage rate, and the supply of labour is also assumed to depend upon the wage rate.

$$Y = f(K, L) \qquad (1.12)$$

Output is a function of capital and labour.

$$L_d = \theta(w) \qquad (1.13)$$

Labour demand depends upon the wage rate.

$$L_s = \mu(w) \qquad (1.14)$$

Labour supply depends upon the wage rate.

The equilibrium in this sector can be illustrated with regard to labour demand and supply alone (see Figure 1.4). Two important points need to be stressed. First, increases in employment will be uniquely associated with increases in real national output and vice versa. This is because we have a given production function (1.12) in which labour is the only variable input. Second, we need to consider whether the labour demand and supply curves depend upon the money wage rate or upon the real wage rate (i.e. the money wage rate deflated by the price index of output).

A moment's thought should make it clear that firms should only be interested in the real wage rate. If the price of output and the money wage

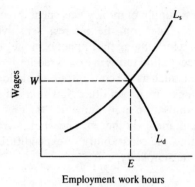

Figure 1.4   Labour market equilibrium.

rate increased together then the levels of real output and employment at which the money wage is equal to the value of the marginal product of labour will be unchanged. Thus it is reasonable to presume that the *demand* for labour depends upon the real wage. So far as the supply of labour is concerned, it would be rational if this depended upon the real wage since leisure is effectively forfeited for the *goods that wages will buy*. However, it is sometimes assumed that workers do not fully appreciate or anticipate the extent to which money wage increases are offset by price increases. Accordingly, it is worth pursuing two alternative assumptions with regard to labour supply. The first is that labour supply depends upon the real wage, and the second is that it depends upon the money wage or, equivalently, that workers offer labour based upon the *expected* price level and expectations lag behind the reality.

If both labour demand and supply depend upon the real wage then output and employment will be determined independently of nominal prices and wages. An increase in the price of output, accompanied by a rise in money wages, would have no real effect since the real wage would not change. However, if labour supply depended upon the money wage, an increase in money wages accompanied by a proportionate rise in prices would increase labour supply. In this case both prices and real output would rise. Workers would, in effect, be suffering from the *illusion* that their real wages had risen and would be acting *as if* labour supply depended upon the money wage.

It is now possible to derive what can be called aggregate demand and supply curves with both price level *and* real income as endogenous variables. The aggregate supply curve is implicit in what has just been discussed. In the case in which labour supply depends upon the real wage, varying the price of output will leave the *real* value of output unchanged. Nothing concrete in the productive sector changes because all nominal values (i.e. prices expressed in terms of the numeraire, money) move together, and there is no change in relative prices. Here the aggregate supply curve, Figure 1.5, is vertical since output is fixed independently of prices.

The situation is very different when labour supply is an increasing function of money wages, or workers act on price expectations which are incorrect. Now *any* rise in money wages is perceived as an increase in real wages so more labour is offered. If prices rise but money wages rise less quickly, there will be an increase in labour supply (money wage has risen) and at the same time an increase in quantity of labour demanded (real wage has fallen). Thus there will be an increase in employment and of real output. In short, on the assumption that there is some money illusion on the labour supply side, as prices rise there will be an increase in supply of output. The aggregate supply curve will be positively sloped. This version we call Model IIIA. Let the vertical aggregate supply be Model IIIB. The latter can be thought of as the long-run situation when workers come to anticipate the price level correctly. The former can be thought of as the short-run case when price rises are not fully anticipated. It is this distinction between anticipated and unanticipated changes in aggregate demand that is central to New Classical economics (see Chapter 4); for a text which develops this approach, see Parkin and Bade, 1982. Their conclusion that only unanticipated aggregate demand policy has real effects depends entirely on this distinction between Models IIIA and IIIB.

Derivation of the aggregate demand curve is entirely from the money-augmented expenditure system Model II (see the appendix to this chapter). It was noted earlier that Model II could be used to determine either real income or the price level but not both. However, it should now be noted that, for given values of all the exogenous variables (especially the nominal money supply), a higher price level will be associated with a lower level of real income. This is not because a higher price reduces the quantity

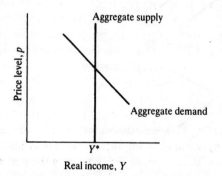

Figure 1.5 Aggregate demand and supply.

demanded as in a single market demand situation. Rather, it is because, for a given nominal supply, a higher price level reduces the real money supply. As a result the LM curve shifts to the left, the interest rate rises and real expenditures fall. Real income therefore falls. Thus, the aggregate demand curve, drawn between the price level and real income, is negatively sloped, Figure 1.5. Higher price levels are associated with lower levels of real income *when Model II is considered alone.*

A simple example will serve to illustrate how the full model works. Anything which in Model II would have shifted the IS curve to the right or the LM curve to the right will shift the aggregate demand curve to the right, i.e. an increase in exogenous expenditures or an increase in the money supply. Only an increase in the supply of factors of production or a technical change in the production will shift the aggregate supply curve to the right. Consider then an increase in exogenous investment in Figure 1.6. The upper half of the diagram shows the IS and LM curves, the lower half shows the aggregate demand and supply curves.

The initial effect of an increase in investment is to shift the IS curve to the right, IS_0 to IS_1. In Model I, income would increase as a result of the simple multiplier to Y_3. In Model II the increase in income is less than this because the increase in income raises transactions demand for money and,

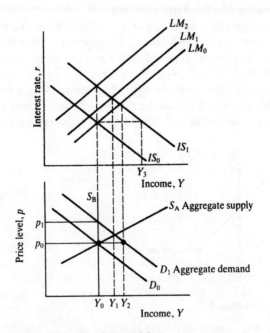

Figure 1.6 The full model.

therefore, bids up the interest rate. This increase in the interest rate reduces endogenous investment, which in turn reduces income. Thus in Model II income increases to Y_2 ($Y_2 < Y_3$).

Y_2 would only be the outcome in Model III if the aggregate supply curve were horizontal, i.e. if all the output demanded were forthcoming at a fixed price level. It has been seen above that this is not likely. For the money illusion or short-run case there will be some increase in both the price level and real output. The aggregate supply curve in this case is S_A. National income will rise to Y_1. This is smaller again than Y_2. The reason for this is that the increase in the price level has reduced the *real* money supply so the LM curve has shifted to LM_1, thereby increasing the interest rate and reducing endogenous expenditures still further.

Where the aggregate supply curve is vertical, S_B (i.e. the long-run case where there is no money illusion on the labour supply side), there is no increase in real national income or output. It stays at Y_0. In this case, the initial increase in exogenous expenditure leads only to a rise in the price level, from p_0 to p_1. As a result the LM curve shifts to LM_2 such that its intersection with IS_1 is at exactly the original level of real income.

Each new model in this chapter represents an extension to the previous one. The above example shows clearly how the predictions change as we move from one model to another. For a given shift in exogenous variables, Model I predicts the greatest effect on real income, since *real* variables are the only ones to adjust. Model II reduces the real effects by adding an interest rate feedback. Model IIIA reduces the real effects still further by adding a price-level feedback. Finally, in Model IIIB, real effects are entirely eliminated and the adjustment is entirely in terms of the price level, interest rates and other *nominal* values.

The term 'Keynesian' in macroeconomics is normally associated with Models I and II (although there is an amorphous 'New Keynesian' school which we consider in Chapter 5). Keynesians presume that increases in aggregate demand will produce significant increases in aggregate supply (except at full employment). Monetarists are associated with the position that, in the long run, increases in nominal aggregate demand will mainly be reflected in prices, with output tending to some 'natural' rate. The main difference between Monetarists and New Classicists is with respect to short-run dynamics. Monetarists believe that prices are sticky so that there are 'long and variable lags' in the adjustment process. A Monetarist would expect there to be temporary output changes in response to aggregate demand increases until prices have adjusted. In New Classical economics the price change is immediate if the aggregate demand change is anticipated. Model IIIA would thus be the Monetarist case during the adjustment period and it would be the New Classical case for unanticipated demand shocks. Model IIIB would be the long-run case for Monetarists and New Classicists, and it would also be the short-run case for the latter when demand changes are anticipated. While New Classical economics assumes price flexibility, it is necessary to adduce other forms of stickiness in order to reconcile their models with real world data which exhibit obvious patterns of persistence. This point is expanded in Chapter 10.

Appendix

In this appendix a derivation is offered of the IS and LM curves as well as of the aggregate demand curve. For simplicity we take a closed economy with no government sector. There are three equations for the aggregate expenditure sector and two for the monetary sector. These are given a simple linear form.

$$Y \equiv C + I \tag{1A.1}$$

$$C = \alpha + \beta Y \tag{1A.2}$$

$$I = \delta - \varepsilon r \tag{1A.3}$$

These are the accounting identity, the consumption function and the investment function. Notation is standard and as in the chapter. The IS curve is derived by substituting for C and I in (1A.1). Thus

$$Y = \alpha + \beta Y + \delta - \varepsilon r$$

$$Y - \beta Y = \alpha + \delta - \varepsilon r$$

$$Y(1 - \beta) = \alpha + \delta - \varepsilon r$$

$$Y = \alpha/(1 - \beta) + \delta/(1 - \beta) - \varepsilon r/(1 - \beta) \tag{1A.4}$$

This is the IS curve. It shows a negative relationship between national income Y and the interest rate r. Notice also that an exogenous shift in consumption, α, or investment, δ, will shift the IS curve parallel to itself by the simple multiplier distance, $1/(1 - \beta)$. The only difference that adding the government sector and foreign trade would make would be to add exogenous expenditures – government expenditure and exports – and the multiplier would become $1/[1 - \beta(1 - t) + d]$, where t is the income tax rate and d is the marginal propensity to import.

The monetary sector is very simple.

$$M_s = M_0 \tag{1A.5}$$

$$M_d/p = \phi Y - \eta r \tag{1A.6}$$

Money supply, M_s, is exogenously determined by the authorities and the demand for real money balances depends upon income and the rate of interest. Rewrite (1A.6) as

$$M_d = p(\phi Y - \eta r)$$

Set money demand equal to money supply

$$M_0 = p(\phi Y - \eta r)$$

$$Y = M_0/\phi p + \eta r/\phi \tag{1A.7}$$

This is the LM curve. It expresses a positive relationship between Y and r, and it shifts as either the money stock, M, or the price level, p, changes. What we now have are two simultaneous equations in two unknowns Y and r. Notice that the price level appears in (1A.7) and is implicitly being held constant.

The aggregate demand curve tells us how changes in Y and p are related. Rearrange (1A.7) as an expression for r and substitute this into (1A.4). This gives

$$Y = \alpha/(1 - \beta) + \delta/(1 - \beta) - \varepsilon\phi Y/\eta(1 - \beta) + \varepsilon M_0/p\eta(1 - \beta) \tag{1A.4}$$

The solution for Y is then

$$Y = \frac{\alpha}{(1 - \beta) + \varepsilon\phi/\eta} + \frac{\delta}{(1 - \beta) + \varepsilon\phi/\eta} + \frac{\varepsilon M_0}{p\eta[(1 - \beta) + \varepsilon\phi/\eta]} \tag{1A.8}$$

This is the aggregate demand curve. A higher level of p will be associated with a lower level of equilibrium, Y. Notice that since this is essentially the 'solution' of the IS–LM system, the effect of exogenous expenditures on Y is now reduced because the 'multiplier' now includes feedback from the monetary sector $\varepsilon\phi/\eta$ as well as marginal expenditure leakages $(1 - \beta)$.

The theory underlying the aggregate supply curve is discussed in Chapter 4.

PART 2
Factions

2

Keynesians

Keynesian economics was what most people understood by 'macro-economics' for the first two decades of the post-Second World War period. By 1969, when President Nixon endorsed the famous dictum 'We are all Keynesians now', it was almost certainly no longer true. The Monetarist camp was sufficiently well established that the illusion of consensus could no longer be sustained. It might be tempting to suggest that the elections of Margaret Thatcher in the United Kingdom in 1979, and Ronald Reagan in the United States in 1980, necessitated a revision of the dictum to 'We are all *Monetarists* now'. However, on the one hand the big turnaround in policy stance, in the United Kingdom at least, came in 1976 not in 1979, and on the other hand, Monetarism in its purest form had been abandoned in the United Kingdom as early as 1983 (see Chapter 3).

The purpose of this chapter is to explain what is normally understood by 'the traditional Keynesian style of economic management'. In a later chapter on 'New Keynesian' economics we will consider some recent attempts to restyle the analysis of aggregate supply in a non-classical framework; but the thrust of this chapter is to do with *aggregate demand*, not supply. The interpretation of Keynes given here came largely from Hansen (1953), rather than directly from Keynes' own writings, though it came to form the basis of the conventional wisdom in the United Kingdom.

The Keynesian revolution and Keynesian cases

The Keynesian model of how the economy works can be thought of either as Model I in its entirety or as special cases of Models II and III. It is convenient to discuss each of these in turn before discussing what the

25

appellation 'Keynesian' normally means in policy discussions, though it is worth pointing out at the outset that the 'Keynesian' model was basically a closed economy model. This made its applicability to Britain doubtful from the start except in very special circumstances.

Consider the simplest possible version of Model I for an economy which has no imports or exports. There are just two equations – the national income accounting identity and the consumption function. Government expenditure and investment are exogenously given.

$$Y \equiv C + I + G \tag{2.1}$$

$$C = \alpha + \beta Y \tag{2.2}$$

$$G = G_0 \tag{2.3}$$

$$I = I_0 \tag{2.4}$$

All the variables are in real terms and all are *flows* of expenditure or income per period. It is presumed that there are unemployed resources, so that a change in the exogenous expenditures will produce an increase in real output and, therefore, of real income. The 'solution' to the model is obtained by substituting for C, G and I in (2.1) and solving for Y. Thus

$$Y = \frac{\alpha + I_0 + G_0}{1 - \beta} \tag{2.5}$$

The coefficient on the exogenous expenditures, $1/(1-\beta)$, tells us how much income will change for any change in exogenous expenditures and is often known as 'the multiplier', a phrase introduced by Kahn, a contemporary of Keynes at Cambridge in the 1930s. It is called this because if the coefficient β were to be of the order of 0.8, which is not unreasonable, then $1/(1-\beta)$ would be 5, i.e. a change in exogenous expenditures would produce a ('multiplied') change in income five times greater.

The diagram used to explain Model I is familiar as Figure 2.1. There is some level of national income at which all resources are fully employed, Y^*. The principal message of the Keynesian revolution is that if aggregate expenditures are insufficient then the system will settle into an equilibrium (at least for a significant period) where resources are less than fully employed. The Classical system, in contrast, was thought to work in such a way that prices adjusted up or down to clear all markets according to whether there was excess demand or supply. If investment and government expenditure are at levels I_0 and G_0, then national income will be Y_0. At this level there is unemployment because the full employment level of national income is higher. There will be no tendency for this unemployment to disappear within the time horizon of the analysis. The major policy significance of this analysis, however, is that there is a simple solution to the problem.

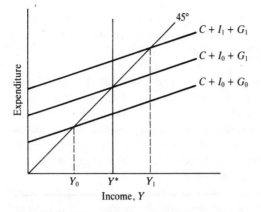

Figure 2.1 The Keynesian 'cross' determination of national income.

The cause of this unemployment is a deficiency of aggregate expenditures. It can be eliminated if the government is prepared to increase its net injection of expenditures into the system. This means that the government should deliberately spend more in the economy than it is raising in taxes. In other words, it should run a budget deficit. Previously, of course, the annual budget was simply a way of raising the revenue to finance government expenditure. Keynesian economics is an intellectual justification for the use of the budget as the major tool for regulating the level of economic activity.

Model I is often referred to as the income–expenditure system or simply the expenditure system, as in Chapter 1. There can be no doubt at all that the formalisation of the analysis of effective demand failure which it presents was a fundamental breakthrough in economics. Economists of nearly all persuasions have added it to their analytical toolbox and would not question its relevance to the problem it was aimed at, i.e. deep and sustained depression. However, it would be foolish to claim that the apparatus is adequate to analyse other economic problems which have a different origin. For example, what if expenditures exceed full-employment real income at $C + I_1 + G_1$? Here it is common to refer to the existence of an inflationary gap (equal to $I_1 - I_0$), but inflation itself cannot remove this gap since all variables are in real terms. The model is incomplete. Macroeconomics today is still largely about what has been left out. Keynesians emphasise what was right with the model; Monetarists (and others) emphasise what was omitted.

The expenditure system is certainly not the model of Keynes' General Theory. This is more usually, though perhaps incorrectly, interpreted as being the money-augmented expenditure system or IS–LM model. This itself was introduced by Hicks in 1939, and although Keynes is on record as congratulating Hicks for his attempt to systematise the ideas contained in the General Theory, the model cannot do full justice to Keynes' work. This is Model II of Chapter 1. The only additions are relationships for the demand and supply of money, and a link from money interest rates to investment expenditures. The Keynesian message above can be shown in an exactly analogous way. Figure 2.2(a), for example, shows an equilibrium for the system at less than full-employment real income, Y^*. Again, the unemployment can be eliminated by an increase in the budget deficit, thus shifting the IS curve to the right. However, in that diagram the same result (with respect to income) could be achieved by increasing the money stock, thereby shifting LM to the right.

The numerical properties of Models I and II are not identical, however. It has already been seen that the multiplier is smaller in II than in I because there is negative feedback from the monetary sector. Higher income increases demand for money, which raises interest rates for a given money stock. Keynesians have justified ignoring the monetary sector by the appropriate use of two specific assumptions, though neither is necessary to an understanding of the views of Keynes himself. Indeed, neither is contained in the General Theory. The first of these is that investment is inelastic with respect to the rate of interest (Figure 2.2(b)). If this were true, Model I could tell us all we need to know about the real economy. Money supply affects interest rates but interest rates do not affect any real

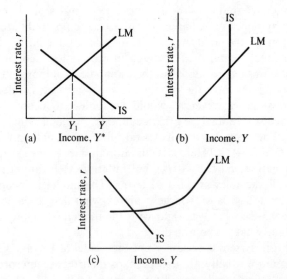

Figure 2.2 The effectiveness of monetary policy in the Keynesian model.

behaviour. The simple multiplier is now appropriate. The second assumption is that there is a liquidity trap so that the LM curve is horizontal (Figure 2.2(c)). This means that changes in the money stock get 'hoarded' and do not influence interest rates so there are no real effects even if investment is interest-elastic. This is the famous case of 'pushing on a string'.

While the latter assumption was used to justify Model I in its early days, British Keynesians increasingly defended their position, in the 1950s and 1960s, by reference to the former. The most influential empirical support for this view of investment behaviour was a survey of thirty-seven businessmen reported by Meade and Andrews (1951), most of whom claimed that the interest rate did not influence their investment decisions. The same survey could in fact be used to sustain the opposite conclusion, since a small number of firms admitted that they were affected, which may amount to a significant effect in the aggregate. Until the 1980s it was difficult to establish the existence of an interest rate effect on investment in the United Kingdom, though this may have been due more to the former policy of pegging interest rates than to investment behaviour itself. However, these debates are now of only historical interest, as there now seems no doubt that interest rates do impact on investment, as well as on other expenditures, including consumption.

There is a special case of Model III which is often called Keynesian. Again it does not appear in Keynes' General Theory but has entered popular discussion as if it did, following Modigliani (1944). This relies upon the assumption that, while there is no general money illusion, money wages are inflexible in a downward direction.[1] If it is assumed that there is an initial equilibrium at full employment, then the aggregate supply curve is vertical above the equilibrium but sloped below the equilibrium, as in Figure 2.3. In effect, the assumption of downward inflexibility of money wages means that there is money illusion in a downward but not an upward

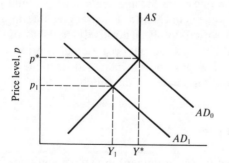

Figure 2.3 Downwardly rigid money wages.

direction. A fall in aggregate demand from AD_0 to AD_1 produces a fall in prices, but, because money wages do not fall, the real wage rises. At a higher real wage, firms employ less labour and, with a given capital stock, produce less output. So national income falls from Y^* to Y_1. Employment will remain at this new low level unless there is a reduction in money wages or an increase in aggregate demand. Above the full-employment level of output an increase in aggregate demand will increase the price level but not the level of real income. We shall see below that the case of real wages being too high is by no means essential for the existence of 'Keynesian' unemployment; the real wage could be below the Walrasian or market-clearing level, and there may still be unemployment in some circumstances. Nevertheless, high real wages may form the basis of what is often referred to as 'Classical' unemployment. Indeed, Keynes himself regarded it as the classical explanation of unemployment.

> Moreover, the contention that the unemployment which characterises a depression is due to a refusal by labour to accept a reduction of money wages is not clearly supported by the facts. It is not very plausible to assert that unemployment in the United States in 1932 was due either to labour obstinately refusing to accept a reduction of money-wages or to its obstinately demanding a real wage beyond what the productivity of the economic machine was capable of furnishing . . . . These facts from experience are a *prima facie* ground for questioning the adequacy of the classical analysis. (Keynes, 1936, p. 9)

What Keynes clearly *did* believe, however, was that it is normally money wage rates that are specified in employment contracts so that, at least in the short run, money wages are more sticky than real wages. This was true for changes in either direction.

> Now ordinary experience tells us, beyond doubt, that a situation where labour stipulates (within limits) for a money-wage rather than a real wage, so far from being a mere possibility, is the normal case. (Keynes, 1936, p. 9)

If this were correct, the implications for aggregate supply would be quite straightforward, as we have seen in Chapter 1. The aggregate supply curve, such as that in Figure 2.3, would simply be positively sloped throughout its length. A rise in AD would increase output because higher prices would be associated with *lower* real wages and an increased demand for labour. Higher money wages would increase labour supply.

The reappraisal of Keynes

The simple Keynesian model was dominant in macroeconomics for three decades after the publication of the General Theory. Eventually its preeminence ceased, as more sophisticated Keynesian models emerged, as well as Monetarist and later New Classical competitors. It may be no coincidence that this decline in regard was accompanied by a theoretical reappraisal of 'what Keynes really meant'. This stimulated an upsurge in macroeconomic theory in what was thought to be the tradition of Keynes. However, by splitting the Keynesians off from Keynes it made them even more exposed to criticism than they were before. After the Reformation came the Inquisition.

At one level, the reappraisal was a response to the Monetarist criticism that all Keynes' insights could be collapsed into the statement that 'wages are too high', in which case he might as well have written a short letter to *The Times*, rather than the six books and 384 pages of the General Theory. The reinterpreters asked the question 'how does the economy behave when prices and/or wages are (temporarily) fixed?'. The answer is that there is thoroughgoing disequilibrium; in general, markets will not clear, and agents will be rationed – in particular, they may not be able to sell all their labour, and will be unemployed. And this turns out to matter; disequilibrium in one market 'spills over' into others. We can find ourselves in a state of 'Keynesian unemployment' where there is unemployment due to a deficiency of aggregate demand, even if the real wage is below the market-clearing Walrasian level. The prime movers in this reappraisal of Keynes were Robert Clower (1965) and Axel Leijonhufvud (1968), and later Barro and Grossman (1976) and Malinvaud (1977), although the work of Patinkin (1956) led the way.

The Classical (Walrasian) model of a market economy was hypothesised to work by means of an imaginary 'auctioneer'. Transactors entered the market at the beginning of each 'week' with a set of goods and services on offer (supplies) and a set of demands which they would communicate to the auctioneer. There would then be an adjustment process (*tatonnement* or 'groping'), starting from some initial price vector, such that the prices of goods that were in excess demand would rise and the prices of goods in excess supply would fall. Trade would take place only when prices had been found which cleared the markets, i.e. equilibrium prices. In this way there could never be an excess supply in equilibrium (e.g. unemployment) because prices would adjust until it was eliminated. This is basically a barter economy since goods would now be exchanged for goods. Every offer of a good is simultaneously a demand for another, so Walras' Law (that the sum of excess demands and supplies is zero) must always hold.

One of Clower's contributions was to point out that in an actual monetary economy Walras' Law need not hold. Suppose an initial price vector exists such that some labour is unemployed. Workers have a supply of labour and a demand for goods. However, the demand for goods cannot be expressed in the market until after workers have received money for their labour. Firms are not going to hire labour until they see the money going down for the goods. It is Catch 22. The actual excess supply of labour is matched by a notional demand for goods, but the *effective* demand for goods is deficient, so the workers do not get employed and the goods do not get produced.

What is shown here is that the existence of unemployment does not necessarily imply that the real wage is too high but rather that the whole price mechanism is at fault. False signals are being transmitted and there is no tendency for these signals to be quickly corrected. Prices themselves are relatively sticky so it is the quantities of employment and trade which have to suffer, but there is no presumption as to which prices are wrong so the mere reduction of money wages will not guarantee full employment.

However, the reappraisal, while stimulating an exhaustive theoretical investigation of macroeconomics when markets fail to clear, eventually came to a full stop. The essential problem was that although we came to discover what would happen *if* prices were rigid, we never understood *why* they were. The informal explanations of why prices might be sticky – for example, the implicit contract approach to labour markets – turned out not to give the right results, as wage stickiness may be quite compatible with market-clearing, given the appropriate environment. We discuss some of these issues further in Chapter 5.

Keynesian economic management

We now turn to more directly practical matters. It is clear that macro-economic management in the United Kingdom during the 1950s and 1960s was governed by Keynesian principles. The exchange rate was fixed, so the domestic inflation rate was clearly related to the world rate which was, in turn, very low. Economic policy was largely a tightrope walk with unemployment on one side and balance of payments deficits on the other. If the balance of payments was in crisis, as judged by the official reserves, the economy would be deflated. As a result, unemployment would rise, so reflation would be undertaken as soon as the reserve position seemed satisfactory. This pattern entered common parlance as the 'stop–go' cycle.

The economic instrument which adopted the centre of the stage was undoubtedly the budget, i.e. fiscal policy. Budgets were normally annual events occurring in April, though it became quite commonplace to have 'mini budgets' in July or November. Detailed expenditure plans were generally set in the autumn.[2] The experience of the time appeared to be that slightly excessive expansion ('overheating') would be associated with lower unemployment but slightly higher inflation and a deteriorating balance of payments. Overheating would be halted by a budget which raised taxes or reduced government expenditure. Slack would be taken up by the reverse. Monetary policy was not non-existent, but it was largely a residual determined either by the necessity to finance the government borrowing requirement or by the imperatives of the external balance. The money stock was definitely not a target. If anything was a target it was the level of interest rates. In normal times the aim of the Bank of England would be to maintain an 'orderly market' for government debt. Any run on foreign exchange reserves would be countered, however, by a sharp upward rise in Bank Rate, later called Minimum Lending Rate. Monetary policy was thus constrained by the fiscal stance of the Treasury and by the commitment to a fixed exchange rate. It is now more fully realised how these two factors severely delimit the possibilities of independent monetary policy, particularly when international capital is highly mobile. Inconsistencies which arose in the 1960s were increasingly resolved by imposing quantitative ceilings on bank lending. These remained until they were swept away by the reforms known as 'Competition and Credit Control' which were introduced in September 1971.

This concentration upon fiscal policy probably explains why (in conjunction with the special assumptions mentioned above) the major forecasting models in the United Kingdom were originally built largely as expenditure systems. Indeed, analysis which focuses upon expenditure changes leading through multipliers to income changes, is the core of what most economists think of as Keynesian analysis. Later chapters will clarify 'the retreat' from Keynesian policies. However, a few points can be anticipated at this stage.

It is very important not to underestimate the importance of the external environment for an open economy like the United Kingdom. During the 1950s and early 1960s there was a steady growth in world trade and virtually no inflation in world prices. However, during the late 1960s world inflation began to accelerate, culminating in the commodity price boom and oil price rise in 1973. This has been attributed by some to US policies in financing the Vietnam War and by others to a series of coincidences. If the United Kingdom had retained a fairly restrictive policy during this period the economy would probably have benefited from exported growth. However, the excessive domestic stimulation associated with the policies of the Conservative Chancellor Anthony Barber[3], accompanied by currency depreciation, guaranteed that the internal inflationary experience would be worse than that abroad, as indeed the 1967 devaluation had led to a deterioration of domestic inflation.

The conventional (Keynesian) macroeconomic theory of the time had incorporated a Phillips curve (see Chapter 7) to explain inflation. This had inflation increasing as the pressure of demand increased. However, in the late 1960s and early 1970s there were periods of both rising inflation and rising unemployment. As inflation accelerated in the mid-1970s, with no obvious rise in the level of activity, the Monetarist criticisms of Keynesian economics began to gain credibility. Controlling the money supply became a dominant policy goal.

The Keynesian era is often characterised as a period when the authorities were most free to pursue discretionary fiscal policies. Nothing could be further from the truth. While maintaining a fixed exchange rate, the authorities were heavily constrained. Any tendency to over-expansion would rapidly lead to a balance of payments crisis because of reserve losses. Money supply targets and self-imposed borrowing limits were unnecessary because such limits were implicit in the commitment to fix the exchange rate. Thus, it was not that there was no monetary policy in the 1950s and 1960s, it was just that the policy took a different form. Fixing the exchange rate, in fact, implies a far more severe monetary control mechanism than most alternatives.

Summary

Keynesian economics is about deficient aggregate demand. The popular analysis of the issue offered the simple solution that the government budget could compensate for these deficiencies. The discrediting of pure Keynesian models has resulted from their inadequacy in inflationary periods, and when the economy is forced into recession not by a shortage of demand, but by an adverse supply shock, like higher energy prices. This inadequacy reflects the profound neglect of supply-side factors in the Keynesian approach. However, the Keynesian insight – that changes in aggregate demand affect output as well as prices – continues to have a contemporary relevance as the United Kingdom limps out of what is arguably the most severe recession in the post-war period. This recession was once again largely caused by deficient demand, stemming from a collapse in consumers' spending and a high exchange rate.

Notes

1. A more sophisticated version of wage rigidity is that wages are temporarily fixed, as wages are typically set in contracts that span several periods – often twelve months in the United Kingdom. This type of model – known under the heading of overlapping or staggered contracts – is discussed further in Chapters 4 and 5.
2. The shift away from fiscal policy may help to explain why the government has now elected to have a single budget in the autumn at which both taxation and expenditure plans are determined.

3. It is the curse of the Conservative Chancellor to be mainly remembered for an imprudent reflation. Barber is associated forever with the 'Barber Boom'; Nigel Lawson, despite his reforming instincts, may also turn out to find immortality only in the phrase 'Lawson Boom'.

3

Monetarists

'Monetarism' is a term first coined by the late Karl Brunner in 1968. It refers to an approach to macroeconomic policy which gives control of the money supply a central role, particularly in the control of inflation. This approach became important in the United Kingdom in the mid-1970s when, after the abandonment of pegged exchange rates, inflation reached its highest peacetime level since the reign of Henry VIII. The cause of this inflation was widely accepted to have been (mainly) the rapid monetary growth which followed the Competition and Credit Control reforms of 1971. Figure 3.1 shows the rate of growth of broad money, M4, and the inflation rate from 1963 to 1992.

Monetary targets were an explicit tool of both the Labour Government after 1976 and the Conservative Government (elected in May 1979). However, faith in the Monetarist approach was severely dented in the early 1980s when financial innovation (see Chapter 8) shifted the underlying money demand relationships. Monetary targets were abandoned in 1985, even by a government committed (allegedly) to a Monetarist strategy. That there followed a renewed bout of inflation may be no coincidence. An exchange rate target was adopted in October 1990, when the United Kingdom joined the ERM of the European Monetary System (EMS). However, the United Kingdom was forced to leave the system by speculative pressure in September 1992. The guiding principles of monetary policy are thus still in doubt.

Monetarists are sceptical about the possibility of successful stabilisation policy. There are 'Long and Variable Lags' involved in policy formation and implementation and there is a good chance that government action to control a cycle will make it worse. The effects of the policy will impact when the condition it was aimed to correct has already changed. In this respect,

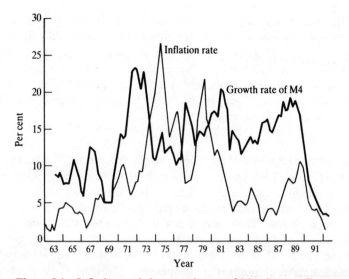

Figure 3.1 Inflation and the growth rate of M4. Source: Datastream.

Monetarists favour rules versus discretion – whether it should be a money supply rule or an external convertibility rule is more controversial (even among Monetarists) though the 'correct' approach will vary from country to country.

Confusion should be avoided between the term 'Monetarism' used here and the popular usage which links it to political leaders like Margaret Thatcher and Ronald Reagan. While Mrs Thatcher claimed to want to use monetary policy to control inflation, in reality her monetary policy was far from what would have been recommended by Monetarists (see Chapter 8). Indeed, her government abandoned monetary targeting in 1986. The distinguishing feature of Mrs Thatcher's ideology was not Monetarism, rather it was *laisser-faire* liberalism. She wanted to disengage government from the economy and wherever possible free up market force. This is discussed further in the last section of this chapter.

Let us now look at Monetarism in the context of textbook models.

Money in static models

Monetarism is first discussed in the context of textbook models, as set out in Chapter 1. Model I has no room for a Monetarist interpretation since it has no explicit monetary sector or indeed assets of any kind. In Models II and III the cases which can be identified with Monetarism are often also called 'Classical' cases.

The orthodox version of the Classical case derives from what can be thought of as a special case of equation (1.9). This special case relates to what is commonly known as 'the quantity theory of money', though in Classical economics it would be better called 'The Monetary Theory of the Price Level'. In modern economics it is part of the theory of the demand for real money balances. The quantity theory was based on an identity known as the equation of exchange:

$$MV \equiv pT \tag{3.1}$$

where M is the number of units of money in circulation; V is the number of times per period each unit is used (velocity); p is the average price level per unit transaction, and T is the number of unit transactions per period. This merely says that the value of money paid out in transactions is equal to the value of goods sold. The theory is achieved by adding the assumptions that V and T are constant, or at least exogenous to the monetary sector. Hence, we have a theory that prices are proportional to the money stock (which in a gold standard model was exogenous).

The modern version of the quantity theory is not based on the turnover of money like the equation of exchange, but rather on the average money balances demanded to be held. The primogenitor of the demand for money function is, ironically, known as the Cambridge Equation, since it was associated with such famous Cambridge economists as Pigou and Robertson. The Cambridge Equation says either that individuals hold nominal money balances in proportion to their nominal income or that they hold real money balances in proportion to their real income.

$$M = kYp \tag{3.2}$$

$$\frac{M}{p} = kY \tag{3.3}$$

where M is the money stock, Y is income, p is the price level and k is a constant. By the late 1950s, however, when Friedman tried to provide empirical support in the United States for a relationship similar to (3.3), this equation was no longer part of the apparatus of Cambridge economists. Indeed, it was complete anathema to most of them.

The only differences between (3.3) and equation (1.11) are, first, that here income is not presumed to be fixed at its full employment level and, second, the interest rate is missing here. The implications of this for the IS–LM diagram are straightforward. If we consider the fixed price level case, it is clear in Figure 1.2 that, if the demand for money does not depend upon the rate of interest, the demand-for-money line is vertical. This means that for each level of the money supply there is only one level of income at which the demand and supply of money will be equal. The implications for the LM curve are shown in Figure 3.2. The LM curve is vertical.

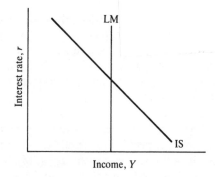

Figure 3.2 LM curve with interest inelastic money demand.

The policy implications of this case of the model should be obvious. Monetary policy means changing the money supply which shifts the LM curve. Fiscal policy shifts the IS curve. If income is the target variable it is clear that fiscal policy will have no effect on income, only on the interest rate. Monetary policy is the tool needed to control income. It is worth noting that, although textbooks often call this the Classical case, it is far from classical in the fixed price level case. Only at full employment could Figure 3.2 represent the Classical case, and as a result monetary policy would only affect the price level and not real income.

It must be emphasised immediately that not even extreme Monetarists would be likely to subscribe to the vertical LM theory today. Although Friedman in his early empirical work in the United States claimed to have estimated a demand-for-money function in which the interest rate was insignificant, the vast bulk of work done since has found the interest rate to be important. So, while this case is of historical interest, it is not to be taken seriously as a practical possibility.

An alternative interpretation of the 'Classical' case, and one which Monetarists may be more likely to subscribe to, can be thought of as being represented by Model IIIB. Here there is a supply side to the economy. Both labour supply and labour demand depend upon the *real* wage. This means that there is no change in aggregate output in response to shifts in aggregate demand. Changes in aggregate demand only affect the price level. This case is illustrated in Figure 1.6 where S_B is the aggregate supply curve. A shift in aggregate demand from D_0 to D_1 will raise the price level from p_0 to p_1 but there will be no change in real income. This is the case in which the price level is proportional to the money stock. An increase in money shifts the LM curve and the aggregate demand curve to the right. Prices rise, as above, restoring the real money supply to its original level – shifting LM back to its original position but with a permanently higher price level.

This is actually a very significant piece of analysis and should be contrasted with the analysis in Model II, though it should be emphasised that even those who do subscribe to this view would regard it as a *long-run* case and not an accurate description of the short-run behaviour of the economy. We shall see in Chapter 7 how short-run behaviour is incorporated into this framework.

In Model II there seemed to be an important distinction between monetary and fiscal policy. However, in Model III monetary and fiscal policy can be seen as complementary aspects of aggregate demand policy. Aggregate demand policy itself is of limited use, especially in Model IIIB, because real output is not affected in the long run by shifts in aggregate demand. Only the price level changes. Thus, even in this simple static model there would seem to be little mileage to be obtained from making a critical distinction between monetary and fiscal policy. This point is reinforced when it is realised that the possibilities for independent monetary and fiscal policies are severely limited anyway. Deficits have to be financed, and this financing has portfolio effects even if deficits do not lead directly to money supply increases.

To summarise so far, monetary policy is of no importance in Model I. In Model II there is a clear difference between monetary and fiscal policy and whichever is the more powerful in controlling national income depends on the shapes of the IS and LM curves. In Model IIIB real national output is independent of both monetary and fiscal policies in the aggregate. It is this last case which comes closest to the spirit of modern Monetarism, though there are many aspects of the latter which have still to be mentioned, especially with regard to the short-run behaviour of the economy.

Indeed, the major distinction between Monetarists and New Classical economics is precisely with respect to the short-run behaviour of the economy. The former would regard aggregate supply as responding to an increase in aggregate demand in the short run, whatever the nature of that demand increase; the latter claim that only 'unanticipated' changes in demand will have real effects. About the long run, there would be little disagreement.

The real balance effect and the transmission mechanism

Important to an understanding of modern Monetarism is the story about how changes in the money supply are transmitted through the economy. The mechanism built into Models II and III is essentially the link proposed by Keynes which many would now see as insufficient. Basically, this relies upon changes in money stock first causing a portfolio disequilibrium.

There is an excess money supply in portfolios and, therefore, excess demand for bonds. This leads to a rise in the price of bonds, which is equivalent to a fall in the rate of interest. The fall in the rate of interest then produces an increase in investment which through the multiplier effect influences income. As we have seen, much of the Keynesian disregard for monetary policy arose from the failure to find convincing evidence of a significant interest elasticity of investment expenditure. Many in the Monetarist camp, however, believe that the link from money to expenditure is much more direct. The direct link is often called the 'real balance effect'.

The earliest form of real balance effect was known as the Pigou Effect. This was usually applied to the behaviour of an economy in a depression when the price level was low. The effect arises because the low price level means that the real value of money balances is high. Consumers, in effect, make a capital gain on their money holdings and as a result spend more than they otherwise would for a given real income. The Pigou Effect was originally presented as an analytical device which would stabilise the macroeconomy, since it meant that prices would not fall indefinitely.

The real balance effect is more general than the Pigou Effect, though it relates to the same behavioural phenomenon. Anything which causes real money balances (or perhaps real liquid assets) to deviate from their desired level will cause a change in expenditures while the desired level of real balances is out of equilibrium. Thus a rise in the money supply could lead directly to an increase in expenditure. Instead of the excess money balances being reflected entirely as an excess demand for bonds, there would also be an excess demand for goods. The system as a whole cannot reduce its holdings of nominal money balances, so the excess real money balances have to be eliminated by either price level or real income increases until the nominal money supply is just demanded. Friedman has summarised this process as follows:

> If individuals as a whole were to try to reduce the number of dollars they held, they could not all do so, they would simply be playing a game of musical chairs. In trying to do so, however, they would raise the flow of expenditures and of money incomes since each would be trying to spend more than he receives; in the process adding to someone else's receipts, and, reciprocally, finding his own higher than anticipated because of the attempt by still others to spend more than they receive. In the process, prices would tend to rise, which would reduce the real value of cash balances, that is, the quantity of goods and services that the cash balances will buy.
>
> While individuals are thus frustrated in their attempt to reduce the number of dollars they hold, they succeed in achieving an equivalent change in their position, for the rise of money income and in prices reduces the ratio of these balances to their income and also the real value of these balances. The process will continue until this ratio and this real value are in accord with their desires. (M. Friedman, 1959, p.609).

There are considerable theoretical problems in specifying a real balance effect in a static macro model, since it must of necessity be a disequilibrium phenomenon. The simplicity of the Keynesian model derives in large part from the separability of expenditures from the choice of financial assets. However, in empirical work there is strong evidence that asset effects are important in explaining consumption, especially in the late 1980s when wealth effects were of substantial size. Muellbauer and Murphy (1989), for example, include liquid and non-liquid assets in their preferred consumption function. They also make an important distinction between households who are credit rationed (i.e. cannot borrow all they might want). The unwinding of these credit restrictions is an important part of the financial innovation of the 1980s. (See also Deaton (1992) for a discussion of liquidity effects on consumption.)

The modern literature incorporates the real balance effect as part of a two-stage process. First, there is an underlying long-run demand function for real money balance. This is the equilibrium relationship specified by the theory. Second, there is an 'error correction' mechanism (ECM) which determines the dynamics of adjustment. In response to shocks, such as a money supply change, the ECM determines the speed at which the disequilibrium is eliminated (see Hendry and Ericsson, 1991).

Modern Monetarism

The focus of attention of modern Monetarism has moved on from the framework of the IS–LM model. There are a number of reasons for this including:
(a) the lack of dynamics,
(b) the absence of a supply side to the model,
(c) the absence of a government budget constraint and
(d) the inappropriateness of the model to an open economy.
The lack of dynamics is particularly crucial since it is now the rate of inflation rather than the price level which is judged to be important and expectations come to have a central role in behaviour. Consider, for example, the following statement by Laidler.

> An increase in the rate of expansion of the money supply to a pace faster than that necessary to validate an ongoing anticipated inflation will first lead to a build-up of real money balances, whose implicit own rate of return will therefore begin to fall relative to that on other assets. As a consequence, a process of substitution into all other assets and into current consumption will be set in motion, with interest rates, both observable and unobservable, falling. The ensuing increase in current production will set in motion a multiplier process . . ..

Along with the increase in output just postulated goes a tendency for firms to increase their prices and for money wages to rise to levels in excess of the values these variables were initially expected to take. Given that there initially exists an expected rate of inflation, this involves an acceleration of the actual inflation rate relative to that expected rate. If the actual rate influences the expected rate, the latter must also begin to rise. In its turn, an increase in the expected rate of inflation has two inter-related effects on variables involved in the transmission mechanism. It puts upward pressure on the rates of interest that assets denominated in nominal terms bear, and in increasing the opportunity cost of holding money, accentuates the very portfolio disequilibrium which sets going the first stage of the transmission mechanism and which accelerating inflation begins to offset. It also causes the inflation rate to accelerate further through its effect on price setting behaviour . . . ..

Because . . . the expected and actual inflation rates will differ so long as output is not at its 'natural' level, the new equilibrium, like the initial one, will see the economy operating at such a level of real output. The expected rate of inflation will be higher in this new equilibrium, and so the quantity of real balances held by the public will be smaller. *If* money is 'super-neutral' so that the 'natural' output level is independent of the inflation rate, and of any past history of disequilibrium in the economy (both of these being dubious assumptions supported by no empirical evidence of which I am aware, and the former being contradicted by a good deal of theoretical argument), then we would also expect to find real rates of interest returning to their initial levels, with nominal rates having increased by the same amount as the inflation rate. If money is not 'super-neutral' then we might find real rates either higher or lower in the new equilibrium. In either event, though, a higher and more rapidly rising volume of nominal expenditure would be associated with higher nominal interest rates. If real balances are to be lower in the new equilibrium, then, on average, during the transition towards it the rate of inflation must exceed the rate of monetary expansion. Moreover, if nominal interest rates at first fall, but end up at a level higher than that ruling initially, they must on average rise during the transition. (Laidler, 1978, pp. 170–1).

This statement of the transmission mechanism may have been controversial in the 1970s, but it would be considered 'mainstream' today. It raises several important issues which will be pursued in detail in later chapters. The most important of these are the 'natural rate' hypothesis, which is discussed in Chapter 7, and the implications of a floating exchange rate of a 'process of substitution into all other assets', including foreign assets (discussed in Chapter 6). Also important, of course, is the issue of 'expectations'. It is the hypothesis of 'rational expectations' in the presence of continuous market-clearing that distinguishes 'New Classical' macro-economics from Monetarism. Chapter 4 is largely concerned with this issue.

Demand for money

It would be a misrepresentation of the Monetarist story to move on without saying something about the demand for money. One major tenet of the Monetarist tradition is that the demand for money is a stable function of a few variables. This contention was supported by a considerable amount of empirical work. There has been a huge amount of empirical work in this tradition in the last twenty years and we can only give a flavour of this here. (See Cuthbertson (1985) for a survey of this area and Cuthbertson and Barlow (1991) for an update.)

A typical functional form for the underlying behavioural relationship is:

$$\frac{M}{p} = \alpha Y^{\beta} r^{\gamma} \tag{3.4}$$

which, when all variables were transformed into logarithms, could be estimated as:

$$\ln \frac{M}{p} = \alpha + \beta \ln Y + \gamma \ln r \tag{3.5}$$

where M is the nominal money stock, p is a price index, Y is real GDP and r is an interest rate on a substitute asset. Recent methodology would treat (3.4) as the long-run demand function and would use cointegration techniques to test for the existence of a long-run relationship.

Whether or not equation (3.5) can be estimated directly as a demand function depends upon what supply conditions are presumed to be. In principle, equation (3.5) alone could be a demand function, a supply function or some combination of the two. The assumption usually used to 'identify' equation (3.5) as a demand function was that money supply was demand-determined. Under fixed exchange rates or where the authorities are pegging interest rates, the assumption that money is demand-determined may be appropriate, but it is not universally suitable. (However, in modern methodology, if (3.5) is a cointegrating vector, estimation is appropriate anyway.)

The empirical problem, which has led to a decline in interest in Monetarism in the United Kingdom, is that demand for money functions have not turned out to be stable – at least not convincingly so. As a result, the stability of demand for money has not proved to be the foundation of successful monetary targeting. In each of the last three decades major shifts have occurred which create work for econometricians but do not give confidence in the generality of their estimated equations.

Relationships such as equation (3.5) estimated on 1960s data broke down in the early 1970s. This followed both a change in exchange rate policy and the change in domestic monetary policy known as Competition and Credit Control. (Indeed, several major macroeconomic relationships broke down in the 1970s, including the consumption function and the simple Phillips curve.) The breakdown was particularly bad when using M3, the broader definition of money, which includes interest-bearing time deposits as well as current account deposits. However, this is not surprising in the period when banks started to use interest rates to attract deposits. The mere fact that money demand equations which fitted well on earlier data broke down in the early 1970s should not be taken as evidence that such functions no longer exist. The truth may be simply that structural changes made the old estimation techniques inappropriate.

It was shown by Artis and Lewis (1976) that a stable relationship of sorts could be fitted. They dropped the assumption that the money stock is demand-determined and substituted for it the assumption that supply is exogenous. The equation estimated is then an interest rate adjustment equation rather than a money demand equation. Its form is

$$\ln r = \alpha + \beta \ln Y + \gamma \ln M + \delta \ln r_{t-1} \qquad (3.6)$$

They showed that this fits well for periods which included data from after 1971 as well as from before. However, Hendry and Ericsson (1991) present estimates of a demand for money function fitted over a long run of data. This has a more complex dynamic form than equation (3.5) and it appears to fit the data well, without making any allowances for structural change.

Even greater challenges to the notion of a stable money demand function arose out of the events of the 1980s. While money supply targeting had become the central tool of counterinflation policy in 1976 (and given even greater importance by the post-1979 Thatcher Government) the financial innovations (see Chapter 8) of the 1980s led to declining confidence in the significance of the targeted aggregates. The abandonment of the 'Corset' in 1980 and subsequent innovations in the banking system (such as interest on cheque-book deposits) created swings in velocity which raised further doubts about the stability of underlying demand. (This change in velocity can be seen implicitly in Figure 3.1. Broad money growth well into double figures continued right through the 1980s but inflation only rose noticeably at the end of the decade.) Charles Goodhart argued that any relationship that was used for policy targeting would break down. This became known as 'Goodhart's Law'. The law makes obvious sense if quantitative restrictions such as the Corset are used to achieve the target, but there is no reason to suppose that targeting is always the wrong thing to do.

Taylor (1987) claimed to have found a stable demand function for M3, even when data for the 1980s were included, when allowance was made for interest payments on deposits. Hall, Henry and Wilcox (1989) were able to estimate stable equilibrium relationships for all the main UK monetary aggregates on data including most of the 1980s, but only with the help of considerable ingenuity in constructing special variables to capture 'financial innovation' and other effects. Whether their elaborate specifications will prove robust remains to be seen, but it is certain that the monetary authorities could never have deduced these relationships *ex ante*, in order to use them as a basis for policy. Indeed, in the face of instability of traditional relationships the authorities abandoned even token targeting.[1] Some academics meanwhile had been looking for an alternative approach which could cope explicitly with the changing nature of 'money'.

William Barnett (1982) suggested that the measurement of 'money' was fundamentally flawed. Standard measures of money supply add up assets which are intrinsically different (such as currency plus cheque accounts plus savings accounts). Aggregation theory suggests that assets can only be aggregated by simple addition if they are perfect substitutes. This does not hold in the case of the components of broad money. This aggregation error will be especially serious when there are significant changes in the relative returns on different components – such as when interest is introduced on current accounts.

The solution proposed by Barnett is to construct an index of 'monetary services' in which the weights on potential components are variable and related to the interest yield (or user cost) of each component. (See Barnett, Fisher and Serletis (1992) for a survey of the micro-foundations of aggregate money demand.) The methodology favoured by Barnett for construction of indicators of monetary conditions was first set out by a French mathematician named François Divisia. Hence the resulting index is known as a 'Divisia' index. Belongia and Chrystal (1991) find that the Divisia aggregate outperforms standard simple sum aggregates as an indicator of monetary conditions in the United Kingdom. Other evidence supporting the Divisia approach can be found in Drake and Chrystal (1994). Chrystal and MacDonald (1993) find that the Divisia money measure gives superior performance in exchange rate models compared with simple sum aggregates.

A variant on the Divisia methodology was suggested by Rotemberg (1991). He called his measure the 'Currency Equivalent' or CE aggregate. It varies slightly from Divisia in the way in which the weights are calculated but conceptually it is very similar. The CE aggregate has an advantage over Divisia in that it can easily incorporate new assets while Divisia requires continuity. Also the calculations required to construct a CE aggregate are even easier than those for Divisia.

The Bank of England has recently taken an interest in Divisia aggregates (see Fisher, Hudson and Pradhan, 1993) so it is possible that they will be used as an indicator for official purposes. However, it seems unlikely that they will become the main targeted indicator.[2]

The whole structure of traditional monetary systems may change in

Europe if the European Community goes down the route of introducing a single currency as agreed in the Maastricht Treaty of 1992. This single currency may appear as early as 1998 but its introduction is supposed to be mandatory by 1999. There is now considerable doubt surrounding this timetable. However, if a single currency were ever adopted, and Britain signed up for it, then the monetary policy problem will change fundamentally. It will be the European Central Bank which will be charged with the task of maintaining stable prices in Europe, and to achieve this it will have to develop monetary indicators at the EC level. Hence, it will be EC money demand that is of central interest rather than that in the United Kingdom alone. Studies of demand for money in the United Kingdom will no doubt become as rare as studies of money demand in Yorkshire! (See Chapter 9 for a discussion of the single currency.)

Money and economic policy

The perception of money and its role in the economy has changed somewhat over time. It is important to realise that changing views about money are related to changing institutional structures which, indeed, imply a varying position for money and monetary control. It is, for example, no coincidence that the period in which Keynesians were able to relegate money to a passive and subsidiary role (at least in small open economies like Britain) was a period of fixed exchange rates and stable world prices. As we shall see in Chapter 6, a fixed exchange rate is a very rigid form of monetary control. Let us, then, consider briefly the changing view of the appropriate macroeconomic policy with special reference to monetary policy.

A hundred years ago there was no real macroeconomics. The economy as a whole was not seen to be something over which the government had any control. Prices in markets were determined by forces of demand and supply. If there were an excess supply of anything, its price would adjust downwards until the market cleared (at least in theory). The only macroeconomic relationship that was widely accepted was the so-called Quantity Theory of Money. Recall that, for the most part, we are talking about a world in which the amount of money in the economy was related more-or-less directly to the amount of gold in the country. Although paper money circulated, this was exchangeable into gold with the bank issuing the paper. This meant that the amount of paper currency banks were prepared to print was limited by the gold they held in their reserves. If there was an inflow of gold into the economy this meant that banks would be prepared to print more currency as they now had bigger reserves. Two important points should be emphasised.

First, in the 'gold standard' system the supply of money in the economy was determined automatically by the combination of inflows from abroad and the behaviour of a large number of banks. The government had no direct role in this story, even for some time after the note issue was centralised. Second, it was obvious to all observers that periods of inflation followed periods of gold inflows, i.e. rises in the money supply – hence the formulation of the Quantity Theory of Money.

In its simplest form this says that the aggregate price index will be proportional to the money stock. This should not be objectionable since a 'price' is the number of units of money that exchange for a unit of a good. If there is twice as much money for the same volume of goods you would expect prices, on average, to double.

Figure 3.3 shows index numbers for the broad money stock M4 and the retail price index (RPI). While there may have been some relationship between these two series in the past, it is precisely the dramatic growth in M4 relative to prices in the 1980s which has raised doubts about the monetarist strategy and led to the abandonment of monetary targeting. This does not mean that there is no connection between money and inflation, only that innovations in the financial system have made these connections harder to identify (see Chapter 8).

In the Classical system causation ran from money to aggregate prices, but money was not in the control of the government. Relative prices adjusted in individual markets to equate demand and supply, so here again there was no role for government in general. What of the 'budget' in this world? The answer to this is very simple. Budgets were entirely an exercise

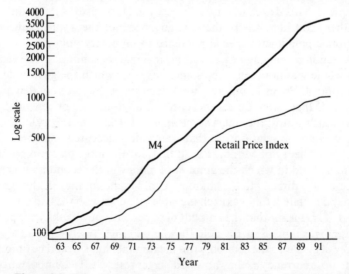

Figure 3.3 Money stock and the price level (1963 = 100). Source: Datastream.

in raising revenue to pay for the government's expenditures. The guiding principle was the 'balanced budget' so that taxes were set to raise just enough money to pay for the government's intended expenditures. Clearly something changed. What was it? There were, in fact, two major changes – one was structural and the other was intellectual.

The important structural change was the break from gold. This happened piecemeal, but was completed by the time the post-Second World War domestic and international monetary system was established. In place of gold in the reserves of the banking system were the liabilities of the Treasury and the Bank of England. The fact could not be avoided that monetary policy was now a matter of central policy concern. For twenty years or so, however, monetary policy seemed to take a back seat to fiscal policy.

Fiscal policy, as we have seen, was the product of the Keynesian revolution in economic thought. Monetary policy in the two decades after World War Two was largely passive. This arose from the commitment to fix the exchange rate. The connection may not seem obvious, but it is very important. If there was too much money circulating in Britain people would want to spend more abroad – either on goods or on investments. To spend abroad domestic residents had to buy foreign exchange. To stop the price of foreign exchange rising, the Bank of England had to buy the extra pounds offered *with dollars*. In other words, if too much money were generated the Bank had to buy it back with reserves of foreign exchange. Hence, even if too much money was 'printed' this would lead to a loss of reserves and a subsequent reversal of policy long before it has caused inflation of prices. In a sense, fixing the exchange rate *is* a rule for controlling the money supply and, in effect, ties domestic inflation to that in the world economy.

The only monetary problem that governments had was how to finance the budget deficits that fiscal policy required without leading directly to a loss of reserves. The problem arises from the fact that short-term government debt is a reserve asset for the banking system. So government borrowing from banks can lead directly to banks increasing the money supply. This is what is normally meant by the government 'printing' money. Inconsistencies in this area of policy were met in the 1960s by the imposition of quantitative ceilings on bank lending which, in effect, swept the problem under the carpet by inhibiting the major clearing banks and stimulating the growth of uncontrolled 'secondary' banks.

The groundwork for early Monetarism was laid by two separate areas of academic work, both contributed to by Milton Friedman. The first was the demonstration that the aggregate demand for money in the economy was a stable function of a few variables. This underlay the analysis which was offered on the effects of increasing the money supply. The rule of thumb was that a rise in the money stock would have transitory effect on output after about a year and a permanent (upward) effect on prices after about two years. Other important ideas were developed in the context of the famous Phillips Curve (see Chapter 7). This had become widely accepted in the early 1960s as establishing that there was a stable trade-off between inflation and unemployment. If the government were prepared to accept an increase of inflation it could achieve a reduction of unemployment. The revised theory, however, held that if unemployment was reduced below what Friedman called the 'natural' rate, this would not lead to stable inflation, but *ever-accelerating* inflation.

The combined effect of these two developments was to reassert the validity of the Quantity Theory, at least in the long run. Expanding the money stock could stimulate employment and output temporarily, but ultimately this effect would be reversed (or even more than reversed) and the only lasting effect would be a rise in prices in proportion to the rise in money stock. However, the relevance of these ideas was not generally appreciated in the United Kingdom in the late 1960s when they hit the academic community because, as we have seen, the money supply was effectively controlled by the commitment to pegging the exchange rate as well as by direct controls on the banks. Indeed, it is ironic to recall that after the election of 1970 an incoming Tory government inherited a balance of payments surplus, a budget surplus and a controlled money supply. The next three years changed all that in a way that was little short of disastrous.

Again, a structural change was integral to what followed. In fact, there were two important changes in 1971. The first was the floating of the dollar which was implied by the Nixon speech of 15 August. The second was the domestic reform known as Competition and Credit Control, introduced in September. This removed the direct controls on the banking system and had the effect of allowing the money supply, as measured by M3, to grow at a rate in the order of 25 per cent per annum until the end of 1973 (see Figure 3.1, this shows M4 growth which is now the standard broad money series; M3 growth was faster than that of M4 in the 1971–73 period). It should be no surprise to find that inflation reached about 25 per cent in 1975 (the highest level of peacetime inflation in the United Kingdom since the sixteenth century). The reason that this was now possible was that the pound was floating. Why did floating the pound have anything to do with it?

Monetary expansion with fixed exchange rates did not lead to inflation because, as we have seen, the Bank of England would buy back pounds with dollars to stop the exchange rate falling. Another way to think of this is that tying the value of our money to that of the dollar also ties our inflation rates together within limits. Monetary expansion with floating rates, however, is very different. Since the central bank does not buy back the pounds, people who find they have too many pounds spend them. If the economy as a whole is spending more than its income, this means there is a balance of payments deficit. The value of the pound *vis-à-vis* the dollar starts to fall. This leads directly to the sterling price of imports rising and prices in the shops soon follow. Under fixed exchange rates a monetary expansion leads directly to a reserve outflow. With floating exchange rates it leads to a depreciating currency and a build-up of domestic inflation as price rises feed through in wage rises and so on.

The expansionary monetary policy of 1971–73 was accompanied by a major fiscal stimulus following the March 1972 Budget of Mr Barber which set the course for the massive budget deficits of the late 1970s. There can be no serious doubts that the policies of the 1971–73 period were irresponsible or incompetent (or both) and Britain suffered from them for at least the next decade. The central Monetarist proposition is substantially borne out by the evidence of this period, as Figure 3.1 (see also Figure I.2) demonstrates. A massive monetary expansion led first to a short-lived boom and later to rapid inflation. This would have been true with or without the Oil Crisis which just made things a little worse. (One of the great myths which survives from this time is that British inflation was caused by the oil shock. West Germany had the same oil shock but did not have inflation above 8 per cent. Britain's inflation was undoubtedly dominantly home grown.)

Another irony of the 1970s experience is that the Labour Government of 1974–79 was the first to admit that the Monetarists were basically right. It was the Labour Chancellor of the Exchequer, Denis Healey, who intro-duced cash limits on Government expenditure as well as money supply targets. In this sense, at least, everybody became Monetarist for a while. Without fixed exchange rates or the gold standard, there has to be *some* method for controlling the money supply to avoid runaway inflation. There is still disagreement, however, even within the Monetarist camp, about how rigid monetary control needs to be. More importantly, perhaps, there is disagreement about how fast an ongoing inflation can be brought down by monetary control. Many, including Friedman himself, have argued for gradualism on the grounds that very tight monetary policy has severe real effects before it works to control prices. Others, such as Hayek, favour a 'short, sharp, shock'. Those in the latter category would now be more likely to fall into the New Classical camp which will be discussed in Chapter 4.

Monetary policy targets were central to the policy strategy of the Thatcher Government after 1979. A gradual tightening of monetary growth rates was intended to bring down inflation over time. In practice, however, the Thatcher Government did not stick to its monetarist strategy very long. There is a continuing controversy as to what extent monetary policy was genuinely the cause of the 1980 recession (see Chapter 12 and Chrystal, 1984). However, in practice, monetary targeting was abandoned by the

Thatcher Government in the early 1980s and, partly as a result of this, inflationary forces were allowed to build up again. (For an extended discussion of the financial innovation of the 1980s and the problems of monetary policy in the late 1980s see Chapter 8.) Broad money growth of 15–20 per cent per annum was permitted for several years in the mid-1980s (see Figure 3.1). Eventually, money supply targets were replaced by exchange rate targets. However, even the exchange rate target had to be abandoned in September 1992 as a result of speculative pressure.

The reasons for the abandonment of monetary targeting were that the favoured measures of money – originally M3 and later M4 – ceased to have the same stable relationship with the economy as had existed in the 1970s (apparently). Hence, discretion dominated rules in monetary affairs. Unfortunately judgement has to be good for policy to be good. Such was not the case in the late 1980s.

In 1993 the United Kingdom found itself again in search of a guiding principle for monetary policy, having suffered over 550 per cent cumulative inflation in two decades, but seemingly having learned very little from the experience. Chancellor of the Exchequer, Norman Lamont, adopted guiding ranges of M0 and M4 as potential indicators of monetary policy, notwithstanding the fact that M4 had been abandoned earlier as an indicator because of the instability of its link with the economy (velocity). Meanwhile, the United Kingdom had lurched from the excessive looseness in monetary policy of 1988 to the excessive tightness of 1990–92. The Monetarist concern that discretionary monetary policy would add to cycles in the economy rather than smooth them was substantially supported by the UK experience. This is particularly alarming given that the government which delivered these extreme lurches in policy was meant to be sympathetic to Monetarism.

Thatcher and Monetarism

The Monetarism that has been outlined above can be associated with statements such as 'There is a stable demand function for money' or 'Inflation is always and everywhere a monetary phenomenon'. It is possible to agree with these and yet disagree with the policies pursued by Prime Minister Margaret Thatcher in the years 1979–91, though she was commonly labelled 'Monetarist'. Indeed, many true Monetarists doubt that Mrs Thatcher was a Monetarist at all. Her government largely ignored its own monetary targets even when it had them, abandoned monetary targeting and rekindled inflation, and then opted for a very costly exchange rate target. As the aim of Monetarism is to achieve a stable monetary environment without recourse to big swings in policy stance, the Thatcher incumbency would score very low in Monetarist popularity polls. The guiding principles of Thatcherism were in fact much more closely related to nineteenth-century liberal *laisser-faire* economics. It is based on a belief in the benefits of the outcome of the working of free market forces, with government participation reduced to a minimum. It is true that many Monetarists, including Milton Friedman, would support the liberal agenda. This is, perhaps, the reason for confusion of terminology. However, this is the Friedman of *Capitalism and Freedom* and *Free to Choose*, rather than the Friedman of *Monetary History of the United States* and *Monetary Trends in the US and UK*.

Thatcherism, then, is associated with a particular view about the role of government in the economy. It is the minimalist view – the 'get Big Government off the back of the People' approach and the 'Taxation is theft' view. Questions as to the appropriate role of government in a market economy and questions about monetary institutions and their control are quite separate. The underlying theory of relevance to the former is not traditionally regarded as part of macroeconomics. Accordingly, a full discussion goes beyond the scope of this book. An introduction to the main issues is available in Alt and Chrystal (1983), especially Chapter 1.

Summary

Monetarism, as the name implies, stresses the role of money in the economy. The link between money and inflation is particularly strong, especially in the long run, when the economy has fully adjusted. In the short run, money can have real effects. However, the presence of 'long and variable' lags makes the use of monetary policy as a control instrument inappropriate – hence the recommendation of rules for the control of monetary growth. The exchange rate regime makes a big difference to the way money should be viewed. With a fixed exchange rate the money stock is demand-determined. Floating exchange rates make money supply an issue for the domestic authorities to determine.

In 1993, after a two-year period when an exchange rate target was adopted, the United Kingdom found itself with the need to reestablish guiding principles of monetary policy. In the longer term this need may be removed by the creation of a single currency for Europe.

The aim of Monetarism was to create policy rules which would generate a stable low inflation environment. There have been three major recessions (and inflationary booms) in the United Kingdom over the last two decades, in all of which irresponsible monetary policy had a role. The promised land has, thus, not been reached. Monetarism may be blameless but the politicians who campaigned under the Monetarist banner cannot be.

Notes

1. After departure from the ERM in September 1992, the authorities established an inflation target but continued to monitor M0 and M4.
2. The Bank of England now publishes a Divisia series for the United Kingdom in its Quarterly Bulletin.

4

New Classical macroeconomics

For about a decade from the mid-1970s, the bulk of theoretical macro-economic attention was directed towards the work of the New Classical School of economists. What is vitally important is to make a clear distinction between this group and Monetarists, with whom many have confused them. It is certainly true that New Classical ideas evolved out of Monetarism and that many former Monetarists have travelled on. What is not true is that it is safe to subsume one set of ideas within the other set.

The distinguishing feature of New Classical economics is often said to be the 'rational expectations hypothesis'. This is indeed important, but it is clear that three other assumptions also play crucial roles in the typical New Classical analysis. These are the assumption of clearing markets, the natural rate hypothesis and the nature of the aggregate supply curve. Logically, these three are really only two independent assumptions (i.e. about the nature of the supply curve, and whether the economy is on both the demand and supply curves at all times). However, they are stated this way for ease of recognition. The natural rate hypothesis in its stronger version requires both long-run market-clearing and a specific supply structure to the economy.

The main drift

For the New Classical economist the economy is made up of actors who consistently pursue the maximisation of some clearly-defined objective function. The actors trade with one another in well-organised markets. Trade takes place at market-clearing prices such that all who wish to trade at the going prices are able to do so. This far, the framework would be recognised by a Classical economist. Novelty arises from the fact that the *New* Classical economist will not locate these actors in a static world, but rather in a stochastic environment. The world is one in which there are *recurrent shocks* to the system – bad harvests, earthquakes, sunspots, policy shifts, exogenous taste changes, wars, etc. In other words, while actors are rationally trying to respond to the price signals of the market, these signals are 'noisy'. The fact that they are noisy has important implications. The New Classical world is often characterised as being 'perfect' in the sense of full information and costless adjustment. Some New Classical models are like this, but these are not the interesting ones. It is central to the New Classical explanations of macroeconomic fluctuations that information is incomplete and that some adjustments are costly – that is, prior commitments are recurrently made.

An individual does not wait to find out the complete set of prices and then make all the supply/demand decisions at those actual prices (as might be the case in the presence of a Walrasian auctioneer). Rather, some decisions have to be made before the price which would affect it has actually been determined. For example, a wage contract may be entered into before work begins and a factory must be built before it can produce. These commitments must be made on the basis of the *expectations* of what the relevant prices will be, but it is to be emphasised that these expectations can, and will in general, be incorrect because the actual outcome is affected by current disturbances.

The rational expectations hypothesis simply amounts to the assumption that, in forming their expectations of what these prices (and perhaps other variables) will be, actors *do the best that they can*. This means that, given the information available at the time the forecast is made, no better forecast could be made on the basis of the same information. This does not imply either that the rational forecast will be correct or that some other guess would not be better for specific episodes. What it does imply is that a 'rational' forecast will, *on average*, be correct and that no other forecasting technique will regularly beat it. If the rational forecast was not correct on average, such systematic error would imply that information was not being fully utilised. This would contradict the notion of rationality. Equally, if there was a way of making forecasts better on average, that information should be included in the rational forecast.

The notion of rational expectations should not be alien to economists. Indeed, since the rational forecast is *defined* as optimal it is hard to support any other. To define the optimal forecast, of course, does not commit us to the view that all actors *actually do* forecast optimally all the time, any more than to define profit maximisation commits us to the view that all firms maximise profits continuously. What it does do is enable us to examine the logical implications of rational forecasts as well as of deviations from full rationality. The New Classical economics has been mistakenly criticised for its use of rational expectations on the grounds that it requires that actors know too much, or more than they can reasonably be expected to know. It is true that some of the literature requires actors to know all that there is to know. However, much of the New Classical literature achieves its mileage precisely by restricting the information available to actors at the time they make their decisions. Lucas (1973) is a good example of this, where actors are presumed to know current prices in the market in which they sell their product, but only to learn about the general price level with a lag.

This far the discussion may seem to have been unnecessarily abstract. These abstract ideas do, however, have powerful implications for the way we view macroeconomic policy. It is these implications which have attracted so much attention to the New Classical economics. Most famous is the result that systematic aggregate demand policies can have no real effect. Recall that Keynesian economics was invented to show ways in which governments could raise the level of activity in the economy. An argument which says that policy can have no effect will obviously be a spark to considerable controversy. The argument will simply be stated here and discussed further below.

Consider an economy which is at full employment in the sense that the labour market clears at a given real wage. The capital stock is held constant. We know that if all prices and incomes double in nominal terms nothing real will change. Suppose the authorities announce that the money stock is about to double. Rational actors would double their prices and so there would be no real effect. However, if the authorities doubled the money stock without telling anyone they were going to do it, firms and workers may think that there is an increased real demand for their services and so increase their supply. Hence, the short-term effect on the economy will depend crucially upon whether the policy change was anticipated or unanticipated. Only unanticipated aggregate demand policies will have real effects.

A useful way to think of the difference between Keynesian and New Classical perceptions of policy is to notice that a Keynesian would consider the policy-maker to be exogenous to the economy, and so all policies would be unanticipated. In the new view, however, to the extent that the policy-maker responds systematically to the state of the economy, actors learn that this is what they will do and change their own behaviour accordingly. More fundamentally, perhaps, it means that the behaviour of the economy will differ with each policy regime. Let us now look at this in more detail.

The New Classical challenge

It has been argued above that Monetarism could be viewed as an evolutionary stage in macroeconomics which started with the simple Keynesian model. While clearly emerging from a Monetarist background, New Classical macroeconomics represents a clean break from the stance of Keynesian economics. The nature of this break is nowhere more clearly evident than in a paper by Robert Lucas and Thomas Sargent (1981a) entitled 'After Keynesian Macroeconomics':

> For the applied economist, the confident and apparently successful application of Keynesian principles to economic policy which occurred in the United States in the 1960s was an event of incomparable significance and satisfaction. These principles led to a set of simple, quantitative relationships between fiscal policy and economic activity generally, the basic logic of which could be (and was) explained to the general public and which could be applied to yield improvements in economic performance benefiting everyone . . . We dwell on these halcyon days of Keynesian economics because without conscious effort they are difficult to recall today. In the present decade, the US economy has undergone its first major depression since the 1930s to the accompaniment of inflation rates in excess of 10 per cent per annum. These events have been transmitted (by consent of the governments involved) to other advanced countries and in many cases have been amplified. The events did not arise from a reactionary reversion to outmoded, 'classical' principles of tight money and balanced budgets. On the contrary, they were accompanied by massive government budget deficits and high rates of monetary expansion, policies which, although bearing an admitted risk of inflation, promised according to modern Keynesian doctrine rapid real growth and low rates of unemployment.
>
> That these predictions were wildly incorrect and that the doctrine on which they were based is fundamentally flawed are now simple matters of fact, involving no novelties in economic theory. The task now facing contemporary students of the business cycle is to sort through the wreckage, determining which feature of that remarkable intellectual event called the Keynesian Revolution can be salvaged and put to good use and which others must be discarded . . . . Our intention is to establish that the difficulties are *fatal*, that modern macroeconomic models are of *no* value in guiding policy and that this condition will not be remedied by modifications along any line which is currently being pursued. (Lucas and Sargent (1981a), pp. 295–313)

What is the basis for such strong claims about Keynesian macroeconomics? The argument is now known as the Lucas Critique after the title of the famous paper in which the argument first appeared ('Econometric policy evaluation: a critique' (Lucas, 1976)). It should be emphasised in advance that these criticisms do not depend in any essential way on the assumptions typically used by the New Classical economists themselves. In other words, it is possible to accept the criticisms without in any way accepting the New Classical view of the appropriate solutions. Before explaining the criticisms, of course, it is necessary to have some idea of what Keynesian methodology was supposed to have been.

Consider the simple expenditure system given by equations (1.1) to (1.6) in Chapter 1. A real model used for policy analysis would be more complicated than this, but the point can be made just as well in this stripped-down version. Let us just take the 'multiplier' equation (1.7):

$$Y = \frac{\alpha + I + G + X - \beta T}{(1 - \beta + d)}$$

The Keynesian strategy would be straightforward. First, estimate the parameters α, β and d from available historical data. Form some view of the likely values of the exogenous variables I and X. Forecast the value of Y on the basis of the estimated parameters and the predicted values of the exogenous variables, assuming the policy instruments G and T are unchanged. Then see what would happen to Y under different assumptions about values of the policy instruments. Choose values of the policy instruments which generate the most desirable outcome by some criterion.

The Lucas criticism is that, while it may produce reasonable short-term forecasts, it is not an appropriate tool for the analysis of alternative policy scenarios. The short-term forecasts are reasonable because actual forecasting models incorporate lots of lagged variables. So forecasting just amounts to an extrapolation of what is going on already. Policy analysis, however, is worthless because the estimated parameters α, β, d, etc. will not be invariant to the policies chosen. Even the assumed values of the 'exogenous' variables may vary with policy if the assumption of exogeneity is not actually justified. It is a complete waste of time for the authorities to predict what will be the result of a change in policy when that prediction relies on the assumption of stability of parameters which will, in fact, change as a result of the policy change.

It may seem to the student that this problem is of minor significance. However, there are several episodes in recent British economic history where it has to be taken seriously, namely the failure to anticipate the inflationary effect of the 1967 devaluation; the misunderstanding of the impact of the 1971 Competition and Credit Control reforms on the monetary system; the Barber 'dash for growth' which had no visible impact on manufacturing investment; the change in the price–output dynamics of the economy which resulted from the adoption of floating exchange rates; the over-appreciation of sterling in 1979–80 which was associated with a 17 per cent decline in manufacturing output in one year; the aftermath of financial deregulation and the asset price boom of the mid- to late 1980s. It is more than bad luck that just about every macroeconomic relationship broke down in the 1970s. Such breakdowns should be expected whenever there is a major change in the policy environment as actors adjust their behaviour to the new environment.

According to the New Classical School, the search should be for 'policy invariant' models; i.e. models which are based upon the optimising behaviour of actors in such a way that the reaction of behaviour to policy changes can be explicitly accounted for. This is one of the reasons for the insistence on 'rationality' as a characteristic of the decision-making of the typical actor. If behaviour was sub-optimal, then presumably reactions to policy changes would be arbitrary and unpredictable.

Once these important lessons were learned, academic and government forecasters did indeed begin to try to model relationships in a way that was immune to the Lucas Critique. To some extent, as Hendry (1988) observed, the proof of the econometric pudding was in the breakdown of relationships, and improvements in modelling technology have led to improvements in this respect. However, it is now routine for estimated macroeconomic relationships to be separated into their expectational and 'structural' components, instead of bundling them together, as was done by default in the past. Price (1992a) is just such an example, where explicit account is taken of forward-looking expectations in a model of UK price-setting. There is now a lot of evidence to support the idea that this approach, desirable on theoretical grounds, is also a *practical* methodology. The foremost UK forecasting model – maintained by the National Institute – is largely constructed on this basis.

Expectations

The importance of expectations has long been appreciated by macroeconomists. In early Keynesian macroeconomics they arose most importantly in the analysis of investment. For example, since building a factory takes time there will be a delay before output is produced. So the entrepreneur has to form expectations about the demand for the product in the future in order to assess the likely profitability of the venture. More recently, an important role for expectations has arisen in the context of wage and price-setting behaviour. This is because in negotiating wage contracts, for example, agents need to have some view about future changes in the value of money in order to assess the real value of any settlement. This issue will be discussed more fully in Chapter 7 below.

The problem posed by the presence of expectations takes the same form wherever it arises in the explicit formulation of testable models. When the expected value of some variable appears in an equation something has to be done about it because that variable is unobservable. A common method of solving this problem has been to extrapolate the past behaviour of the variable itself. In other words, take the past trend in the variable and assume that the trend will continue. A specific form of extrapolation is provided by the 'error learning mechanism' or 'adaptive expectations'. This says that the forecast currently being made of next period's value of the variable in question is a revision of the forecast made last period for the current period. The size of this revision is proportional to the error made last time and is in the same direction. If the expectation was, for example, of the price level, we would write:

$$p^e_t - p^e_{t-1} = \mu(p_{t-1} - p^e_{t-1}) \qquad 0 < \mu < 1 \qquad (4.1)$$

The difference between the expectation of the price level in period t and expectation in period $t - 1$ depends on the difference between the *actual outturn*, p_{t-1} in $t - 1$ and the expectation of what that would be. The time subscripts refer to the period of the outcome. The expectation is formed immediately prior to that.

This may not look very helpful as a way of replacing an unobservable variable by observables. Since

$$p^e_t = \mu p_{t-1} + (1 - \mu)p^e_{t-1} \qquad (4.2)$$

we would be replacing one unobservable with an expression which contains another. However, since it is also true that:

$$p^e_{t-1} = \mu p_{t-2} + (1 - \mu)p^e_{t-2} \qquad (4.3)$$

by continued substitutions we can obtain

$$p^e_t = \mu p_{t-1} + \mu(1 - \mu)p_{t-2} + \mu(1 - \mu)^2 p_{t-3} + \ldots +$$
$$\mu(1 - \mu)^n p_{t-n-1} + (1 - \mu)^{n+1} p^e_{t-n-1} \qquad (4.4)$$

The right-hand side of this expression only contains observables, except for the last term $(1 - \mu)^{n+1} p^e_{t-n-1}$. Since μ is less than unity, $(1 - \mu)^{n+1}$ will become very small as n gets larger. So if a large enough number of lagged values is used this last term can be ignored. The expectation of the variable is then replaced by a weighted average of past observations, the weights being geometrically declining.

One thing to notice immediately about adaptive expectations is that the only information used in forming them is the past observations on the variable in question. No other information is presumed to be of assistance. It would not be permissible, for example, for actors to expect higher prices just because OPEC (Organisation of Petroleum Exporting Countries) announces a substantial rise in the price of oil today. They would have to wait until this had worked through to prices in the shops. The second thing to notice is that until prices have been stable for a considerable time, expectations formed adaptively will be consistently incorrect.[1] This is because there is only a partial adjustment in response to the error in forecasting. Hence, there will be no error in the steady state only when the variable to be forecast is constant for some time.

The rational expectation (Muth, 1961) of a variable is defined in such a way that it cannot be *systematically* incorrect. Formally, the rational expectation is the mathematical expectation given the information available at the time the expectation is formed:

$$p^e_t = E(p_t \mid I_{t-1}) \tag{4.5}$$

where E is the expectations operator, p^e_t is the typical actor's subjective expectation of the price level in period t, formed on the basis of all information available up to and including period $t - 1$, I_{t-1}. In other words, the actors' expectations will be the same as the best forecast that could be made with the information available when the forecast is made. This is what was meant by the statement that actors do 'the best they can'. It does not follow that the rational expectation will typically be correct, but it does follow that over-predictions and under-predictions will average out to zero, unless the information set is changing.

$$p^e_t = p_t + \varepsilon_t \qquad E(\varepsilon_t) = 0, \ E(\varepsilon_t \varepsilon_{t-i}) = 0 \quad \text{for all } i > 0 \tag{4.6}$$

The expectation will be equal to the actual value plus a random ('expectational') error with mean zero. If this error were not random, the actor could improve the forecast by incorporating that information; i.e. they would learn from their mistakes.

It is sometimes argued in criticism of rational expectations that it is unreasonable to expect actors to be able to forecast as well as the best professional. Criticisms of this kind miss the point. Rationality implies no more than that the expectation is formed as the outcome of an optimisation exercise. In this respect it is no more extreme than the assumption of profit maximisation or utility maximisation. If information is freely available people will use it optimally. If information is not freely available they will acquire only just as much as it is worth their while to acquire. *It is only in specific applications of the idea that it is possible to say if the information required is in excess of that which it is reasonable to believe actors have.*

Aggregate supply

While most of the early arguments between Monetarists and Keynesians were about the determinants of aggregate demand (although see Modigliani (1977) for another interpretation), an important characteristic of the New Classical School has been their formulation of the aggregate supply curve. A fairly standard version of this would be:

$$Y_t = Y^* + \eta(p_t - {}_{t-1}p^e{}_t) \tag{4.7}$$

where Y_t is the level of output (national income) in period t; Y^* is the constant 'natural' level of output[2] associated with the vertical Classical aggregate supply curve; p_t is the price level or the rate of inflation in period t and ${}_{t-1}p^e{}_t$ is the price level or the rate of inflation expected to hold in period t, when that expectation is formed on the basis of information available in period $t - 1$. This says that there will be a fixed level of output except to the extent that actors make errors about prices. Notice that we can talk equivalently about inflation or the price level because

$$(p_t - p_{t-1}) - ({}_{t-1}p^e{}_t - p_{t-1}) = (p_t - {}_{t-1}p^e{}_t) \tag{4.8}$$

and these variables are normally written in natural logarithms so that $p_t - p_{t-1}$ is the rate of inflation.

There are two somewhat different approaches in the literature which can be used to justify an aggregate supply curve of the form above. The first is due to Lucas and Rapping (1969) and underlies many of the New Classical explanations of the business cycle (see Chapter 11). It focuses explicitly on labour supply behaviour. Workers are presumed to have some notion of the normal wage, which may be thought of as the expected average wage. They have some flexibility as to how much they work, but in any given period more work means less leisure. Leisure yields positive utility, but so do the consumer goods they buy with their wages. In each period they have to decide how much to work, and they do so by comparing the current wage with the expected or normal wage. If the current wage is higher than the normal wage they will work more now in the expectation of taking more leisure in the future when the reward for working is expected to be lower. If the current wage is lower than normal they will take leisure now and expect to work more in the future when the reward is higher – in other words, there is intertemporal substitution. This behaviour may reasonably be called 'speculative' labour supply. (Keynesian 'speculative' demand for money depends on comparing the current interest rate to the 'normal' interest rate.)

Thus, if the current wage is higher than expected more labour supply will be forthcoming and vice versa. The wage in question in both cases is presumed to be a real wage. The only way the price level (as compared to its expectation) enters into the Lucas/Rapping analysis is through its effect on the real interest rate. The real interest rate is important in its role as a way of discounting utility tomorrow into utility today. The expected real interest rate is defined as $r_t - \ln(p^e{}_t/p_t)$, where r_t is the current nominal interest rate,

p^e_t is the expected price level and p_t is the actual price level. Lucas and Rapping argue that labour supply will be positively related to the expected real interest rate, and it is from this that labour supply would rise with ($\ln p_t - \ln p^e_t$) for a given nominal interest rate. This connection must surely be extremely tenuous. It is hard to believe that labour supply is much affected by the real interest rate and it is far from obvious what the sign of that effect would be. It is even far from obvious what the effect of a change in expected inflation would be on the expected real interest rate. Indeed, the weight of the econometric evidence is against this kind of model.

While the precise link between the Lucas/Rapping analysis and 'un-anticipated price changes' is somewhat implausible, the spirit is less so. This is that a demand shock which is perceived to be temporary will have an effect on current supply which is greater than that which would result from a permanent demand shift. This is because of the inter-temporal substitution of work into the period when demand is high and away from the (future) period when demand is (expected to be) lower. We shall return to this issue in the context of discussions of the business cycle below. Notice in passing, however, that the Lucas/Rapping analysis depends in no way on rational expectation; indeed, Lucas and Rapping themselves use adaptive expectations to determine the 'normal' level of wages and prices. What they do assume, however, is that prices and wages clear markets in each period. So changes in employment are perceived as 'voluntary' in the sense that everyone who would choose to work at current wage rates can do so. This is a source of some controversy which we shall return to below.

The second approach to aggregate supply is that found in Lucas (1972, 1973). Here the focus is directly on goods markets rather than on labour markets. Sellers are presumed to be located in one of a large number of 'local' markets which are segregated, though within each market there is perfect competition. The local price is known for the current period, but the general price level across all markets is only learned with a lag. The problem for the seller is to decide how much to sell (and produce) on observing the current price. This is difficult because a change in price could reflect a shift in demand towards their own market (which requires a rational response) or merely a change in the value of money (which needs no response). Part of the decision, therefore, depends upon a single comparison of the current local price with the *expectation* of the general price level for the same period. If they are the same there is certainly no reason to change the supply. If they are different then the setter may wish to change the supply. However, the size of the response will depend upon perceptions of variability in the price level compared with the variability of relative price changes. It is here that rational expectations enter the scene, since the actor is presumed to respond optimally to this price signal in the light of knowledge of the 'true' probability distribution of price level changes and real demand shifts. If the variance of price level changes is high relative to the variance of demand shifts (they are assumed to be statistically independent), the price signals should be distrusted and the supply response should be small. If the reverse is true a change in current price is more likely to reflect a real shock to which supply should respond. Therefore, η above (equation (4.7)) will be close to zero if price level changes have a high variance relative to the variance of real shocks. It will be significantly above zero if the reverse is true.

While providing a formal justification of the 'surprise' aggregate supply curve, this argument is not entirely convincing either, even though the supply curve itself has almost become 'conventional wisdom'. One problem is that the restriction of information it requires is just as *ad hoc* as many of the alternative Keynesian stories such as sticky money wages. Why should a seller perceive the demand price for the product earlier than perceiving the general price level? It is quite possible that the reverse would be true. Aggregate information and forecasts are much more widely available than information on specific markets.

An alternative explanation of this supply curve is based upon an asymmetry of information between workers and firms. This is the approach mentioned in Chapter 1 above. Demand for labour by firms depends upon the real wage where both the money wage and the price of output are correctly perceived. Labour supply depends upon the real wage. Workers perceive the money wage correctly, but their belief about the purchasing power of that wage depends upon their *expectation* of the price level. An unexpected increase in aggregate demand will lead to an increase in aggregate supply. Initially, prices will rise by more than money wages. Firms will correctly perceive this as a fall in the real wage and will demand more labour. Workers will *incorrectly* perceive a rise in the real wage and will supply more labour. The higher input will be associated with higher output, that is, greater aggregate supply. Whether or not expectations are rational, this effect can only be temporary as workers are unlikely to be fooled for long.

Again, this seems a somewhat tenuous basis for the theory of aggregate supply. Supply will only change if someone is tricked. However, some thought about the supply-side structure within which this result is derived will show why it must emerge in that framework. It is the characterisation of the economy which must be challenged to overthrow the result, not the internal consistency of the analysis itself. In an economy with one input and one output there is only one relative price – the real wage. The market-clearing real wage is unique (if both labour supply and demand depend on it) and that is all there is to it. Without more structure to the economy there is no scope for real changes in output and employment, especially in response to nominal expenditures. This, of course, is why Keynes thought Classical economics to be unsatisfactory. The real problem is to explain why output and employment do actually fluctuate. We shall return to this central question in the next chapter, and again when discussing business cycles in Chapter 11.

Policy ineffectiveness

One of the earliest claims made by the New Classicists was that '[macroeconomic] policy is ineffective'. Systematic demand management will have no real effects. This dramatic result created extraordinary controversy, and may indeed have temporarily set back the adoption of rational expectations because of the extremity of the conclusion. The first proponents of this idea, Thomas Sargent and Neil Wallace, now claim their seminal model was designed mainly as a vehicle to demonstrate the importance of taking expectations seriously; but even if this were the intention, their work was not interpreted in this light at the time. The supply function assumes great importance in this debate, because the claimed ineffectiveness of systematic aggregate demand policy is crucially dependent upon it.

Consider Figure 4.1: the economy is initially at $p_0 \, Y^*$, with aggregate demand D_0. The level of income Y^* is the 'natural' level of output which is defined to be that sustainable in the long run. Any greater level will be associated with rising prices. The supply curve S_A will be the response to an unanticipated shift in D. This is because, with p^e held constant, the curve of equation (4.7) has a positive slope with respect to p_t. However, as p^e_t is revised upwards S_A will shift to the left. With rational expectations, p^e_t will not differ from p_t for any reason that could be predicted. Hence, if a shift in

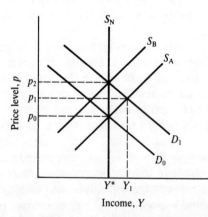

Figure 4.1 New Classical aggregate supply.

aggregate demand is anticipated all its effect will be felt in prices and not in output. The economy will go straight from p_0 to p_2, but Y^* will not change.

In this framework any systematic policy reactions which involve shifting aggregate demand will have no real effect – at least where the authorities respond with a lag and they are not better informed than the actors. Consider again equation (4.7), which is modified only by adding a random supply disturbance e^s_t.

$$Y_t = Y^* + \eta(p_t - {}_{t-1}p^e_t) + e^s_t \tag{4.9}$$

Here and elsewhere we assume that the random error e^s_t takes an average (or expected) value of zero, and is serially uncorrelated. Formally, $E(e_t)$ and $E(e_t e_s) = 0$ $(t > s)$. The price level can be assumed to be proportional to the money stock M_t, plus a random demand disturbance, e^d_t:

$$p_t = \alpha M_t + e^d_t \tag{4.10}$$

Let us suppose that the monetary authorities keep the money stock constant, except that they try to stabilise the economy by changing the money stock in response to deviations of the last period's output from the natural rate. They achieve this with a random error, e^m_t.

$$M_t = \beta_0 + \beta_1(Y^* - Y_{t-1}) + e^m_t \tag{4.11}$$

With rational expectations, actors will expect the price level to be proportional to the *systematic* component of the money stock (where we have used the assumption that $E(e_t) = 0$).

$$p^e_t = \alpha(\beta_0 + \beta_1(Y^* - Y_{t-1})) \tag{4.12}$$

The *actual* price level will also depend on the error in (4.11) and the demand disturbance.

$$p_t = \alpha(\beta_0 + \beta_1(Y^* - Y_{t-1})) + \alpha e^m_t + e^d_t \tag{4.13}$$

So the error in price expectations just depends on the disturbances – subtract (4.12) from (4.13).

$$p_t - p^e_t = \alpha e^m_t + e^d_t \tag{4.14}$$

Substituting this back into (4.9) results in the following:

$$Y_t - Y^* = \eta \alpha e^m_t + \eta e^d_t + e^s_t \tag{4.15}$$

This says that the deviation of current real income from the natural rate only depends upon the random disturbances and not at all upon the systematic component of policy. This is essentially the analysis of Sargent and Wallace (1975), which leads to the conclusion that only unanticipated policy matters.

An obvious comment on this result is that if deviations from the natural rate (of output or unemployment) were really random then stabilisation policy would not be necessary anyway. It is persistent deviations that have to be explained and, of course, corrected for. New Classical economists would all accept that there has to be persistence and, indeed, assume it (and discover it) in their empirical work. If they did not do so their case would hardly be credible. Lucas (1973), for example, writes his aggregate supply curve:

$$Y_t - Y^*_t = \eta_0(p_t - p^e_t) + \eta_1(Y_{t-1} - Y^*_{t-1}) \qquad (4.16)$$

where the term $\eta_1(Y_{t-1} - Y^*_{t-1})$ reflects persistence, though this persistence is not justified explicitly and must, therefore, be considered *ad hoc*. However, even though random shocks lead to sustained output changes this does not restore a role for systematic stabilisation policy, as repeating the above exercise with (4.16) instead of (4.9) will demonstrate.

One line of argument that will restore at least partial policy effectiveness is that of long-term overlapping wage contracts, a point made early on in the debate by Gray (1976) and Fischer (1977) (see also Taylor (1979, 1980)). This works by creating some stickiness in money wages and thereby allowing some temporary real wage changes which can be exploited by the authorities. Suppose, for example, that money wage contracts are set for two periods and the authorities continue to operate the rule (4.11). Wage contracts will presumably reflect price expectations over the subsequent two periods, but they cannot anticipate the systematic reaction of the authorities in the second period because this depends on the outcome in the first period which has not yet happened. Thus, aggregate demand policies will exert some leverage over aggregate supply in the short term. This effect will die out over time as the longest contract matures and money wages catch up with prices. But this approach is essentialy *ad hoc*; we return to the issues in the next chapter.

However, even if wages are fully flexible, it soon became clear that the Sargent and Wallace case is very specific, and quite small changes in the specification, on either the demand or supply side, can reintroduce effective policy. Effectiveness will be restored if there are non-linearities in the model, for example, or if supply is forward-looking so that *next* period's price is what matters. The issues are discussed further in Minford (1991) and Pesaran (1987).[3]

Turning to the evidence, the proposition that 'only unanticipated policy has real effects' seemed initially to gain powerful support from work by Barro (1977, 1978). On annual data for the United States for the period 1941–73, Barro showed that the unemployment rate was significantly affected by unanticipated money growth, but that it was either unaffected or affected perversely by actual money growth. Unanticipated money growth was measured as the difference between the actual and fitted values of an equation in which money growth depends upon its own lagged values, the deviation of the Federal budget deficit from normal and lagged unemployment. This is a mixture of a kind of reaction function and budget constraint. Unanticipated money growth has effects not only in the same year, but also in two subsequent years and, thus, illustrates the importance of persistence. Actual money growth has no significant negative effect on lowering unemployment, except a marginal one after four years. The overall fit was much worse than for unanticipated money.

Impressive as these results seemed, they were not in the end convincing. To begin with, the method of generating 'unanticipated' money growth is inconsistent with rational expectations. Information should only be used which was available at the time. There may be no relation between the residual in 1948 of an equation estimated with a sample for, say, 1946–73 and the forecast error that would have been made in 1948 based only upon information available in 1947. My forecast of next year cannot be dependent on information that will only become available subsequently. Barro noted this, but did not cope with it.

Simple as this point is, it opens a can of worms that has not yet been successfully untangled. The issues go beyond the question of empirical tests. The point is that although rational expectations offer a coherent theory of expectations conditional on a given information set, it offers no explanation of how this information is acquired. Perhaps we need a theory of *learning* to complement our theory of expectations. This observation has spawned a highly technical literature exploring the changes that learning brings. The results tend to be specific to the model – sometimes learning makes the existence of a rational expectation equilibrium more likely, sometimes less. What is clear, though, is that no tractable ways of modelling learning have yet appeared.[4] This is something of a disappointment, as the great advantage of the rational expectations (RE) approach was its apparent conceptual simplicity.

There is a further, very deep, problem with the tests. This can be appreciated by noting that the news that the rate of growth of money does not explain unemployment will be quite happily received by Keynesians, Monetarists and New Classical economists alike – but for very different reasons. A wide variety of models may yield the same predictions. Going beyond this, the evidence that only *unanticipated* money matters is at first sight rather harder for a non-New Classicist to explain, until it is realised that this is consistent with a completely different scenario. Suppose the authorities are pegging interest rates rather than controlling the money stock (fixing the exchange rate will do just as well). *Real disturbances* will then *cause* monetary changes rather than *vice versa*. In so far as the real disturbances are uncorrelated with earlier monetary growth, the current monetary change will be unpredictable by any monetary rule. Here, of course, causation runs exactly in reverse and so constitutes a very different kind of explanation. This substitute explanation must have some *prima facie* plausibility in the light of the widespread practice of stabilising both interest rates and exchange rates in the bulk of the sample periods studied so far, though this evidence is at least consistent with the New Classical view. So quite disparate models predict the same qualitative results.

Pesaran (1982, 1987) showed that while the method employed by Barro could show the data were consistent with the RE/ineffectiveness model, it could not *reject* the Keynesian model, for the simple reason that there are well defined Keynesian models with 'observationally equivalent' specifications, as discussed above. A better approach is to test the RE and surprise supply parts of the model separately, and then to test the implied cross-equation restrictions. Attfield, Demery and Duck (1981) find that the restrictions are (just) accepted by this method; but the observational equivalence problem remains. What is really needed is a well defined (Keynesian) alternative against which the model may be tested. When Pesaran used such a framework, he found the Keynesian model outperformed the New Classical version.

Perhaps unsurprisingly in view of the theoretical arguments against ineffectiveness, the weight of the evidence is now opposed to the proposition. However, there is more evidence from individual survey data supporting rational expectations in (for example) consumption decisions, and financial markets appear to act in a way that is at the very least extremely close to full rationality. This is quite fortunate for the theoretician, as there is no obvious alternative to the notion of rational expectations. It is almost as basic as the notion of maximising behaviour; but, at the risk of labouring the point, this does not automatically support the New Classical doctrine of policy ineffectiveness, which is a *joint* hypothesis.

Policy games

Perhaps the most profound insight that the New Classicists brought to macroeconomics was that agents will try to predict the actions of governments. As we saw, one of the initial consequences was the ineffectiveness proposition, which in the end did not stand the test of time. Once we realise that agents are trying to predict the actions of government, the nature of our models shifts in a fundamental way. The point is that behaviour will in general be affected by one agent's guess ('conjecture') of what the other will do. Models of this kind, where agents have to react to other agents on the basis of their conjectures about the other party's behaviour, are known as 'games'. It turns out that the implications for macroeconomics go very deep. What is more, this insight helps us to understand the operation and formation of key economic institutions in our society, such as the Exchange Rate Mechanism of the European Monetary System, or the Bundesbank in Germany.

To understand the issues, we will first look at a one period game between the public and the government. The fact that the game is only for one period is not as severe a restriction as one might imagine, as we will explain below. The game is about inflation. The government chooses the level of inflation, given what it believes the public's *expectation* of inflation will be; in turn, the public chooses its expectation, given its belief of how the government will act. We assume that both players have rational expectations, so an equilibrium can only exist if both party's expectations about the other are correct.

Figure 4.2 shows aggregate supply in the short and long run. The only difference between this and the set-up in Figure 4.1 is that we have inflation on the vertical axis, not the price level. As equation (4.8) reveals, the two ways of drawing the diagram are perfectly equivalent. The short-run supply curves are all drawn for different levels of inflation expectations. Only where they cut the long-run supply curve S_N are expectations correct; thus all rational expectations equilibria must be at output Y^*.

Suppose that the public dislikes inflation. If so, then the best possible equilibrium is at point A, where we enjoy zero inflation and the long-run level of output. If both government and the public have the same preferences, the game is trivial. Both parties will want to be at A; as it is in both parties' interest to be there, this is what both will expect, and A is where we will end up. However, suppose that the government, while disliking inflation, would also prefer to have output higher than Y^*. One way of formalising this is to define a government cost function, C:

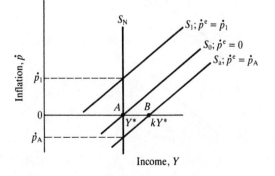

Figure 4.2 Short- and long-run supply curves.

$$C = a\dot{p}^2 + b(Y - kY^*)^2; \ k > 1 \tag{4.17}$$

The government cost function C is equal to a times the square of inflation $\dot{p}$ plus b times the square of the deviation of output Y from kY^*.

For simplicity, C is defined as a quadratic. The function puts a specific cost on deviations from either zero inflation or the target output level, kY^*. As k is greater than one, this target exceeds the long-run rate. The function is smallest (actually zero) when inflation is zero and output is equal to kY^* – say, at B. As can be seen from the diagram, in order to get to B, the public would have to expect inflation to be negative (so that we were on S_a). The problem with this is that the public is assumed to know what the government's preferences are (i.e. equation (4.17)), so if inflation were expected to be $\dot{p}_A$ they would expect the government to set inflation at zero; but this is greater than $\dot{p}_A$ – so an equilibrium at B is inconsistent with rational expectations. The government could promise to fix inflation at $\dot{p}_A$ of course, but no-one would believe them. In the jargon, the promise would not be *credible*. B is the government's *first best* position; but it is unattainable. Given this, the *second best* position would be A where the government meets its inflation target, and we are also at the long-run level of output. Unfortunately, this is also unattainable. Suppose the public expects zero inflation, so that we are on S_0 in Figure 4.3. We have now sketched in the government 'indifference curves' implied by equation (4.17). They give the trade-off between inflation and output; *ceteris paribus*, (for positive inflation) lower indifference curves are preferred. Clearly, if $\dot{p}^e$ is zero (so we are on S_0), then the government will want to set inflation at the level corresponding to point C on the diagram, where the indifference curve is tangential to the supply curve. This is the best the government can do,

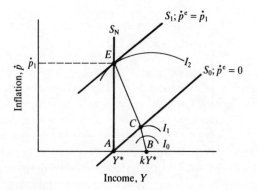

Figure 4.3 A policy game.

given the short-run supply curve. Inflation will again be at a higher level than the one expected. *C* could be called a 'cheating' equilibrium, as it requires the government to fool the public into thinking inflation will be lower than it actually turns out to be. There is a whole set of such points that minimise the cost function given the public's expectations; this is the government's *reaction function*, though there is only one position where the government's optimal inflation choice (given the public's expectation) is identical to the actual expectation (itself formed given the public's knowledge of how the government behaves). That point is where the government's indifference curve is tangential to a short-run supply curve *and* is on the long supply curve – where the reaction function crosses the long-run supply curve, at *E*.[5] So this unique point, *E*, characterised by high inflation, is the only possible rational expectations equilibrium.

Thus we have an apparent paradox. If the government and public could somehow agree to be at the zero inflation point *A*, both would prefer the outcome to the high inflation outcome *E* (which is at the same level of output, and therefore unambiguously worse). Somehow, this obviously desirable outcome cannot be achieved. Why is this?

The basic problem stems from the timing. In effect, the public chooses its expectations *before* the government sets inflation. As there is always an incentive for the government to cheat, the public always assumes it will do so, unless inflation is expected to be so high that there is no incentive to cheat (as at *E*). If the public and government could somehow make their moves simultaneously, there would be no problem. However, this is not possible. The general problem is one of *time inconsistency*. The rationale for this phrase is that although *ex ante* it is rational for (in this case) the government to go for zero inflation, when time has moved on and the public has irrevocably set its expectations (via wage contracts and the like), the world has changed, making it optimal to cheat. It is as if the structure of the problem changes with the passage of time. Although this idea has been extant in dynamic programming for some time, it was Kydland and Prescott who first pointed out the dramatic implications for macroeconomics in 1977.

Fortunately there may be ways out of this bind. One way is to repeat the game an infinite number of times. Barro (1983) showed that in this case a government may be able to acquire an anti-inflationary reputation which can be sustained in equilibrium. The idea is that the public can impose costs on the government by 'punishing' governments which spring inflation surprises by setting their inflation expectations high. While this sounds arbitrary, it is possible to show that this is in fact an optimal strategy for the public. This punishment can make it optimal for the government to keep inflation low (though not zero). The key idea, to which we return below, is that an outside force is imposing extra costs on the government if it lets inflation rise. This makes it in the government's own best interest to control inflation. So low inflation equilibria are possible. The problem, however, is that repeating the game 100, 1000 or even 10,000 times is not enough. In finite cases, no matter how many times the game is repeated, there is always a last game when the government has an incentive to cheat. As this effectively wipes out the last period, the last game moves back to the period before last (as we know the government will try to cheat in the last game and cannot keep its reputation). However, in this new 'last' game the government will again have an incentive to cheat, so the next-to-next last game now becomes the effective last game and so on. All finite games unravel to the current period.[6] Only in infinitely repeated games can reputations be sustained.

As no government in history has yet been seen to last for ever, this is not a very helpful approach. However, Backus and Driffil (1985) showed that uncertainty can help. If there are two types of governments – one tough on inflation and one soft – then it may pay the soft type to pretend to be tough. By doing this they can build up some anti-inflation credibility which it may be useful to cash in later, possibly in a severe recession, or just before an election. So if there is uncertainty – as there surely is – then low inflation equilibria become more likely. This approach has a distinct appeal to the observer of the recent economic scene in Britain. It is certainly possible to tell a story about the Conservative administration that follows the line set out above. Between 1979 and 1984 the Government undoubtedly acted as if it were tough on inflation, allowing unemployment to rise to record levels at an unprecedentedly rapid rate, and presiding over a proportionately greater decline in manufacturing output between 1979 and 1981 than between 1929 and 1931. Yet in 1986, with inflation screwed down to $2\frac{1}{2}$ per cent, the pound was allowed to float down and the scene was set for a tax-cutting budget before the 1987 election. These policy choices undoubtedly contributed towards the subsequent unsustainable boom and inflation of the late 1980s. We shall have more to say about the political business cycle in Chapter 11.

There may be more direct routes towards a low inflation world. The basic problem facing governments is to acquire some anti-inflation credibility. As governments are never held to the implicit contracts they form with the electorate (manifesto pledges are not enforceable in the courts), this is difficult. The key ways that have been proposed to circumvent this problem all involve 'tying the government's hands', in Giavazzi and Pagano's (1988) graphic phrase. Paradoxically, by deliberately restricting the scope for independent action, it may be possible to achieve better outcomes. The issue is one of 'pre-commitment' to a policy. One way of doing this is to make the central bank, the institution that is directly responsible for monetary policy, constitutionally independent of the government. This is the German model, where the Bundesbank is not only independent, but also has as its overriding aim the explicit maintenance of price stability, or zero inflation. When the German government pursues potentially inflationary policies, the Bundesbank will step in to raise interest rates to offset this. That it will indeed act in this way has been dramatically confirmed during the process of German reunification, where, arguably, some distinctly imprudent policies were pursued by the German government. Despite intense international pressure, the Bundesbank kept interest rates at such a high level that the domestic tensions in some ERM members like Britain and Italy came close to destroying the system; indeed, it is not clear at the time of writing that the ERM will survive.

The ERM effectively ties participant currencies to the Deutschmark (DM). Historically, German inflation has been very low; indeed, in 1986 German prices actually fell. So locking on to the DM is a way of imposing an external discipline. There is nothing strictly to prevent governments from allowing inflation to rise, but if they do, exports become uncompetitive, manufacturing suffers, unemployment rises; these are unwelcome costs that make governments unpopular. So ERM membership imposes extra costs on governments when inflation rises. This is just what is needed to make low inflation equilibria possible.

The problem, as shown by the dramatic events on 'Black Wednesday'[7] in September 1992 when Britain was summarily booted out of the ERM by a tidal wave of speculative pressure, is that the need for credibility is simply pushed sideways. Before ERM entry, there was a problem maintaining a credible anti-inflation stance; after entry, the problem was to convince observers that continued membership in the teeth of a deepening recession at a time of high real interest rates was itself credible. We return to the wider issues of international policy coordination and exchange rate regimes later in the book.

Summary

New Classical economics is a major source of ideas which are a challenge to both Keynesians and Monetarists alike. As advocates of rational expectations New Classical economists are on strong ground, especially if the notion is applied carefully (i.e. with limited, or even endogenous, information). One important area of application is that of exchange rates which will be discussed below. Rather harder to accept is their portrait of the supply structure of the macroeconomy. Here, the insistence of continuous market-clearing in a 'natural rate' framework so that only 'surprises' matter seems unnecessarily nihilistic. We shall have more to say on these subjects below. However, one insight that continues to illuminate our view of how macro policy operates is given by the policy game approach to macroeconomics, where the public plays a kind of game with the government. These models undoubtedly help us to understand more clearly why actual economic institutions evolve, and why the battle against inflation may be more difficult to win than we might at first think.

Notes

1. In fact there is one case where adaptive expectations are 'correct', in the sense of giving the best possible forecast, and where expectations will not suffer from this systematic bias. This is when the true model generating the relevant variable can be expressed as a first difference in the variable with a first-order moving average process. While some variables may be characterised in this way, the vast majority cannot.
2. The 'natural' rate is a term introduced by Friedman to describe the long-run equilibrium level of unemployment. See Chapter 7 for more discussion.
3. It should perhaps be noted that even if government policy is effective, it need not be *optimal* to intervene; but this is not the point.
4. One approach to modelling expectations that goes some way to addressing this issue of learning is to use the Kalman filter to generate expectations. The Kalman filter can be thought of as a rule to be used to update expectations in the light of new information; thus it does not suffer from the problem of using information which was never available to economic agents. See Chapter 7 of Cuthbertson, Hall and Taylor (1992) for some more discussion and a description of the Kalman filter.
5. Technically, this is the Nash equilibrium of the game.
6. It is impossible to fault the logic of this unravelling process. However, it must be said that not everyone is convinced by the argument.
7. Not everyone agrees that this particular Wednesday was 'black'; some, believing the United Kingdom to be better off outside the ERM, prefer the sobriquets 'white' or even 'golden'.

5

New Keynesians

Keynesians, discussed in Chapter 2, were concerned with aggregate demand. Supply was considered only cursorily, if indeed at all. New Classicists (and to some extent Monetarists) hold that with market-clearing and rational expectations, there is no role for demand to affect anything except the price level (especially in the long run). By contrast, New Keynesians noticed that fluctuations in aggregate demand seem to have real effects, and asked what models of aggregate *supply* are consistent with this. So this chapter is about some new approaches to aggregate supply, that move away from the Classical view of the world.

At the end of the 1970s, most economists could be classified into one of the camps described in the previous three chapters. The old, un-reconstructed Keynesians differed from the Monetarists on empirical issues such as the interest elasticity of money demand and the practical problems associated with interventionist policy; the fundamentalist New Classicists differed profoundly from both, in believing that the analytical roots of the old schools were severely deficient. New Classicists simply did not believe that economic agents could act in the irrational, non-optimising way that previous generations of economists had allowed. This retreat to fundamentals struck a deep chord among economists, who prefer to assume that agents always act in their own rational interest. The problem for some, however, was that the evidence seemed to conflict with the theory. As we saw in the last chapter, after a promising start, the weight of the formal econometric evidence piled up against the New Classicists.[1] There was also the informal testimony of everyday experience. Although anecdotes cannot replace proper econometric evidence, it certainly *looked* like the world had some distinctly non-Classical features. For example:

- Wages and prices are usually set for relatively long periods, typically a year in the United Kingdom and often longer in the United States.
- Tight government fiscal and monetary policies and other demand shocks *appear* to have real effects long after they are public knowledge, as in the 1980–81 and 1990–93 recessions in the United Kingdom.
- Fluctuations in unemployment do not appear to be voluntarily induced, dominated as they are in the United Kingdom by unemployment spells of very long duration.

Thus, some economists applied US President George Bush's 'duck test' to the economy; if it looks like a duck, walks like a duck and sounds like a duck, it's a duck. In our case, the 'duck' is a Keynesian model; but at the same time, to satisfy economists' basic requirement, economic agents must be rational maximisers. This rules out the most direct route to Keynesian results, arbitrarily fixing money (or real) wages.

The research agenda of the New Keynesians can be outlined as follows: construct rigorous models of rational maximising agents where it is *optimal* to act in such a way that the economy has Keynesian features. This broadly defined agenda has many paths, some of which have already turned out to be dead ends. It is impossible to single out one approach. Nevertheless, several themes have emerged, which we discuss below. We do not attempt to make a comprehensive survey of an extremely diverse and eclectic field; instead we try to pick out some broad themes and ideas which have emerged in the past few years. A good introduction to the area is given in the two volumes edited by Gregory Mankiw and David Romer (1991), and in the winter 1993 issue of *The Journal of Economic Perspectives* Vol. 7, No. 1.

Wage contracts

Long before Keynes, it was appreciated that if wages were insufficiently flexible to clear the labour market, demand shocks would have real effects. Even with rational expectations, as we saw in Chapter 4, the existence of wage contracts lasting longer than one period is sufficient to induce a role for activist macroeconomic policy. What is more, Taylor (1980) showed that where contracts depend on future relative wages, the effects of shocks could last far longer than the duration of the wage contracts. However, the problem with this approach, from the point of view of *both* the New Classicist and New Keynesian research paradigms, is that lengthy overlapping contracts – wage rigidity itself, in other words – are never derived from theory. Originally, two justifications for these contracts were put forward. First, it was argued that setting contracts is costly. It is unclear to what extent this is true, but it must also be said that economists have an inbuilt resistance to explanations appealing to 'adjustment costs', usually described as *ad hoc*. The second justification was an appeal to the implicit contract literature of the early 1970s.

The theories of implicit contracts were a microeconomic response to the observation that firms do not usually change their wage scales when demand meets a downturn; wages remain constant while employment and output vary. The ideas were first explored by Azariadis (1975), Baily (1974) and Gordon (1974). The basic insight of the models was that contracts may consist of two elements: an explicit wage, and a (possibly implicit) commitment about employment. The latter effect was hypothesised to work via the employer contracting to lay off workers in bad times at agreed rates. In an uncertain world, a risk-neutral firm would be indifferent between a wide range of wages for good and bad times. For example, if there is an equal chance of good and bad times, *ex ante* a firm expects to make the same profits (on average) for a given work force if 'good' and 'bad' wages were £170 and £10 respectively (average £90), or £100 and £80 (also an average of £90). If workers dislike risk and there is a basic level of unemployment benefits, then workers are best served by constant wages in good and bad states with some random layoffs. Firms are effectively acting as insurance agents for risk-averse workers in this set-up. What is more, despite the apparent constancy of the wage, the level of employment that results is the efficient level, that which would hold if wages were free to fluctuate, though it is this last result that gives the game away. The point is that in these models, although wages are indeed constant over the cycle, wages are a veil, in the sense that firms and workers have agreed *ex ante* to effectively disregard the fact that *ex post* wages may differ from the marginal product. The macroeconomic significance of this is that fixed wage contracts do *not* necessarily imply the existence of a simple Keynesian aggregate supply relationship. Later refinements (see Grossman and Hart, 1981) incorporating the possibility that firms may cheat by lying about whether they face a good or bad state led the models away from the efficient outcome; but the basic insight endures, that rigid wages over lengthy contracts may not be all they appear to the naive observer. Alternative explanations were required.

Efficiency wages

Another explanation for wages failing to move to clear the labour market is that they perform more than one function. That is, wages are set not only in order to attract a supply of workers, but also to induce those workers to supply a particular level of *effort*. As soon as this holds, the wage will in general not be able to clear the market. We have two targets – high effort and full employment – but only one instrument with which to attain them.

The explanation for the existence of efficiency wages may lie in one of two possible areas. The first is to do with *recruitment and retention*. Most firms have at least a little monopsony power in relation to the labour market, if only because searching for and moving between jobs is costly. This means that to some extent they must decide on the optimal (*efficient*) wage to offer. If wages are high, vacancies will be filled more quickly and fewer workers will quit in any period. Both these phenomena lower costs, and firms will balance a higher wage bill against lower turnover costs. If workers differ in ways hard to measure before hiring, a higher wage will tend to attract applicants who are more productive, on average. Furthermore, the best workers will not leave so readily, as they will be less likely to be poached by higher wage offers elsewhere.

The other area has to do with direct effects on efficiency. This may work via non-economic routes; if a firm pays more than is strictly required by the market, this 'gift' of higher wages may be reciprocated by the employee with loyalty and higher effort (Akerlof, 1982). An alternative story, somewhat less sanguine about human nature and therefore more to the taste of economists, revolves round the idea that firms cannot easily measure effort. (If they could, they would simply demand minimum effort levels from workers and dismiss workers who failed to deliver.) In this case (explored by Shapiro and Stiglitz, 1984) firms set wages high enough to make workers regret being laid off – even though workers would find a new job eventually, the wage would be lower – and (imperfectly) monitor workers. Some slacking workers will be picked up by the firm's monitoring process and be sacked. The high wage makes this a real threat, and if *all* firms set high wages, as they must in equilibrium, unemployment results.

These models do offer an explanation for unemployment and rigid wages, but *by themselves* they are not the missing Keynesian link we are searching for.[2] The point is that although wages are higher than the competitive level, they are not 'too high' in the usual sense, based as they are on optimising behaviour. In Chapter 2 we looked at a Keynesian special case, where money wages are fixed at too high a level – that is, above equilibrium. Unemployment results. In that model, expansionary policies raise the price level and therefore reduce real wages, increasing employment and output. In the efficiency wage model we also have high wages and unemployment; but if prices rise, employers will want to offer proportionally higher wages, as the (real) efficiency wage is indeed efficient for them. Thus efficiency wages, or other stories with similar consequences, do not yet offer a direct connection between aggregate demand and output, which is the characteristic Keynesian proposition. We have part of the jigsaw, but there is a missing piece that connects non-competitive wage setting and output fluctuations. It is to that issue we now turn.

Menu costs and near rationality

In this section we examine two ideas which seek to explain how fluctuations in nominal demand can cross over into output, despite the fact that firms are acting rationally (or vanishingly close to rationality). Both mechanisms revolve round the notion that the advantages of adjusting wages (or prices) to a small demand shock can be extremely small, so that firms may find it more profitable to meet demand by quantity adjustments – changing output – than by altering prices.

Menu costs, as the name suggests, refers to the costs associated with changing prices (printing new menus, in other words). These costs may be quite small, but as Caplin and Spulber (1987) argued, in the presence of imperfect competition, their existence may have a disproportional effect on aggregate demand – and in fact the costs may be larger than we might expect. Although the physical cost of altering price lists is trivial in many cases, these are not the only considerations. Customer goodwill and loyalty may well be more important factors; higher price lists may encourage existing customers to start searching for better deals elsewhere. In the end this is an empirical question. Carlton (1986) examined detailed data on individual buyers' prices in US manufacturing. He found that although there is evidence that the physical fixed cost of changing prices is low for many buyers, it is also the case that 'The degree of price rigidity in many industries is significant. It is not unusual in some industries for prices to individual buyers to remain unchanged for several years' (Carlton, 1986, p. 638). There is also some econometric evidence on the matter. Price (1992a) estimates a model of UK manufacturing price-setting which tests a model with explicit costs of adjustment. The model performs very well, and price-setting occurs with a high degree of persistence, implying relatively large adjustment costs.

The easiest way to see why menu costs matter is in the context of a monopolist. Take the standard textbook model of a monopolist, illustrated in Figure 5.1. Suppose that the firm's demand curve is affected by the aggregate price level P so that the firm's price p is given by

$$p = D(Q)P \tag{5.1}$$

> The firm's price p is proportional to the aggregate price level P but is also affected by other factors summarised in $D(Q)$, where Q is the firm's output. The firm's price and output are negatively related (the demand curve slopes down).

So if q is the real price (p/P) and MC is real marginal costs, we have the situation illustrated in Figure 5.1.

At the optimum, output and price are Q^* and q^* respectively. Now

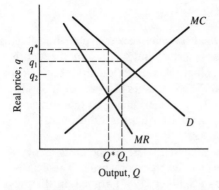

Figure 5.1 Monopoly: real demand and costs.

suppose aggregate demand rises, so P increases. If real industry demand is unaffected, the optimal price is unchanged. However, if the *nominal* industry price is fixed, the real price falls to q_1 and output rises as demand increases. If so, the firm will necessarily make less profit than before. Nevertheless, because of menu costs, it may not be worthwhile for the firm to raise the price. What is more, the firm will still want to satisfy the higher demand as the extra revenue exceeds the extra cost at this point $(MR > MC)$. This is crucially different from what would happen under perfect competition, where the firm will lose even more if it increases output, as the rise in output will generate less revenue than the extra cost. The key insight is that for small changes in P the profit loss is 'second order' (very small, in other words) as q is still very close to the optimum. Figure 5.2 illustrates the point.

At the optimum, the objective function is horizontal. In terms of calculus, for a maximum we require that $d\pi/dQ = 0$. So a small nudge away from equilibrium, say to Q_1, will have next to no effect on profits; firms will not change prices. If every firm acts the same way, we find that aggregate demand will affect output – just as in a Keynesian model. Similarly, the same type of argument applies to wages if, as in the efficiency wage model, the firm sets their level. Wage effects are not theoretically necessary, but as Ball and Romer (1990) show, they help to make the resulting effects more plausible from an empirical point of view.

Akerlof and Yellen (1985) had a very similar argument with their concept of 'near rationality'. They argue that in the region of the profit maximisation point wage-setting rules of thumb lead to only second order (i.e. tiny) costs. In a similar manner to menu costs, nominal disturbances are thereby transmitted to output.

The problem is that menu costs do not really work as a mechanism for explaining *large* changes in aggregate demand. For example, if demand

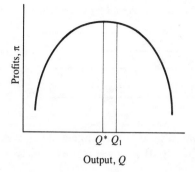

Figure 5.2   Profits for a monopolist.

were to rise to the point where q fell to q_2 in Figure 5.1, the lost profit might exceed any menu costs. Furthermore, we have only considered a one-off change. A more realistic model would allow for a succession of shocks over time, and allow different firms to be in different positions relative to their optimal price. It turns out that if the direction of shocks is always upward (not too restrictive an assumption given some inflation) then the effect of aggregate demand on output washes out on average (Caplin and Spulber, 1987). On plausible assumptions firms will find it optimal to adjust their price when they hit a particular threshold value for the real price; in expecting the shocks to continue, they raise the price 'too high', above the optimum in the absence of shocks. So on average just as many firms have prices above the optimum as below. An increase in demand pushes some off the top of the distribution – their real price hits its floor – but simultaneously others are entering at the bottom. On average, the real price remains unchanged.

Insiders and outsiders

An alternative explanation for non-competitive or sticky wages is that 'insiders' – those already in employment at firms – selfishly disregard 'outsiders' – the unemployed and those in low paid jobs – when setting wages. The insiders are often thought of as members of unions. This need not necessarily be the case as most workers have special skills and knowledge that give them some bargaining power, but it is convenient to think in terms of a 'union' bargaining with an employer. Certainly, unions are important in Britain, despite the efforts of the Thatcher and Major governments to reduce their power. Unionisation has declined in the United Kingdom so that less than 50 per cent of workers are now unionised, but this may understate their significance. Table 5.1 shows that in 1984

Table 5.1 Percentage of workers covered by collective agreements in Britain, 1984.

| | Private | | |
	Manufacturing	Services	Public
Manual	79	53	100
Non-manual	79	40	100

Source: Layard, Nickell and Jackman (1991).

two-thirds of workers were covered by collective agreements, well above the proportion unionised, although the figure varies widely between industries.

The important issue to grasp is that in the existence of unions, wages and possibly employment are the outcome of a *bargaining* process, in which neither unions nor firms are likely to get exactly what they want. The first authors to explore this properly were McDonald and Solow (1981), although Leontief (1946) anticipated the fundamental results. The firm's objective is simple: it wants to maximise profit. Things are not so straightforward for the union. Unions may care about a wide range of issues, including personal power and job security for union bosses, political aims, as well as the conventional issues of working conditions and remuneration. However, we focus on the narrowly economic objectives of wages and employment. There can be no doubt that *ceteris paribus*, unions prefer higher wages to low. Indeed, that may be all they care about; Oswald (1987) offers some evidence for the United Kingdom that is consistent with this view. Yet wages cannot be increased indefinitely without consequence. Eventually, jobs must go. So if unions do consider employment consequences, which the balance of the evidence suggests they do, then they must take this into account when bargaining over wages.

We can express this somewhat more formally. The union's objective function ('utility') is given by

$$V = V(N,W) \tag{5.2}$$

V is the union's objective function; it is increasing in employment N and real wages W.

A popular version of this general function is that the union maximises the expected utility of its members. The utility that members get will depend on whether they are in or out of work. In work, they receive the wage rate; out of work, they receive unemployment benefits.[3] The probability of being employed is simply $(1 - u)$, where u is the proportional unemployment rate.

We can simplify by making a number of assumptions. If union members are risk-neutral then we can treat money returns as equivalent to individual utility. A closed shop makes the identification of unemployment rates and probabilities exact, and assuming that the return to unemployment is zero simplifies the analysis without any loss of generality. Under these circumstances, union utility is given by

$$V = (1 - u)MW \tag{5.3}$$

where M is the union's membership. With the closed shop,

$$u = (M - N)/M \tag{5.4}$$

so

$$V = NW \tag{5.5}$$

In other words, unions aim to maximise the wage bill. Some union indifference curves are sketched in Figure 5.3, showing the trade-off between wages and employment.[4] A higher wage can compensate for lower employment. Union utility rises as we move to the right or upwards. Although (5.5) guarantees the standard convex shape, it is natural to assume that the corresponding curves from the general case in (5.2) would also look like this.

Next we consider the firm. If there were no union, firms would simply maximise profits subject to the market wage. Figure 5.4 shows how the demand curve for labour may be derived, using the (possibly unfamiliar) device of *isoprofit* lines. An isoprofit line shows the combinations of wages and employment yielding particular levels of profit. Maximum profit is at the point where the standard textbook condition holds, namely, that the real wage equals the marginal revenue product. As we move away from this point (which marks the maximum of the isoprofit line) in any direction, with higher or lower employment, the wage must be lower in order to maintain the same level of profits. For any level of employment, lower

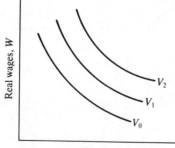

Figure 5.3 Union indifference curves.

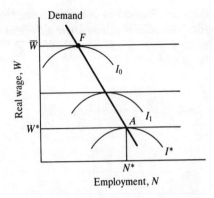

Figure 5.4 Isoprofit lines and the demand for labour.

wages mean higher profits, so the lower the isoprofit line, the higher is profit. Thus the firm will choose the lowest possible curve given the wage, and the tangency points for all the possible wages map out the (profit-maximising) demand curve. If W^* is the market wage, the firm is on I^* at N^*, point A on the diagram. F marks the zero profit point. This may seem like a long winded way of deriving a downward sloping demand curve, but the derivation has the great advantage of telling us what happens when we are off the demand curve.

We are now in a position to put the firm and union together. In Figure 5.5, the union's preferences are again summarised in the indifference curves, of which V^*, V_1 and V_2 are shown. If the bargain is restricted to the demand curve, then the best point for the union – the highest attainable utility – is at B. Notice that (in general) this will not be the zero profit point. This point is

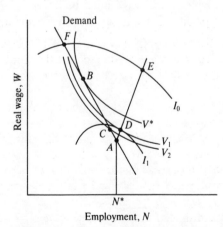

Figure 5.5 Firm and union bargains.

that which would be chosen in the extreme *monopoly union* case where the union has all the bargaining power. In general, in this *right to manage* set-up where the firm and union bargain over the wage but the firm chooses employment, the wage will end up at some intermediate point, such as *C*. The precise position will depend on relative bargaining power. As union power falls (affected by legislation, for example), the outcome will shift to the right and employment rises.

One problem with this model is that, as Leontief observed in 1946, these bargains are inefficient. Starting from *C*, both parties can do better by lowering the wage and raising employment. This violates the basic principle of Pareto efficiency, where efficiency is defined (rather weakly) as a situation where no-one can be made better off without making at least one other person worse off. Only points like *D*, where the isoprofit and union indifference curves are tangential, constitute *efficient bargains*. The locus of these, *ADE*, defines the *contract curve*. On the face of it, this is a remarkable result. Notice that the contract curve lies to the right of the competitive outcome.[5] Also notice that if the union becomes more powerful, it will push the bargain up and to the right. So if unions and firms bargain over employment, not only is employment higher (and unemployment lower) than in the competitive case, but *an increase in union power will raise employment*! In fact, appearances are misleading here, as this is a *partial* equilibrium model. In *general* equilibrium, as Layard and Nickell (1990) show, a rise in union power will lower aggregate employment; but the result still holds for a particular industry.

Whether bargains are efficient or not is an empirical problem. It may be that because of imperfect information or high bargaining costs efficient outcomes are unattainable, and this seems to be the case for the United Kingdom: see Layard, Nickell and Jackman (1991) for some evidence on this.

So far there is no particular macroeconomic consequence. Employment may be less than or greater than the competitive outcome. In special cases shifts in demand may leave the real wage unaltered; but this does not by itself lead to aggregate demand affecting output. As before, we need (for example) menu costs.

One basic deficiency of the simple models presented above is that they involve *static*, one-shot bargains. In reality, unions and firms repeat the bargaining process year after year – a *dynamic* problem. This leads to several considerations, among which is the growth or decline of union membership. The most dramatic assumptions are, first, that membership is equal to the last period's employment, and, second, that insiders care only about their own expected welfare.

This leads to two apparently contradictory phenomena. First, the insiders want to consider their future probability of being employed. Lower employment now will tend to imply lower employment in future (as the small membership has no incentive to enlarge the pool), and thus a higher probability of being out of the inside group. This gives an incentive to lower wages in bad years – real wage flexibility is higher than in the static case; but there is a second effect working in the opposite direction. If employment does fall, the reduction is likely to persist for a long time. In the extreme, as in Blanchard and Summers (1986), there is pure *hysteresis*.[6] That is, a shock to employment will persist forever; unemployment is permanently higher. The mechanism is that if demand and employment fall in any period, the 'insiders' left in employment are happy to negotiate higher wages reflecting the smaller sized workforce, ignoring those of their previous colleagues who are now outside the bargaining process. If the world is like this, then it becomes very important to avoid adverse demand shocks, as the consequences may be very severe.

To some extent these results conflict. The insider–outsider models have tended to emphasise the second effect, but it is by no means clear that unions will want to act in this way. However, the hysteresis model based on the insider–outsider approach does offer an explanation of one of the great macroeconomic puzzles; that is, the stubborn refusal of real wages to fall during the two crushingly severe recessions that the United Kingdom has been subjected to since 1979. Indeed, the period since 1979 has seen a combination of very high unemployment (by both historical and international standards) *and* high real wage growth (again, on both comparisons). We return to some related issues in Chapter 7.

Imperfect competition

We have already seen how imperfect competition is important in the approaches set out above. Models with menu costs require marginal revenue to exceed marginal cost, which is incompatible with perfect competition, and unions are inherently uncompetitive. Beyond this, the theory of imperfect competition can help to explain *directly* why firms respond to demand shocks by expanding output, not raising prices, as Weitzman (1982) was among the first to show. This is not enough by itself to generate real effects from changes in aggregate demand, but it helps generate large changes if any exist at all.

One story is that when the demand for output increases, firms lower their profit margins. This could follow if firms and customers have a long-run relationship, encouraging the formation of implicit contracts to keep prices constant. Like the literature examining implicit wage contracts discussed earlier in the chapter, this indicates that rigid nominal prices have no particular macroeconomic consequences, and does not help us in our search for Keynesian mechanisms. Another argument is that competition tends to be procyclical – firms price compete more in booms, cutting margins (Rotemberg and Saloner, 1986). More straightforwardly, the elasticity of demand may be procyclical. Standard micro theory tells us that the mark-up of prices over marginal costs is inversely related to this elasticity, so profit margins will fall in booms. More subtly, firms may find it optimal to attract new customers in booms, hoping they will remain attached in the downturn.

Another approach follows from an idea introduced by Sweezy in 1939. This is that firms adjust their prices asymmetrically, leading to a kinked demand curve, as shown in Figure 5.6.

The original rationale for this was based on firms' conjectures about their competitors' behaviour. If a firm expects that other firms will match price cuts, but will hold prices constant when its price rises, then the expected demand curve takes the form in the figure, with a kink at the current price. This creates a 'hole' in the marginal revenue schedule, so that a (small) shift in demand may leave output unaffected. An alternative justification is given by Stiglitz (1979), based on costly customer search. Lower prices will not attract many new customers (who are not looking for new suppliers) but higher prices will put off existing customers. The implication for macroeconomics is that if aggregate demand increases, shifting sectoral demands to the right, the price will remain constant (so long as the change is not too large). Thus aggregate demand can have real effects.

Conclusions

The problem with Keynesian economics has always been that it lacked a proper treatment of supply. This laid Keynesians wide open to the New

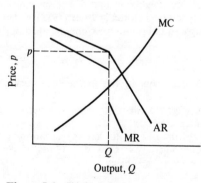

Figure 5.6 Kinked demand curves.

Classical counterrevolution. Thus New Keynesian theories are in part a reaction to the powerful intellectual thrust of the New Classical equilibrium business cycle theorists, who attempt to explain business cycles purely in terms of optimising equilibrium behaviour. Using the New Classicists' own tools, the aim is to generate Keynesian style effects. Ultimately, the motivation for this task is the common sense observation that even if we are not sure why, to many observers the economy does *look* as if it has Keynesian characteristics. In contrast to the clearly defined approach which underlies Chapter 4, there is no single model we can point to as the central case which captures the main issues. There are many possibilities on the agenda, and no doubt still more to come. While the dust has not yet settled to reveal the true picture, it seems at least possible that one or some of the approaches set out above will ultimately be seen to afford a sensible underpinning for the naive Keynesian policies that the policy-maker on the street pursues, regardless of whether academic economists approve or not. However, these are still early days. We shall allow Lawrence Summers the last word:

> While words like menu costs and overlapping contracts are often heard, little if any empirical work has demonstrated connections between the extent of these phenomena and the pattern of cyclical fluctuations. It is difficult to think of any anomalies that Keynesian research in the 'nominal rigidities' tradition has resolved, or any new phenomena that it has rendered comprehensible. (Summers, 1988)

Notes

1. The New Classicists' descendants, real business cycle theorists, also turned out to offer less than was initially promised (see Chapter 11).
2. An exception to this may hold if the existence of efficiency wages leads to multiple equilibria. If there are high or low output equilibria, a severe demand shock may bounce the economy away from the neighbourhood of a stable equilibrium to another. Some models of this type are explored in Price (1988). Other models may generate this kind of multiple equilibrium – see Cooper and John (1988) for a unifying framework.
3. More generally they also enjoy more leisure, or may obtain employment (at a lower wage) in a non-union sector.
4. If unions do not care about employment, the indifference curves will be horizontal.
5. Strictly, if unions maximise the wage bill, the contract curve is vertical. In more general cases it will take the shape shown.
6. 'Hysteresis' is a term borrowed from physics to describe situations where the current state depends on the route whereby we arrived. R. Cross (1988b) gives a wide-ranging collection of papers on the subject.

PART 3

Issues

6

Balance of payments and exchange rates

This chapter is concerned with analytic approaches to the balance of payments and also to the exchange rate. The dominant constraint on macroeconomic policy in the United Kingdom during the 1950s and 1960s was perceived to be the balance of payments. The nature of this constraint changed in the early 1970s as a result of major industrial countries adopting floating exchange rates. The sterling exchange rate was floating from June 1972 until October 1990. Then the United Kingdom joined the Exchange Rate Mechanism of the European Monetary System, though it was forced to leave in September 1992. (The issue of regime choice is discussed in Chapter 9.)

The importance which should be attached to balance of payments questions cannot be detached from the regime within which the country is operating. So it is important to remember that institutional changes may seriously affect the way in which these problems are viewed. For example, there is a possibility that the European Community will adopt a single currency by the end of this century. In this event, if the United Kingdom were a member of this currency area, the balance of payments of the United Kingdom would cease to be of great significance – just as the balance of payments of Yorkshire or Devon has had little policy significance in the past (see Chrystal and Wood, 1988).

The Keynesian or structural approach

The Keynesian approach to the balance of payments is based upon an analysis of the balance of trade. In its simplest form it relies on a single import function and a single export function such as equations (1.3) and

(1.4). If we specify the import function so that imports are proportional to income as in equation (1.3),

$$P = \mathrm{d}Y \tag{6.1}$$

while exports, X_0, remain exogenously determined, then the balance of payments can be analysed simply in the context of Figure 6.1. Since exports are constant and imports rise with national income, the balance of payments gets steadily worse as national income rises. Beyond a national income of Y_1 the balance of payments is in deficit.

While this model is a gross over-simplification, it represents a view of the economy which was widely held and which would appear to have been justified by UK experience. Any tendency for over-expansion in the UK economy produced balance of payments problems. The experience of the Stop–Go cycle in the United Kingdom throughout the 1950s and 1960s seemed to confirm the story that domestic expansion increased imports faster than exports, so the balance of payments inevitably deteriorated. As a result, the expansion had to be reversed. One curiosity, however, to which we shall return, is why it is that this pattern did not seem to apply to other countries? How was it that countries like West Germany and Japan had sustained and rapid economic growth without running into balance of payments problems? Indeed, Japan has recently had exactly the opposite problem – its economic success was associated with an almost perpetual balance of payments surplus.

Most empirical Keynesian models of the balance of payments, such as those used for forecasting, would, of course, have been more complex than that above. Exports and imports would typically be broken down into several different categories and there would be a term to capture relative price effects. The form of equation would, however, be similar for each category. Exports depend upon foreign demand and relative prices, and

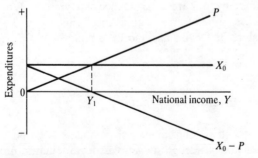

Figure 6.1 Keynesian view of balance of payments.

imports depend upon domestic demand and relative prices. The overall balance of payments forecast would be obtained by combining all of these import and export categories which had been forecast separately. These categories normally represent different industrial sectors. Hence, this can be thought of as a 'structural' approach.

Many operational models of the balance of payments had similar properties to the aggregate expenditure model above. An expansion of domestic aggregate demand worsens the balance of payments and the addition of a relative price effect can only serve to reinforce this. However, the structural approach to the balance of payments does allow a bias to develop in attributing blame for balance of payments problems. Since the core of the balance of payments is the real trade account, failure here must be due to 'inadequate' export performance, these inadequacies being attributable to inefficient domestic industries (perhaps due to under-investment or excessive wage settlements) which are 'uncompetitive'. An alternative approach points the finger directly at government macro-economic policy as the source of the problem. This is the monetary approach which is discussed below.

Mundell's assignment problem

One major inadequacy of the Keynesian approach to the balance of payments is that it focuses entirely upon the current account. Systematic interactions between the capital account and the domestic economy are thereby completely ignored. A simple rectification of this omission, in the IS–LM framework, was proposed by Mundell (1968). This treatment still provides the basis of many textbook models of the balance of payments. Ignoring capital flows was, perhaps, excusable in the 1950s since there was no general convertibility of major currencies and, as a result, private capital flows were of minimal significance. However, by 1971 financial capital movements were potentially so large that many observers attributed the breakdown of the fixed exchange rate system to their very size and volatility. The liberalisation of capital controls continued to such a degree in the 1970s and 1980s that it is common to talk about 'globalisation' of finance.

The Mundell model is achieved by adding to Model II of Chapter 1 a relationship between net capital flows and the domestic interest rate:

$$K = f(r) \tag{6.2}$$

Net capital flows depend upon the interest rate.

Capital flows should not be thought of as sales of machines to foreigners, rather they are net sales to foreigners of domestic bonds. There is a problem in drawing the line between the current and capital accounts. In this case 'capital' includes only financial assets. Assuming foreign interest rates to be fixed exogenously, as the domestic interest rate rises foreigners will buy more domestic bonds so the capital account of the balance of payments will improve. In effect, foreigners are lending more to the domestic economy. Initially, we assume imperfect capital mobility, so that a rise in domestic interest rates leads to a finite increase in capital flow. The implications of perfect capital mobility follow later.

The overall balance of payments is the current account plus the capital account. The current account gets worse as national income rises just as in the Keynesian model. Thus, if balance of payments equilibrium is to be maintained (at zero overall) as national income rises, the domestic rate of interest must also rise so that the improved capital account compensates for the worsening current account. In other words, the locus of zero overall balance of payments positions will be a positive relationship between national income and the interest rate, like BB in Figure 6.2.

Equilibrium for the system as a whole requires that all three lines BB, LM and IS should intersect at the same point. Consider the policy choices in the initial situation depicted in Figure 6.2. The IS and LM curves intersect at *A* where there is full employment. However, this is not a point of balance of payments equilibrium, since *A* is to the right of the BB curve. In fact there is a balance of payments deficit at *A* equal to the horizontal distance between *A* and BB multiplied by the marginal propensity to import. It is open to the authorities to correct the deficit by appropriate use of monetary and fiscal policy, but it is not obvious which to use.

A fiscal deflation would move the economy to point *C*, whereas a contraction of the money supply would move it to point *B*. Mundell's suggestion is that the best response is to react with monetary policy to the

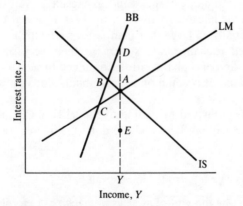

Figure 6.2 The Mundell model.

balance of payments and with fiscal policy to output (and thus to unemployment). Consider the contrary. Initially we react to the balance of payments deficit by shifting IS down until it passes through *C*. This has corrected the balance of payments but caused unemployment. An increase in money supply now designed to eliminate unemployment would shift the LM curve down to the right. The economy would then be at a point like *E* where the balance of payments deficit is worse than it was originally. If, however, starting from *A* we change the money supply in response to a balance of payments deficit and fiscal policy in response to unemployment, the economy would converge on point *D* at which there is full employment and balance of payments equilibrium. This is the reason for Mundell's assignment of monetary policy to the balance of payments and fiscal policy to output and employment.

An alternative version of the Mundell model gives an even better insight into the interaction between policy and external balance when capital is perfectly mobile. This version involves drawing the BB line as horizontal – see Figure 6.3. The interpretation of this is that interest rates are set in world financial markets. Minor deviations of the domestic from foreign rates set up massive inflows or outflows. The domestic economy is effectively a price-taker in the market for bonds. Let us consider how monetary and fiscal policy work under fixed and floating exchange rates.

Consider first fixed exchange rates. An increase in the money supply leads the LM curve to shift right (LM_0 to LM_1). This puts downward pressure on domestic interest rates but as soon as they start to fall there is a capital outflow. This leads to selling of the home currency in the foreign exchange market. In order to stop the exchange rate falling the central bank

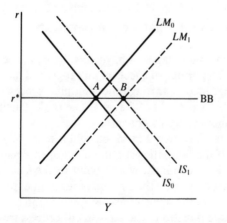

Figure 6.3 Effects of monetary and fiscal policies with perfect capital mobility.

has to buy it back (because they are pegging the exchange rate). This purchase of the home currency reduces the money supply until LM returns to the original position. Hence a monetary expansion under fixed exchange rates has had no real effect. The monetary expansion has to be reversed in order to maintain the value of the currency.

A fiscal expansion by contrast shifts the IS curve to the right. With a given money supply, this puts upward pressure on domestic interest rates and, thereby, causes capital inflows. The central bank has to sell domestic currency to stop the exchange rate rising. This increases the domestic money supply, so the economy goes from *A* to *B*. Hence, fiscal policy does succeed in generating an expansion where monetary policy failed.

Under floating exchange rates the outcome is reversed. A monetary expansion leads to capital outflows which now cause a depreciation of the exchange rate. The exchange rate depreciation stimulates export demand which shifts the IS curve to the right, so the economy moves from *A* to *B*. In contrast, a fiscal expansion leads to upward pressure on interest rates. This causes capital inflows and an exchange rate appreciation. The exchange rate appreciation leads to a fall in export demand which shifts the IS curve back to its original position. In effect, the increased budget deficit is exactly offset by a current account deficit (equal to the capital account surplus). See Chrystal (1989) for a more detailed exposition of this analysis.

In short, monetary policy is redundant under fixed exchange rates (fixing the exchange rate is a monetary policy) but useful under floating rates. The reverse is true for fiscal policy. In this context it is easy to explain the apparently active role of fiscal policy in the 1950s and 1960s, while monetary policy became more important in the 1970s and 1980s.

The monetary approach to the balance of payments

It has been seen that Keynesian balance of payments theory concentrates on the market for goods. The principal effects of an exogenous increase in exports would be to change income through the multiplier process. It was not always thus. In the classical world of David Hume trade deficits were associated directly with money supply changes.

Consider a pure gold standard world in which gold is both the internal and the external money. If the domestic economy developed a balance of payments surplus, a classical economist would point to the fact that the domestic gold stock would be rising by the amount of surplus per period. In other words, any imbalance in the value of goods flows is matched by net money flows in the opposite direction. The adjustment process from here on would be automatic since the rise in the domestic money stock would raise domestic money prices and cause a substitution of foreign for domestic goods. Thus the balance of payments surplus would disappear. This is the 'price-specie flow mechanism' of Classical economics.

Notice that where the internal and external money is the same, the balance of payments is not a problem *per se*. Outflows of bullion may have caused banking crises and contraction of the money stock may have caused unemployment, but the balance of payments was no more a problem in the pure gold standard world than the balance of payments of East Anglia is today. There was, of course, a problem when paper backed by gold began to circulate as money, because external payments required bullion. As a result, the reserve ratios of banks came under pressure whenever gold left the country. However, this was not an 'official sector' problem as reserve outflows under fixed exchange rates would be today.

In the modern world, where each nation state has its own fiat money, it might be thought that there has ceased to be a connection between the domestic money stock and the balance of payments. However, this is not generally true if the authorities are intervening to support the domestic exchange rate.

The process of pegging an exchange rate means that, in the UK case, the Bank of England takes up the residual excess demand or supply of foreign exchange at or close to the pegged price. If the United Kingdom has a balance of payments surplus, the authorities would buy foreign exchange with newly issued sterling. The foreign money would go into reserves and the sterling would go into the domestic money supply, so long as it is spent on UK goods (as opposed to being held overseas). The new increase in the money supply could be 'sterilised' by open market bond sales but this is of limited effectiveness where capital is perfectly mobile, since the process of selling more government debt would raise domestic interest rates and thereby induce additional capital inflows – thereby putting further upward pressure on the currency and requiring further purchases of foreign exchange.

The monetary approach points out that since the balance of payments has monetary effects, and is indeed a monetary 'problem', the domestic demand for money (or indeed other assets) should be an integral part of balance of payments analysis. If money continues to flow across the international exchanges then domestic money markets cannot be in equilibrium. An excess supply of money domestically will be reflected in an outflow across the exchanges. As the earlier 'absorption approach' (Alexander, 1952) emphasised, the balance of payments on current account is by definition equal to the difference between what the economy earns (output) and what it spends (national expenditure). Any group or individual for whom income and spending differ will be changing asset holdings. The decisions to spend or save out of a given income are not independent. However, specifying asset choices and expenditure decisions simultaneously offers important insights. The Keynesian approach focused explicitly on expenditures. The monetary approach emphasised asset stocks, especially money.

The most influential single contribution to the monetary approach is that of Johnson (1976). He considers a highly simplified world in which there are rigidly fixed exchange rates and all goods are traded at a single world price. Real income growth is exogenous. The domestic money demand function is given by:

$$M_d = pf(Y, r) \tag{6.3}$$

Real money demand depends upon real income and the rate of interest.

and the money supply is given by definition as the sum of money domestically created and money associated with international reserve changes.

$$M_s = R + D \tag{6.4}$$

Money stock is equal to reserves plus domestic credit.

If the system is in static equilibrium money demand will equal money supply and there will be no reserve changes. If, however, domestic income is perpetually growing, with constant world prices and interest rates, Johnson shows that the growth in reserves will be positively related to domestic income growth and negatively related to domestic credit expansion.

$$g_r = \alpha_0 n_y g_y - \alpha_1 g_d \tag{6.5}$$

where g_r, g_y and g_d are the growth rates of reserves, income and domestic credit respectively, and n_y is the income elasticity of demand for money.

This is a remarkable conclusion which implies that real income growth alone improves the balance of payments and is in stark contrast to the Keynesian model above, where a rise in income has exactly the opposite effect. How does this result come about? Very simply, if there is real income growth, at constant price and interest rate levels, then there will be growing demand for money for transactions purposes. An excess demand for money can be met in one of two ways, either through domestic credit creation or through a balance of payments surplus. If there is no domestic credit expansion, reserves will grow in line with the growth in money demand. The existence of an excess demand for money means that people will be spending less than their income. For the country as a whole there will be a balance of payments surplus. If, on the other hand, domestic credit expands faster than money demand, then there will be a loss of reserves through a balance of payment deficit. The problem, then, which causes balance of payments deficits and associated reserve losses is not income expansion itself but rather the authorities' policies with respect to domestic credit expansion. If domestic credit expands faster than demand for money balances, there will be a balance of payments deficit and associated reserve losses.

The monetary approach under fixed exchange rates should be thought of as a theory of reserve changes rather than the trade balance, since it is not clear from the literature whether the effects will appear in the current or capital account. However, it should be obvious that many of the simplifying assumptions in the Johnson model are not at all critical. Indeed, a wide range of possible macroeconomic models will have similar properties, at least in the long run, so long as they include a monetary sector which generates a stock demand for money.

The monetary approach does, however, resolve for us the apparent paradox of fast-growing countries which appear to have perpetual balance of payments surpluses, though it does not tell us where this growth comes from. Indeed this approach predicts exactly this outcome, so long as the domestic monetary authority restricts the growth of domestic credit to less than the growth in money demand. Thus, in countries like West Germany in the 1960s, since fast growth in real income caused a growth in demand for money for transaction purposes, the economy induced an inflow of money via the foreign balance to the extent that this money was not created by the Central Bank. Since the economy was trying to acquire financial assets it would be spending less than the value of its output which is identical to running a balance of payments surplus. This surplus could be sustained because growing income required ever-growing money balances. The United Kingdom was the opposite – slow real growth and faster domestic credit expansion leading to perpetual balance of payments problems.

Flexible exchange rates

Much of the above discussion has presumed the existence of fixed exchange rates. The widespread variability of exchange rates since 1971 has required a great deal more attention to be paid to flexible exchange rates and their policy implications. An endogenous treatment of the exchange rate, of course, requires an explicit model of the market in which it is determined – the international money market. Modern literature on the exchange rate developed out of the monetary approach to the balance of payments. A collection of early work in this area is provided in Frenkel and Johnson (1978) and a recent survey is available in MacDonald (1988).

The traditional textbook analysis of the exchange rate derives certain propositions about the flow demand for foreign exchange from the demand for imports and exports. Suppose there are two countries, the United

Kingdom and the United States. There is trade in goods between them. Each has a different domestic currency and the domestic currency price of domestic output is assumed to be fixed. The United Kingdom demands US goods but the sterling price in the United Kingdom depends upon how much UK citizens have to pay for dollars. The higher the price of dollars, the more expensive will be US goods in the United Kingdom, and vice versa. UK citizens demand a flow of dollars to pay for their imports and US citizens demand a flow of sterling to pay for UK exports.

In Figure 6.4 the vertical axis shows the price of $1 in pounds, so going up the axis is devaluing the pound. The horizontal axis shows the quantity of dollars demanded or supplied in exchange for pounds. As the price of dollars rises UK citizens find the price of US goods has gone up, so they buy less of them. If demand is elastic they will buy both a smaller quantity and a smaller value and will, therefore, demand fewer dollars. In that case the demand curve for dollars D will be downward sloping with respect to the exchange rate. Even if the underlying demand curve for goods were negatively sloped, the demand curve for dollars would be upward sloping if the demand for goods were not elastic.

The supply of dollars, S, is upward sloping so long as US demand for UK goods increases, as the pound is devalued. This is basically the 'elasticities approach' to the balance of payments and it leads to the Marshall–Lerner condition. This is that for a devaluation to improve the balance of payments, the sum of the elasticities of demand for imports and exports must exceed one in absolute value. This is really the stability condition for the market depicted in Figure 6.4, since if D were upward sloping and S downward sloping the market would be unstable in the sense that there would be excess demand above the equilibrium price and excess supply below.

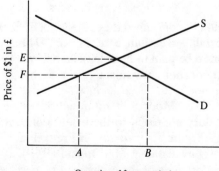

Figure 6.4 Exchange rate determination.

This model is extremely helpful in illustrating why the balance of payments is such a problem when the authorities are trying to peg the exchange rate in an over-valued position, such as at F. Here there is an excess demand for dollars, which in this model is the same as a current account deficit, equal to $B - A$. The only way that price F can be maintained is by the domestic authorities providing $B - A$ dollars per period out of reserves by, in effect, buying back sterling of equivalent value. Reserves are finite so this position is not sustainable indefinitely. A short-term solution is to borrow more reserves. A devaluation would involve changing the intervention price to E; but the conventional response in the 1950s and early 1960s was to depress domestic expenditures so that the D curve would be shifted to the left.

The monetary approach is critical of treating exchange rates as solely determined by flow demand for currencies derived from flow demands for goods. Exchange rates are the relative price of two moneys, so conditions in money markets must have some part to play. In a world of mobile financial capital the critical condition to be met is that all money stocks and financial asset stocks must be willingly held, at the margin. If there are excess money supplies or portfolio disequilibria, then financial capital will be flowing internationally and, in the absence of central bank intervention, exchange rates will be changing.

The principal difference between the fixed and floating exchange rate cases of the monetary approach is that, in the former, the price level was fixed to that of the rest of the world and the nominal money supply could change through induced reserve changes. In the latter there are no reserve changes and the nominal domestic money supply is fixed by the authorities. However, the real money supply is determined endogenously because domestic prices are no longer tied to foreign prices. Monetary expansion by the authorities now leads to downward pressure on the exchange rate and upward pressure on the domestic price level. The exchange rate measures the value of domestic money in terms of other moneys. The price level measures the value of domestic money in terms of goods. They are both indicators of the same thing – declining value of the domestic money. Neither is the cause of inflation, both are different aspects of the same inflation.

The monetary approach to the exchange rate does not claim that only monetary factors are important, but it does stress the importance of money markets in the short-run determination of exchange rates. This is because it may take a long time for price changes to influence goods markets, but the international 'wholesale' money markets are highly sensitive to minute interest differentials and expected exchange rate changes. If these markets anticipate an exchange rate change, as a result of some policy change, holders will tend to move immediately out of the currency which is expected to decline in value. Floating currencies do not move smoothly in line with inflation differentials. They adjust quickly to new information, but with a tendency to overshoot. The cause of overshooting will be discussed below.

Finally, it is important to avoid confusion about whether the monetary approach is a long-run or short-run theory. The fixed rate case was criticised by some for only explaining the long-run situation, while the proponents of the floating case espouse it as providing the dominant short-run explanation of exchange rates. It would seem that the behaviour of the authorities can change a model from long run to short run or vice versa. The answer to this paradox is very simple. In both cases demand for money for transactions purposes for most individuals and non-financial firms can be out of equilibrium for long periods. International goods arbitrage is also slow, so that the 'law of one price' or purchasing power parity are at best long-run equilibrium conditions. However, interest arbitrage equilibrium conditions between financial firms such as international banks hold almost exactly even in the very short run. The monetary approach in both fixed and floating exchange rate cases is a theory of short-run international portfolio adjustments, i.e. capital flows. These markets adjust most quickly and can thus dominate exchange markets in the short run. They are thus vital components to the explanation of short-run exchange rate changes in one case and reserve changes in the other.

Exchange rate models: An introduction

Considerable effort has been devoted in the last two decades to analysing the behaviour of floating exchange rates. Some of the most important theoretical work in this area is due to Dornbusch (1976a,b). Before discussing this theoretical work, however, it is important to emphasise that this area is not of peripheral importance for an understanding of recent UK economic history. Indeed, it would be hard to explain the dramatic rise in unemployment in the United Kingdom in the early 1980s without reference to the exchange rate. Entry into the ERM in October 1990 at a high exchange rate was also perceived to have exacerbated the 1991–93 recession. Let us now devote attention to explanations of the exchange rate itself.

There is an important analytical distinction between models of the long-run behaviour of exchange rates and the short-run. For the long run, purchasing power parity (PPP) is presumed to hold, so that prices of traded goods are the same in all countries (when converted at the existing exchange rate). There is no reason why PPP should hold in the short run, since it may take considerable time for goods arbitrage to react to price differentials. It is interest parity that ties down the exchange rate in the short run. The long-run case will be examined first.

Consider a two-country world where all goods are traded. Purchasing Power Parity holds so that prices in the domestic country will equal those in the foreign country when converted by the exchange rate

$$p = Ep^* \tag{6.6}$$

where p is the domestic price, p^* is the foreign price level and E is the domestic currency price of one unit of foreign currency (pounds per dollar). Each economy has a demand for real money balances which depends upon real income.

$$\frac{M}{p} = KY^\alpha \text{ and } \frac{M^*}{p^*} = K^* Y^{*\beta} \tag{6.7}$$

where $*$ denotes values for the foreign economy; K is the inverse of the velocity of circulation and α and β are the respective income elasticities of demand for real money balances.

Rearrange (6.7) as expressions for p and p^* and substitute into (6.6) so

$$M/KY^\alpha = EM^*/K^* Y^{*\beta}$$

This gives

$$E = \frac{M}{M^*} \frac{K^*}{K^*} \frac{Y^{*\beta}}{Y^\alpha} \tag{6.8}$$

The exchange rate, therefore, depends upon relative money stocks, relative velocity and relative real income. Converting all variables into growth rates (log differentials) we would have

$$e = (m - m^*) + (k^* - k) + (\beta y^* - \alpha y) \tag{6.9}$$

This focuses attention for explaining the percentage rate of change of the exchange rate on differences in monetary growth rates, velocity changes and income growth. This is the floating rate analogue of equation (6.5). If the rate of monetary expansion at home, *ceteris paribus*, is faster than that overseas e will rise. This is a devaluation of the home currency. Notice that the derivation depends critically upon (6.6) (purchasing power parity) holding.

Equation (6.9) provides the framework for much of the recent empirical work on exchange rates (see Frankel (1979) and MacDonald (1988)). However, a framework based upon PPP is unlikely to be very helpful in explaining short-run exchange rate movements. It is well known that exchange rates can move substantially and rapidly so that PPP is violated for significant periods. There may also be permanent shifts in PPP due to structural shifts, such as an oil discovery. (See Figure 6.5 for a chart of the UK real exchange rate and Figure 6.6 for a chart of the UK effective (nominal) exchange rate.) The problem is to explain these short-term movements of exchange rates without relying on the assumption of PPP.

If the exchange rate is not tied down by the fact that goods have the same price in all markets, some other condition has to be used. The obvious one is interest parity. Interest parity requires that the expected return on assets of different currency denomination should be equal. If they were not equal funds would be moving and exchange rates would be changing. A full discussion of the nature of interest parity is beyond our present scope. It will simply be presumed to hold in a particular form and the implications will be pursued. Suffice it to say that there are forms of the interest parity

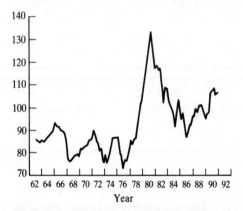

Figure 6.5 UK real exchange rate (series is 'relative normalised unit labour cost') (1985 = 100). Source: Datastream.

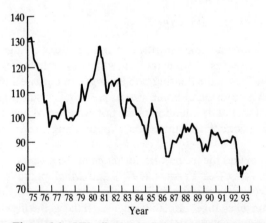

Figure 6.6 UK effective exchange rate 1975–93 (1985 = 100). Source: Datastream.

relationship which do hold more or less exactly, so long as appropriate interest rates are chosen and exchange risk is hedged through forward markets. Critical for what follows is the assumption implicit in the dropping of PPP and adoption of interest parity. This is that asset markets adjust quickly and goods market adjust slowly. Goods prices are sticky, but exchange rates and interest rates can change rapidly. The model to be discussed is essentially that due to Dornbusch (1976b).

Consider an IS–LM type portfolio choice between money and bonds. Domestic bonds and money are denominated in domestic currency (obviously) and foreign bonds and money are denominated in foreign currency. Interest parity requires that the expected return on domestic and foreign bonds be equal. If exchange rates can change, the relative return has two elements – the coupon interest yield and the change in the exchange rate.

$$r = r^* + x \tag{6.10}$$

The domestic interest rate, r, is equal to the foreign rate, r^*, plus the expected rate of depreciation of the domestic currency. If, for example, the sterling bond interest is 5 per cent per period and the equivalent dollar rate is 10 per cent, sterling must be expected to appreciate by 5 per cent per period. If this were not true it would be expected to be profitable to shift funds to where the return were higher. Notice, though, that the mere fact that one interest rate is higher does not indicate inequality of expected return.

The exchange rate is defined to adjust at some rate from the existing exchange rate e to the equilibrium $\bar{e}$.

$$x = \theta(\bar{e} - e) \tag{6.11}$$

where e and $\bar{e}$ are now in logs. Again, we focus on the domestic money market as expressed by the demand for money equation (plus the assumption that supply equals demand).

$$m - p = \alpha y - \lambda r \tag{6.12}$$

where variables are in logs, except the interest rate, r. (This is the same as (6.7) if $K = \exp[-\lambda r]$.) The foreign economy can be assumed to be 'large' relative to the home economy. This enables us to take the foreign interest rate r^* as exogenously fixed. Substitute (6.11) into (6.10) for x and then substitute this combined expression into (6.12) for r. This gives

$$m - p = \alpha y - \lambda r^* - \lambda\theta(\bar{e} - e) \tag{6.13}$$

This is nothing more than the domestic money market-clearing condition when interest parity is imposed as an extra constraint. Notice that in full equilibrium e will equal $\bar{e}$, so equilibrium prices will be:

$$\bar{p} = m - \alpha y + \lambda r^*$$ (6.14)

This enables us to simplify (6.13) by replacing $m - \alpha y + \lambda r^*$ with $\bar{p}$. Rearranging as an expression for the exchange rate gives:

$$e = \bar{e} - \left(\frac{1}{\lambda\theta}\right)(p - \bar{p})$$ (6.15)

This says that the exchange rate will deviate from the long-run level if the price level deviates from its long-run level. This may not seem particularly interesting, but in reality it says a great deal about the behaviour of exchange rates.

Consider Figure 6.7 which plots two relationships between the price level and the exchange rate. The positive sloped (45°) line labelled $p = e$ is equation (6.6). This is determined by purchasing power parity. It is drawn on the assumption that units are chosen so that p^* is unity.

The negative relation between p and e is given by equation (6.15) for given values of exogenous variables (so given values of $\bar{e}$ and $\bar{p}$). It reflects domestic money market-clearing in conjunction with interest parity.

Start at A in full equilibrium and let there be a once-and-for-all rise in the domestic money stock. Let us presume that the domestic economy is at full employment so that income effects can be neglected (a vertical IS curve or a classical aggregate supply curve will do just as well). From (6.14) and (6.6) it should be obvious that in full equilibrium both p and e will rise in proportion to the increase in m. (Recall that e is the domestic currency price of one unit of foreign exchange, so a rise in e is a devaluation of the domestic currency.) This means that the new money market-clearing condition will pass through a point like B which is north-east of A.

However, the economy will only jump straight to B if prices and

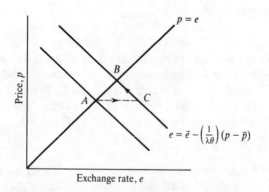

Figure 6.7 Overshooting model of the exchange rate.

exchange rates are perfectly flexible. In that case the excess money stock would be immediately eliminated by higher prices and the real money stock would be unchanged. It is more realistic to believe that the exchange rate can adjust rapidly, but that goods prices (and money wages) are relatively sticky. As a result, the adjustment pressure will be reflected first in the exchange rate. It will jump up to *C* and then gradually fall to *B* as prices adjust over time. This reflects 'overshooting' of the exchange rate, since the initial devaluation is greater than that ultimately required. Further comment on this overshooting is required, since it is fully consistent with rational expectation formation.

What happens after a money supply increase if the price level does not immediately adjust? If domestic output is constrained not to rise, the pressure must be reflected in the domestic interest rate. It will fall. This means that the interest parity condition (6.10) is violated. Since r^* is fixed, only x can now change to restore the equality. The value of r has fallen, so x must be negative if the domestic and foreign bonds are to have the same expected return. A negative x means an expected appreciation of the home currency. Long-run equilibrium requires a depreciation when compared to the initial point. These can only be reconciled if e immediately depreciates to a point from which it can be expected to appreciate during the adjustment of prices to the long-run equilibrium. This appreciation is just sufficient to compensate for the lower domestic interest rate. Hence, when the money stock increases the exchange rate depreciates too far and subsequently appreciates. This is what is meant by overshooting.

Notice that overshooting depends only on the price level being relatively sticky. There is no requirement of absolute fixity. The analysis will be more complex in reality to the extent that real income changes. It should be expected to change because at a point like *C* in Figure 6.7 (indeed, any point off $p = e$), PPP does not hold so there will be expenditure shifts in favour of the economy with lower prices. In the case of domestic monetary expansion, the exchange rate depreciates too far so domestic goods become relatively cheap (temporarily). With a tightening of domestic monetary policy, the home currency over-appreciates and domestic goods become relatively expensive.

The exchange rate overshooting model was widely used to explain the over-appreciation of sterling in 1979–81 (Figure 6.5). Buiter and Miller (1981a), for example, argued that the tight monetary policies of the Thatcher Government were responsible. However, they later (Buiter and Miller, 1981b) had to admit that the interest rate evidence was not consistent with overshooting caused by tight monetary policy. An alternative explanation (or perhaps a complementary one) places emphasis on North Sea oil. Britain was becoming a net exporter of oil at this time and the oil price doubled in 1979 (see Chrystal, 1984). The explanation of these events remains controversial, though the idea of overshooting is now widely accepted.

Besides explaining specific episodes of exchange rate misalignment, this analysis also explains why exchange rates in general have been so volatile. The system is recurrently being hit by disturbances or policy changes. If goods prices are sticky, the adjustment will be reflected in the exchange rate which can easily change from minute to minute. Thus, exchange rates should be expected to bounce about in response to 'news' in a way that is not possible in other markets. At the outset of floating many commentators argued that fluctuations would be reduced as the system settled down. This has not happened. Even (or perhaps, especially) in a model where actors hold rational expectations, there can be exchange rate overshooting so long as goods prices are relatively sticky in comparison to exchange rates.

Wealth and the balance of payments

Major extensions to the Dornbusch model involved the incorporation of fiscal policy effects and the modelling of full asset equilibrium. Fiscal policy effects are hard to simplify because there are many different ways in which fiscal policy can be implemented and most of these have real effects, even in full long-run equilibrium. However, the general result that a fiscal policy stimulus leads to exchange rate appreciation (identical to Mundell's floating case) will be illustrated below.

Asset equilibrium is important in overshooting models because the transition to full equilibrium involves current account deficits and surpluses. A current account deficit necessarily involves an economy running down its net foreign assets (or increasing its net foreign debt). A current account surplus involves the acquisition of foreign assets.

An unexpected monetary expansion at home causes a sequence of events which can be traced out using a model developed by Branson and Buiter (1983). For a simplified exposition of it see Chrystal (1989). Figure 6.8 plots the exchange rate on the vertical axis and holdings of foreign assets (by the home economy) on the horizontal axis.

The economy starts at *A*. The expansion of the money supply leads to an immediate depreciation of the home currency – a rise in *e*. If rational expectations formation is dominant, the economy jumps to a point like *B* which is on the new rational expectations consistent path (see Begg, 1982, pp. 31–41). The exchange rate depreciation is caused by incipient capital outflows and it also causes a current account surplus to develop. While the current account surplus persists, the economy is accumulating foreign assets, so it starts to move from *B* to *D*. Simultaneously there is a rise in domestic prices, not shown in this diagram. When the economy reaches *D*,

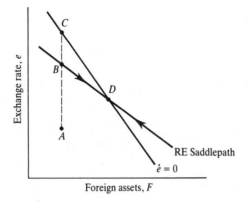

Figure 6.8 Monetary expansion.

the full adjustment has taken place, the current account is back in balance and there are no net capital flows. The domestic price level has fully adjusted to the new higher money supply. However, the economy has a permanent increase in foreign assets.

If the actors in the system had static, instead of rational, expectations, the adjustment process would be similar except that the initial jump would be to *C* instead of *B*. This requires a greater initial overshoot of the exchange rate. The reason for this difference is that rational actors know that the exchange rate is going to appreciate from *B* to *D* and hence they are prepared to hold more money balances than otherwise – they anticipate the appreciation. Those with static expectations, in contrast, think that the exchange rate is going to stay wherever it happens to be so they choose to hold lower money balances after the initial shock. In other words, those with static expectations dump more domestic money and hence drive the exchange rate down further.

The case of a fiscal policy expansion (see Figure 6.9) is more or less the reverse of the one we have just been through – though recall the proviso that fiscal policy can take many different forms. The economy starts at *A*. The government borrowing associated with a fiscal expansion puts upward pressure on domestic interest rates. This attracts capital inflows and appreciates the exchange rate. The current account goes into deficit. Under rational expectations, the exchange rate initially jumps to *B*. It then depreciates back to *D* while the economy is losing foreign assets. Under static expectations the jump appreciation is greater initially, than under rational expectations, because the subsequent depreciation is not anticipated. Full equilibrium is restored in both cases at *D*, where the current account deficit has been eliminated and the country has lost foreign assets.

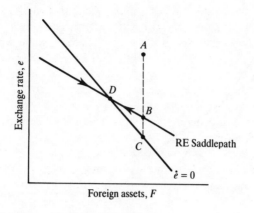

Figure 6.9   Fiscal expansion.

Empirical exchange rate models

An enormous amount of empirical work has been undertaken since the late 1970s in order to test models of exchange rate determination. Initially the exercise seemed fruitful. Models such as Frankel's (1979) seemed to do well in fitting simple models to the data. However, in the early 1980s these models broke down comprehensively (for a survey of much of the 1980s literature see MacDonald (1988)). Likely reasons for this failure were the dominance of real shocks such as North Sea oil and the US fiscal deficit. Also there was a clear breakdown in traditional monetary relationships in several major countries due to financial innovation. Since exchange rate models were built on demand for money equations it was hardly surprising that they would break down too. The key financial innovation in this context has been the payment of interest on current accounts. Chrystal and MacDonald (1993) provide some evidence which suggests that the simple monetary model may be rescued if 'Divisia' monetary aggregates are used instead of the official simple sum measures of the money supply (see Chapter 3).

Exchange rate modellers received another blow from Meese and Rogoff (1983). They compared the out of sample forecasting performance of a wide range of alternative models. The best one period ahead forecast was achieved from a model which says that the exchange rate next period is equal to the exchange rate this period plus a white noise random error. This forecasting rule outperforms all economic models and time series forecasting techniques. The exchange rate, it seems, is a 'random walk'.

The failure of economic models to outforecast a random walk does not necessarily imply that the economics is worthless. Rather it suggests that the foreign exchange market is very efficient (see Levich (1989) for a discussion of efficiency). Efficiency implies that, even if some known economic model were at work in determining the exchange rate, all information relevant to that price (including history and what is predictable about the future) has already been taken into account in setting today's exchange rate. The only thing that can move the exchange rate is 'news' – something that was not expected yesterday. News by definition is random. Predicted events which happen are not news in this sense.

In short, exchange rate models should be seen as something which can be tested against historical data and which will inform our understanding of the forces determining exchange rates. However, they do not provide a tool which can forecast future exchange rate changes in anything like a reliable way. The simple message for businesses potentially affected by exchange rate changes is to hedge exchange risk wherever possible and heavily discount econometric forecasts of exchange rate changes. The actual outcome will be dominated by events yet to happen.

Summary

In the 1950s and 1960s the balance of payments was the problem that dominated British macroeconomic policy. It was a problem precisely because the authorities had to finance deficits out of reserves while maintaining a fixed exchange rate. Keynesian and monetary approaches to the balance of payments offer different insights into the nature of the problem. Floating exchange rates provide a different policy environment. Excessive monetary expansion causes (and caused) currency depreciation and inflation. Excessive monetary contraction causes (and caused) currency appreciation (and unemployment, if prices and wages are sticky). Inflation and unemployment are the subjects of the next chapter. Notice that the analysis of overshooting above offers a very plausible reason as to why fully-anticipated monetary policy will have real effects.

7

Inflation and unemployment

Between 1951 and 1967 the rate of inflation in the United Kingdom never exceeded 6 per cent per annum. In 1975 it was of the order of 25 per cent per annum. It should, therefore, be no surprise that economic policy of the 1970s was dominated by the problem of inflation. By mid-1986 inflation had fallen to nearly $2\frac{1}{2}$ per cent, and although it rose subsequently it was back under 2 per cent in 1993. In contrast, unemployment drifted upwards. In 1955, it was 1.1 per cent of the labour force, but in 1974 it was 2.0 per cent[1] (a level sufficiently high to prompt the famous 'U-turn' of the Conservative administration led by Prime Minister Edward Heath). By 1979 it was at 4.1 per cent, prompting the Conservative opposition to coin the phrase 'Labour isn't working', which, in the light of subsequent events, was to prove highly ironic. From early 1980 unemployment accelerated dramatically, reaching about $10\frac{1}{2}$ per cent by early 1983. Between the beginning of 1980 and the end of 1982 about 1.7 million jobs (net) disappeared in the United Kingdom. When the upturn came, unemployment fell almost as precipitously, from 11.2 per cent in 1986 to 5.6 per cent in mid-1990, but subsequently rose again, to 11.0 per cent in April 1993. It is incumbent upon economists to offer some explanations of these dramatic events which have been variously blamed upon declines in world demand, excessive unemployment benefits, Monetarist deflation, variations in house prices and many others.

In this chapter we concentrate on the period up to 1985, leaving discussion of the more recent past to the following chapter. We begin by examining the development of analytical models of the interaction of inflation and unemployment.

The Phillips curve

One of the most famous relationships in macroeconomics is the inverse relationship between inflation and unemployment identified by A. W. H. Phillips (1958) and hence known as the Phillips curve. This relationship was, however, pointed out much earlier in the United States by Irving Fisher (1973). Further important supportive work on the Phillips curve was done by Lipsey (1960).

The problem Phillips posed for himself was how to explain the dynamic behaviour of a macro model such as Model II when it was close to full employment. The textbook models had real output changing only at less than full employment, whereas at full employment only prices changed. Phillips focused particularly on the labour market and proposed that as the pressure of demand, as measured by unemployment, got greater and greater, the rate of increase of wages would rise. As a zero level of unemployment was approached the rate of increase of wages would approach infinity. Phillips showed that the evidence of nearly 100 years was consistent with the existence of a stable relationship, as depicted in Figure 7.1. The theoretical underpinnings were refined by Lipsey who worked in terms of separate wage and price equations. Wages were determined by unemployment, and prices were determined by a mark-up on wages plus other costs. Followers often dropped this refinement and simply drew Figure 7.1 with inflation,[2] $\dot{p}$, on the vertical axis instead of $\dot{w}$. It is now a commonplace to draw the Phillips curve as a relationship between $\dot{p}$ and U, and this practice will be continued below.

The Phillips curve was widely adopted by economists in the early 1960s as filling in a gap in the standard version of Model II. During this period it was generally accepted that inflation was mainly caused by demand factors, though even Phillips was fully aware that cost factors, especially import prices, *could* exert an independent influence on the price level. However, they had not often done so in the previous 100 years. Recent work on price

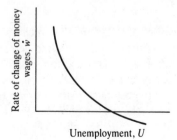

Figure 7.1   The Phillips curve.

determination (for example, Price ⟨⟩ ⟨⟩ ⟨⟩ ⟨⟩s it clear that elements of costs other than wages are importa⟨⟩ ⟨⟩ ⟨⟩ ⟨⟩ ⟨⟩ determination of prices though it is no surprise that the evidence only becomes econometrically visible after the 1970s, as before then there was very little variation in raw material and energy prices.

After devaluation in 1967 the inflationary experience was considerably worse than previously, as Phillips himself would have predicted. Wages, however, lagged behind prices owing to the incomes policy of 1968–69 and also presumably because people did not know what to expect in terms of price rises. The resultant 'wage explosion' in 1969 was widely interpreted as proving the possibility of wage push independent of the level of demand. However, it can also be interpreted as a catch-up of expectations. Laidler (1976) argues that over this period the country was merely reimporting the inflation it had previously been exporting.

Even if the data from the late 1960s could be made to fit with the simple Phillips curve, the data from the 1970s certainly could not. Indeed, the theoretical basis of the simple Phillips curve had been undermined independently by Phelps (1968) and Friedman (1968) long before events had made this reappraisal necessary. The Phelps–Friedman approach forms the starting point for the model to be developed below.

An essential ingredient of the modified approach to the Phillips curve is the idea that workers and firms bargain over *real*, rather than nominal, wages.[3] Thus the Phillips curve has to be shifted up for each level of expected inflation to take account of the anticipated erosion of purchasing power over time. There is then a short-run trade-off between inflation and unemployment for each *given* expected rate of inflation – but the story does not stop there. Not only does the short-run Phillips curve shift over time as inflation expectations change, but the long-run position may also alter. We return to these issues in more detail below.

Aggregate demand and supply

The major disagreement over the causes of inflation is often characterised as being between those who think it comes from aggregate demand and those who think it comes from the supply side of the economy. Most would agree that an expansion of the money stock is necessary to sustain a price-level rise, but those who believe in cost-push usually argue that the money stock has to be expanded in the wake of inflation to avoid unemployment. Both lines of argument could be valid. The question is, what actually happened in any particular episode?

Let us first look at the price level and the level of output in terms of Model III. Following Gordon (1978) it is convenient to combine the two versions of

Model III by a simple modification of the aggregate supply curve. For the short-run case where money illusion was assumed on the part of suppliers of labour, we assume that labour supply depends upon the expected price level p^e. Demand for labour on the other hand depends upon the actual price level. In the short run, while expectations lag behind reality, the aggregate supply curve will be upward sloping but it will shift leftward if expectations are revised upwards. In the long run expectations are correct so the long-run supply curve is vertical at the trend output level – sometimes called the 'natural'[4] output level. In other words, the long-run supply curve shifts rightwards each period because of the underlying growth of the economy.

If we consider the initial position in Figure 7.2 to be at point A then it is clear that a price-level rise can be started by either a rightward shift of aggregate demand AD_1, or a leftward shift of aggregate supply. A cost-induced inflation would involve a supply-side shift and the economy would move from A to C. A move to D would then follow if measures were taken to eliminate unemployment. Eventually the system would settle again at a higher price level on the long-run aggregate supply curve. A demand-induced inflation, however, would be caused by a shift of the demand curve to, say, AD_2 so the economy would move from A to B. Expectations would then be revised so that AS_1 would shift in the direction of AS_2 and the economy would move to a point like D. Whether D is in this case to the left or right of long-run AS does not matter – either is possible. The point is that a demand-induced inflation will move the economy through an anticlockwise arc initially. A supply-induced inflation will move it through a clockwise arc.

The picture in the United Kingdom in the early 1970s is extremely clear, as Figure 7.3 shows, so long as it is appropriate to start the cycle in 1971. The end of 1971 marks the beginning of a major expansion of the money

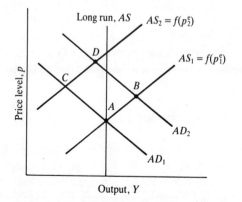

Figure 7.2 Aggregate supply and demand with price expectations.

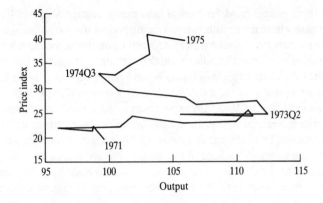

Figure 7.3 Producer prices and manufacturing output in the United Kingdom, 1971–75 (1985 = 100).

supply associated with Competition and Credit Control, and March 1972 was the date of Mr Barber's famous expansionary budget. Hence a shift of demand moves the economy along a short-run supply curve, which incidentally appears to be fairly flat. After the oil shock (and a further supply-side squeeze following from a spectacularly badly timed attempt to introduce indexed wage contracts just when retail prices were unexpectedly rising steeply) there is a dramatic leftward bounce in output to the trough in late 1974. While the adverse supply shift does not go away, the effects of the Barber boom persist and the economy slides up the short-run supply curve as demand recovers.

Notice that while the movement from 1973 to 1975 must involve a shift of the supply curve, some such shift would be an essential part of the demand-induced story. The economy cannot stay at a point like *B* in Figure 7.2 because it is beyond the long-run supply curve. Price expectations will necessarily shift the supply curve leftward sooner or later. It is quite likely that the oil price rise induced the shift of supply between 1973 and 1975, but it is important to realise that after the events of 1971–73 some such shift would have occurred anyway due to the behaviour of expectations.

The expectations-augmented Phillips curve

The above analysis is couched in terms of the price level and the level of output. An analogous argument can be developed in the more familiar dimensions of inflation and unemployment. It was seen above that a single stable Phillips curve is incapable of reconciling the observation of both high inflation and high unemployment. However, once it is admitted that there is a new higher Phillips curve for each higher expected rate of inflation events become easy to explain.

To see this, suppose curve PC_1 in Figure 7.4 is the Phillips curve for zero expected inflation. If the level of unemployment is U^*, this expectation will be fulfilled and nothing need change. However, if unemployment were U_1 inflation would be greater than zero at $\dot{p}_1$. In effect, the wage bargainers made a mistake setting wages – inflation turned out to be higher than they expected (the expectational error is positive). Friedman, using a form of adaptive expectations, argued that having underestimated inflation, the next period expectations would be revised upwards. This generates a higher Phillips curve, say PC_2. Again, inflation would be higher than expected and, so long as unemployment stayed at U_1, inflation would accelerate. So long as we remain to the left of U^*, inflation carries on increasing. Consequently, we call this the 'accelerationist' hypothesis. We can think of the long run as the period within which expectations are fulfilled. As a result, the *long-run Phillips curve* traces out the point on each short-run curve where expectations will be fulfilled and where inflation is consequently stable. The dramatic conclusion is that the long-run Phillips curve is vertical *by definition*. There can be no long-run trade-off between inflation and unemployment.[5]

Friedman referred to the unique level of unemployment at which expectations turn out to be correct as the *Natural Rate of Unemployment*, also known as the equilibrium rate. He made very large claims for this rate, which we now know to be unjustified:

> The natural rate of unemployment . . . is the level that would be ground
> out by the Walrasian system of general equilibrium equations, provided
> there is embedded in them the actual structural characteristics of the labour
> and commodity markets, including market imperfections, stochastic

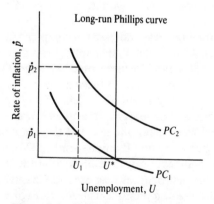

Figure 7.4 Shifting Phillips curves.

variability in demands and supplies, the cost of gathering information about
job vacancies and labor availabilities, the cost of mobility, and so on.
(Friedman, 1968, p. 8)

'Natural' carries with it the implicit connotation that it is also 'best'; but the
equilibrium rate, even in the absence of powerful unions, will generally be
inefficient. This is not the place to rehearse the arguments, but it turns out
that the natural rate may be too high or too low, as the factors pushing us
away from efficiency can go either way; see Pissarides (1990) for an
exhaustive discussion of the issues. Thus a preferable, less value-laden, term
for the unique long-run level is the NAIRU, or *Non-Accelerating Inflation
Rate of Unemployment*. However, the term 'Natural Rate' is still a useful
one to keep. As we see below, the concept of the NAIRU can be fitted into
the wage bargaining model set out in Chapter 5, and it is useful to think of
the natural rate as the level of unemployment that would prevail in the
absence of any union bargaining power. It is important to bear in mind that
it is unlikely to remain constant over time. For instance, if unemployment
benefits fell it is likely the unemployed would want to spend less time
searching for work, and the natural rate would fall. This will affect the
NAIRU. However, as we will see, other factors (such as trade union
legislation) can also affect the NAIRU, even if the natural rate is constant.

Wage bargains and the Phillips curve

Friedman had in mind a competitive world where atomistic firms compete
and individual workers search for work. What drove his version of the
Phillips curve were unemployed workers mistakenly accepting high money
wage offers, wrongly thinking that they were high *real* wages. In order to
understand how the Phillips curve shifts in a unionised economy like the
United Kingdom, we have to consider the bargain struck between firms and
workers.

The issue of firm/union bargaining was addressed in Chapter 5, and this
section builds on that analysis. As argued in that chapter, firms and unions
both have ideal targets for the real wage. The firm would like wages to be set
at the minimum market rate. This sets a floor; if the wage were any lower,
the firm would be unable to employ enough workers. *Ceteris paribus*,
unions want a higher wage, but as they recognise that higher wages imply
lower employment, their ideal wage takes into account the consequences
for jobs, balancing higher wages with laid-off union members. We assume
that firms have the 'right to manage', so we are always on the demand
curve. While this is technically inefficient, as discussed in Chapter 5, the
evidence is that it is the realistic assumption. This leads to Figure 7.5.

The figure assumes there is only one (representative) firm so we can work

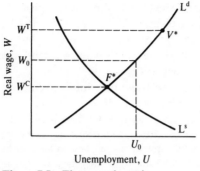

Figure 7.5 The wage bargain.

directly with unemployment. Thus L^d is the conventional labour demand curve, which slopes upwards when unemployment (rather than employment) is on the horizontal axis as drawn here, and L^s is labour supply.[6] V^* is the union's ideal point, with associated real wage W^T; F^* is the firm's ideal at the competitive wage W^C. The actual outcome is at W_0 and U_0. The determinants of W_0 (and therefore U_0) are the factors that affect the target wage, the competitive wage, and the union's relative bargaining power. The *competitive wage* can be thought of as being determined by the natural rate of unemployment; if this increases, effective labour supply falls and the competitive wage rises. So anything that affects the natural rate affects the competitive wage. Factors likely to increase the natural rate are the degree of mismatch or 'noise' in the labour market, like the disparity between the type of jobs available and the skills of those unemployed; the level of unemployment benefits, which affects the length of time the unemployed spend hunting for a job; and institutional factors like the social stigma attached to unemployment, or the administrative structure of the government employment services.

The *union wage* will similarly be affected by several factors. These include union preferences; if unions become more 'militant' it may be reflected in a push for higher wages. Other factors include the level of unemployment benefits or wages in any non-union sectors, which soften the impact of job losses on union members, and the level of aggregate unemployment itself. The higher is unemployment, the more serious is the effect of a lost job, as laid-off workers tend to spend longer between jobs.

The *actual outcome* will depend on the relative bargaining strength of the two parties. This will be affected by legislation, and also by the ability of one party to impose costs on the other. For example, a high level of capital intensity makes it easy for workers to impose large costs on employers in the event of a strike, as although there are no wage costs during a strike, capital and other fixed costs are still incurred. Strikes might also be more effective when demand for the product is buoyant, as lost profits are high. Finally, note that a contraction in demand (a rightward shift in L^d in Figure 7.5) will tend to lower the bargained real wage, as the competitive wage is lower and higher unemployment for any given wage will tend to lead to a downward shift in the union target wage.

Putting these factors together, the wage bargain is given by:

$$W = Pf(u,z) \tag{7.1}$$

The nominal bargained wage, W, is proportional to the price level, P, negatively related to the unemployment rate u, and affected by other factors, z, including the level of unemployment benefits and aggregate demand.

However, we need to recognise that firms and unions must form expectations of the price level. We begin, where lower case letters indicate logs, by rewriting (7.1) as

$$w = p^e + g(u,z) \tag{7.2}$$

The log of the wage, w, is equal to the log of the *expected* price, p^e, and negatively related to the unemployment rate and other factors, z.

Next, note that the actual price differs from the expected price by an error term, ε:

$$p = p^e + \varepsilon \tag{7.3}$$

The log of the actual price, p, is equal to the expected price, p^e, plus the expectational error, ε.

Next, we need a story about what determines prices. It is natural to assume that prices are a mark-up over wages, so

$$p = w + h(z) \tag{7.4}$$

The price level is a mark-up over wages. The mark-up, h, is affected by a range of factors including aggregate demand.

We have again used a log–linear form to simplify the equation here, and abstract from other costs (such as energy, import prices and taxes), although in practice these are potentially very important. Putting prices, wages and expectations together, we get

$$p = p^e + j(u,z) \tag{7.5}$$

where $j(u,z)$ conflates $g(u,z)$ and $h(z)$. Equation (7.5) is about the price level, not inflation, but we can easily transform it into a Phillips curve. Recalling that $\dot{p}_t = p_t - p_{t-1}$ and $\dot{p}^e_t = p^e_t - p_{t-1}$ (as p_{t-1} is known at time t), subtracting p_{t-1} from both sides of (7.5) yields

$$\dot{p} = \dot{p}^e + j(u,z) \tag{7.6}$$

This tells us that for given z there is a *unique* level of unemployment at which expectations are correct – where $\dot{p} = \dot{p}^e$ – defined by the value of u that satisfies

$$0 = j(u,z) \tag{7.7}$$

given z. This is the NAIRU,[7] and varies as z changes. Later in the chapter we look at what actually happened to z and the NAIRU in the 1970s and 1980s.

Phillips curves and the growth of aggregate demand

In order to understand what happens to the course of inflation and unemployment in reality, it is necessary to add to this picture a means of analysing the growth of aggregate demand.

There are really two separate relationships that can be identified between aggregate demand growth and inflation/unemployment. These are illustrated in Figure 7.6. Let us assume for simplicity that there is no productivity growth, so that output is constant at the NAIRU. With output fixed, it follows that the long-run budget constraint (LRBC) of the economy is determined by the nominal growth in aggregate demand. This is no more than an accounting identity – hence the use of the term 'budget constraint'. Thus the inflation rate (at a constant NAIRU output level) will be equal to the growth rate of aggregate demand. If aggregate demand in money terms is growing at 10 per cent per annum the long-run budget constraint will be a horizontal line at a 10 per cent inflation rate (or lower if the productivity assumption is changed).

Naturally, there is no reason why the economy should be on the

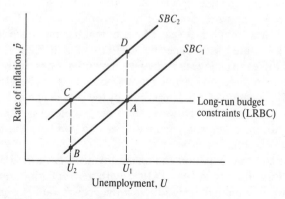

Figure 7.6 Budget constraints.

long-run budget constraint in each period. It will only be on LRBC when the economy is on the long-run aggregate supply curve, that is, when output is not changing. Take the growth rate of *money* income as being exogenously fixed by policy. Then the short-run budget constraint that has to be satisfied is given by the fact that the rate of growth of money income is equal to the sum of the rate of growth of *real* income and the rate of inflation. Again, this is a matter of accounting that must hold by definition. So if there is some real income growth during the current period the inflation rate must be lower than the growth rate of money income. Let us also presume that there is a one-to-one relationship between real income (output) and unemployment. (A specific form of this relationship is known as Okun's Law.) Higher output will be associated with lower unemployment. This means that we can express the short-run budget constraint as a relationship between inflation and unemployment.

To see what the short-run budget constraint must look like, start at point A in Figure 7.6 on LRBC. If there is no real income growth, inflation will equal the growth of money income so the economy will stay at A. However, if there is real income growth in the current period, unemployment will fall and inflation will *necessarily* be less than the rate of growth of money income. The economy will go to a point like B. The short-run budget constraint is, therefore, positively sloped in inflation/unemployment space, SBC_1.

Notice that point B is not sustainable for a second period. The move from A to B required real income growth and, therefore, a *fall* in unemployment from U_1 to U_2. If unemployment now stays at U_2, real income must be unchanged and so in the second period inflation must be equal to the rate of growth of money income – the economy would then be at C. This demonstrates that the short-run budget constraint for the second period must pass through C. In general, the SBC for a specific period cuts LRBC at the unemployment level achieved at the end of last period. This is because it depends upon the growth of real income when the base from which growth is measured is last year's level of real income. Each level of real income is associated with a specific level of unemployment.

Of course, if there is a change in aggregate demand policies, LRBC itself will shift and the exercise will start again at a point such as A on the new LRBC curve. The location of A is determined by the level of unemployment at the beginning of the period. However, in order to determine the actual course of inflation and unemployment we need to combine the budget constraints with the Phillips curves.

Consider the course of inflation and unemployment that would occur if the economy were initially at the NAIRU with zero inflation and zero growth of aggregate nominal demand. Now the growth rate of aggregate demand is raised to 10 per cent. What happens? The long-run budget constraint becomes a horizontal line at the inflation rate of 10 per cent, as depicted in Figure 7.7. The new short-run budget constraint SBC_2 passes through the long-run budget constraint at the initial level of unemployment, i.e. at G. The short-run Phillips curve is PC_1 so the economy moves from the initial position $(U^*, \dot{p} = 0)$ to A. Next period, the new short-run budget constraint will be SBC_3 and, if the short-run Phillips curve did not shift, the economy would go to B and then converge on C. However, expected inflation will now start to shift the short-run Phillips curve up to the right. If it now intersects SBC_3 at D the budget constraint will stay put for one period but the short-run Phillips curve will continue to move to the right.

Once the intersection of PC and SBC is *above* the long-run budget constraint, the SBC curve will now start to shift back down to the right. Once the economy is to the *right* of the long-run Phillips curve, the PC curve will start to shift back down to the left. Thus from a point such as E which is on PC_2 and SBC_3 we move to F on PC_2 and SBC_2. From F both the SBC curve and the PC curve will shift down, so the next position could well be southeast of G. Clearly, the economy will home into the long-run equilibrium point G in a clockwise cycle, presuming, that is, that the expectations feedback is reasonably stable, so that the economy does not explode.

It is important to notice that, while we have conducted the simplest possible experiment of raising demand growth from zero to 10 per cent, we have discovered a pattern of response which includes periods of rising inflation and rising unemployment, falling inflation and rising unemployment, as well as rising inflation and falling unemployment. The economy has moved through a clockwise convergent cycle from the initial position through A, D, E and F, and eventually to G.

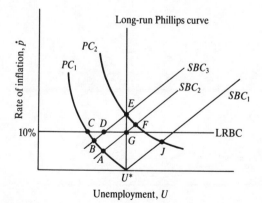

Figure 7.7 Short- and long-run Phillips curves and budget constraints.

Figure 7.8 plots the actual course of the UK economy during its inflation cycle of 1971–76. The movement from 1971 to 1972 can be regarded as the tail of the previous cycle. From 1972 there is a clear clockwise cycle which is entirely consistent with a demand-induced inflation as above. Specific factors such as the oil price rise and incomes policies will no doubt have an influence on the numerical size of various shifts, but it is hard to see how these specific factors could explain the pattern as a whole. For example, if the 1973 oil crisis had struck at the initial position in Figure 7.7 and the authorities had maintained the level of domestic demand constant, the economy would initially have moved north-east to a point like J.

On the basis of Figure 7.8 the NAIRU looks to be of the order of 3 or 4 per cent. Indeed Sumner (1978) estimated it at 3.2 per cent for this period and Batchelor and Sheriff (1980) estimate the 'equilibrium' level for this period to be 4 per cent.[8] More recently, Layard, Nickell and Jackman (1991) estimate the rate to be around $3\frac{3}{4}$ per cent for the period 1969–73 (using Organisation for Economic Co-operation and Development (OECD) definitions of unemployment). As a result of this analysis one would have concluded that the economy should home in on an unemployment rate of 3–4 per cent at some stable inflation rate. The latter should have been reasonably low given the adoption of fairly restrictive aggregate demand policies in late 1976.

This, of course, did not happen. The above analysis has been deliberately retained from the first (1979) edition of this book because it is instructive about the conventional wisdom of the time. The policies pursued by both the Labour Government of James Callaghan after 1976 and the Conservative Government of Margaret Thatcher after its election in May 1979 should have had a better effect on the British economy. Subscribers to the

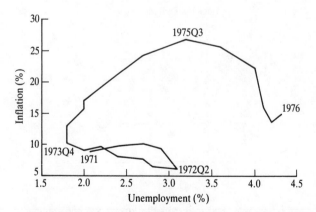

Figure 7.8   Retail price inflation and UK unemployment: 1971–76.

above view of the world should not have viewed their policies with total disfavour. It should have been possible to have unemployment in the region of 4 per cent, with inflation below 10 per cent by 1980.

The economics of 1978–82

As Figure 7.9 graphically demonstrates, the economy did not home in on 4 per cent unemployment. Rather, unemployment accelerated dramatically from early 1980 to reach a level of nearly 12 per cent in early 1983. It is true that inflation had also come down to about 5 per cent by early 1983, but on the basis of previous patterns this should have been possible at very much higher levels of employment. The rise in inflation from 1978 to 1980 may be explicable in terms of a number of temporary factors such as the 1979 oil price rise and the increase in VAT resulting from the June 1979 Budget. The real problem, however, is to explain the massive rise in unemployment.

Earlier in this chapter we set out a bargaining model of the labour market which is now more or less the conventional view. It offers a synthesis of demand and supply-side effects; we can analyse changes in unemployment in terms of either demand or supply-side forces. For example, if the demand for output and therefore labour collapses *and* if wages do not immediately respond to the changed conditions, then unemployment will rise. Alternatively, if (say) there were an increase in the mismatch betweeen the unemployed and vacancies, then the natural, NAIRU and subsequently actual rates would rise. Which factors matter is an empirical question. The most comprehensive (and comprehensible) account of the UK experience is given in Layard, Nickell and Jackman (1991), where the results from the

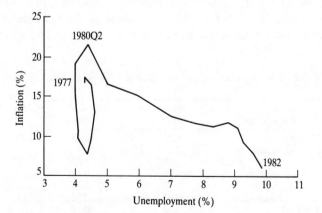

Figure 7.9 Retail price inflation and UK unemployment: 1977–82.

LSE Centre for Labour Economics (now Centre for Economic Performance) research programme into the causes of unemployment are set out. Broadly speaking, a given rise in unemployment can be broken down into three components: a rise in equilibrium unemployment (the NAIRU), a fall in demand, and dynamic effects (which can be very long lived, more so in the United Kingdom than in many other countries). Table 7.1 summarises their findings with respect to the first component.

The table shows that one popular explanation of the rise in unemployment can be dismissed straightaway. That is, that high unemployment benefits shifted the natural rate of unemployment so that millions of workers *chose* to be out of work, the utility of not working being greater than that in work. This explanation, although popular, was always preposterous. It is undoubtedly true that the level of unemployment benefits has a marginal effect on the level of measured unemployment, but it is absurd to suggest that this can explain job losses in Britain in recent years. As the table shows, the effect is absolutely minimal; but other supply-side effects do not really add up to much either. There appears to be a small effect arising from mismatch[9] and from an improvement in the terms of trade (import prices) which drive a wedge between producer and consumer prices, but the total effect (comparing the period 1974–80 to 1980–87) is less than $\frac{1}{2}$ per cent, compared to a rise of nearly 6 per cent in the actual unemployment rate.[10]

This means we must look elsewhere for an explanation of the rise. On the supply side, Layard, Nickell and Jackman (1991) believe that their econometric results exclude two crucial variables. First, they argue that there has been an increase in the degree of skill mismatch in the 1980s which is not picked up by their indicators. As evidence, they give the ratio of firms reporting shortages of skilled to unskilled labour (from the Confederation of British Industry (CBI) survey). This ratio was 2.73 in the 1960–74 period, but rose to 6.92 in 1981–87. The other factor is the treatment of the unemployed. They believe that compared with the 1950s and 1960s, the

Table 7.1 A breakdown of changes in the UK NAIRU.

Percentage points	1967–73 to 1974–80	1974–80 to 1980–87
Effect of: oil	−0.28	−2.58
mismatch	0.55	1.54
import prices	1.49	1.27
benefits	−0.29	0.48
unions	0.82	0.08
tax wedge	0.03	−0.32
Total effect	2.32	0.46
Actual rise	1.84	5.91

Source: Layard, Nickell and Jackman (1991), p. 446.

unemployed were treated more leniently by the social security and unemployment registration systems in the 1970s. Society was also more tolerant towards individuals who found themselves unemployed. These changes were due partly to institutional changes like the separation of unemployment benefit administration and registration for job search; the former is administered by the DSS, while the latter takes place at Department of Employment job centres. Another hard to quantify factor is the insidious effect of the growth in unemployment itself, eroding the work ethic (and also general skills).[11] So unemployment became less of a threatening experience, and less pressure was placed on the unemployed to search for new jobs.[12]

Yet no-one argues that the exceptionally rapid rise in unemployment between 1979 and 1981 was mainly caused by supply-side phenomena. The culprit must be demand. This raises the question of where the impetus came from. One suggestion is that Britain suffered from a decline in world trade. There is a modicum of truth in this, but it can explain only a tiny fraction of the problem. World trade in manufactures, in fact, continued to grow in volume terms until some time in the middle of 1981. Indeed, British exports of manufactures in volume terms were virtually constant in the four years 1977–80, and declined by only about 4 per cent in 1981 to then level off for 1982. The events of importance for employment precede this drop in exports by between one and two years.

Another explanation which has more widespread support is that the British economy suffered a massive ('Monetarist') deflation of domestic aggregate demand through cutbacks of domestic expenditures. Perhaps surprisingly, this is also hard to sustain. Table 7.2 shows the breakdown of expenditures in constant (1985) prices. The two major categories of spending – personal consumption and government current expenditure on goods and services – have a rising trend throughout the period. Investment declines but only latterly, and there is a running down in the last two years of the stocks built up in the 1976–79 period.

Table 7.2 Expenditures (£M 1985 prices).

Year	Total	Consumers' expenditure	Government expenditure	Investment expenditure	Change in stocks
1974	300 057	178 216	63 598	54 465	2980
1975	294 668	177 500	67 147	53 383	−3402
1976	302 547	178 279	67 977	54 277	1622
1977	301 583	177 483	66 855	53 307	3416
1978	314 247	187 510	68 400	54 914	2867
1979	325 813	195 664	69 776	56 450	3328
1980	316 602	195 825	70 872	53 416	−3371
1981	311 634	196 011	71 086	48 298	−3200

Source: *Economic Trends* (1974–80) HMSO, London.

It could be argued that this shows that the 'transmission mechanism' is through high real interest rates causing a fall in investment and a rundown of stocks. This is certainly contributory, but it is not the main event. Notice that the volume of demand in 1981 is about the same as in 1978 and yet between those two dates unemployment more than doubled. Notice also that the rundown of stocks in 1980 and 1981 was still less than the build-up in the previous four years. This suggests that we look to these earlier years and ask why it was that stocks of unsold goods were building up. Domestic consumption was rising steadily and yet domestic manufacturers were producing more than they could sell. How can these apparent inconsistencies be reconciled?

A major part of the answer turns out to be remarkably simple. It is that there was a substantial *shift* of domestic demand away from domestic manufactured goods towards imported manufactured goods. This is graphically illustrated by Table 7.3. There was a 66 per cent increase in the volume of imports of manufactures between 1975 and 1982, with the bulk of the rise coming before the end of 1979. Notice that manufactured imports and exports move together until after 1977 when exports level off and imports accelerate. The switch does not produce an immediate decline in production by domestic industry. Rather, they build up stocks of unsold products, as we have seen. As Figure 7.10 reveals, the production pattern changes dramatically after 1979. Between late 1979 and the end of 1980 there is a massive fall in industrial production of the order of 15 per cent. This fall is largely over by 1981, though the annual average figures look like they continue to fall (the average index for 1980 is higher than the index at the end of the year). This fall in production is clearly correlated with the period of rapidly rising unemployment and precedes it by some months. Production starts to dive in late 1979 and unemployment starts to accelerate in early 1980.

Table 7.3 Imports and exports of fuels and manufactures (1985 = 100).

Year	Imports		Exports	
	Fuels	Manufactures	Fuels	Manufactures
1973	227.9	45.2	22.5	74.1
1974	213.1	48.3	21.0	79.2
1975	173.7	43.5	19.3	76.8
1976	174.0	48.3	23.2	83.2
1977	143.7	52.3	32.1	88.3
1978	139.1	59.7	40.4	89.8
1979	137.0	69.1	58.4	88.5
1980	115.4	65.1	58.2	87.2
1981	94.3	68.3	70.2	84.7
1982	86.0	75.9	77.6	85.2

Source: *Monthly Digest of Statistics* (1973–82) HMSO, London.

Figure 7.10 Index of industrial production (excluding energy and water supply), 1970–84, 1985 = 100.

The speed of this adjustment presumably owes something to high interest rates, but it should be clear by now that this is not the major cause. There had been overproduction for some years. The problem was that domestic firms had, over successive years, lost their grip on the home market. There was no compensating expansion of exports. This increase of import penetration was not due to an upsurge of incompetence on the part of domestic producers. Rather, the explanation is to be found in the fact that this is the period of maximum expansion of North Sea oil production. Table 7.3 shows the steady decline of fuel imports and rise in fuel exports. This is associated with a substantial appreciation of sterling as we saw in Chapter 6. This appreciation of sterling, remarkably, had only a minor effect on the volume of manufactured exports, but it had a substantial effect on imports of manufactures. Domestic producers were squeezed out of the home market. The effect on *employment* lagged behind output somewhat. The reason is that producers failed to appreciate what was happening to demand; the CBI survey of output expectations shows that expectations were consistently over-optimistic throughout this episode. This also explains why firms found themselves building up stocks at such a rate. Despite the fall in stocks in 1980 and 1981, the ratio of stocks to output was higher throughout 1982 than in any period in 1977 or 1978.

This is the cause of the rise in unemployment. Something like 1½ million jobs were lost in manufacturing industry between 1979 and 1982. Certainly, monetary policies contributed to the problem by increasing the over-appreciation of sterling. However, a major contributory factor must be the changing oil balance of this period. Total imports and exports move more or less in line when oil is included. This suggests that the exchange rate moves to clear the current account in the long run as implied by the analysis of Chapter 6, though at times it may have moved too far.

There is further discussion of the analytics of this problem in Chapter 12.

There is one further point worth making at this stage. This is that if the above analysis is correct, it throws some light on the argument made in some circles that excessive capital outflows are causally related to domestic job losses. We have seen that job losses were due to an appreciation of sterling which made domestic manufactures relatively expensive. In so far as some of this appreciation was exchange rate overshooting of the type discussed in Chapter 6 above, the appropriate policy would have been to *encourage* capital outflows and discourage inflows. It does not make any sense at all to argue that sterling was overvalued and that capital outflows were excessive. They are inconsistent statements. In reality, what is hard to explain is why private sector investment in Britain held up so well in this period. In any event, there is no direct relationship between external financial flows and domestic real investment. And indeed, as we will see in Chapter 12, it made good economic sense to allow capital outflows during this period, essentially to build up savings overseas for the day that North Sea oil runs out.

There is still a mystery remaining to be cleared up, however. We have argued that a major part of the explanation of the rise in unemployment was a supply-side structural shift (oil). This resulted in lower demand for labour, and higher unemployment. It is easy to see why this happened, *ceteris paribus*. What is less easy to explain is why all things *were* equal. In particular, why did wages not adjust? Lower wages would have allowed employers to hire more of the unemployed in plentiful supply from 1980 onwards; but this did not happen. One of the remarkable phenomena of the 1980s was the seemingly inexorable rise in both unemployment *and* real wages. So wages are the macroeconomic dog which did not bark.

In terms of the Phillips curve or the real wage bargaining approach, the problem is that the trade-off between wages and inflation is very steep. It takes a lot of unemployment to reduce inflation. It also seems that the dynamics of the wage/price interaction are such that such adjustment as does occur is very slow. This amounts to simply describing the problem once more. Exactly what lies behind this phenomenon is unclear, but two plausible explanations have emerged. The first is the insider–outsider story set out in Chapter 5. Insiders – those in work – care only about their own prospects, not those of the unemployed and low wage sector outsiders. We consider a possible institutional solution to this problem in the next section. The other explanation may be that, as discussed briefly above, the experience of unemployment itself permanently damages the unemployed, making them practically unemployable, as well as unemployed. In effect, the natural rate is constantly moving toward the actual rate – the opposite to the usual story. If this is the case, there is a strong supply-side case for both intensive training programmes and a job guarantee for the long-term unemployed, as has been advocated forcefully by Richard Layard (1982) of the London School of Economics (LSE), among others. This supply-side solution, by increasing the effective size of the labour force, would not be a political quick fix to an uncomfortable problem, but would instead restore some of the lost potential production of the UK economy.

The implications for traditional macroeconomic management of the economy of the arguments set out above are far from clear. Throughout the 1980s and into the 1990s some have argued that the solution to the unemployment problem is a substantial reflation of aggregate demand. Yet we have seen that in 1980 the problem was not caused by a deficiency of domestic spending. The success of any reflation would depend on the extent to which it could *lower* the relative price of British manufactures. There is also the question of whether the labour force is ready to respond to an expansion of demand, given our arguments about the role of the unemployed. The important point to notice, however, is that traditional macroeconomics – Keynesian, Monetarist or New Classicist – is not much help. The central issue is how to adjust to a change in the structure of the productive sector of the economy. The expansion of a non-labour intensive sector has 'crowded out' the relatively labour intensive manufacturing sector. To what extent has there been 'overshooting' in the adjustment process? Has the 'natural rate' of unemployment permanently shifted? Is the 'natural rate' still a relevant concept? Will the economy adjust automatically to solve these problems or is there some policy that would help? These are some of the important questions, but macroeconomics is not well placed to answer them. Macroeconomics of all flavours has taken the supply structure of the economy to be homogeneous and stable. For Britain in recent years these are not reasonable assumptions. Policy solutions based on these traditional approaches should, therefore, be viewed with suspicion.

Incomes policies

The rise in unemployment in the 1980s caused a resurgence of interest in incomes policies as a way of holding down wages and prices during a reflation of aggregate demand. Incomes policies have been tried from time to time in the United Kingdom, but they are generally viewed with scepticism by professional economists.

The academic objection to incomes policy is usually based upon three propositions. The first is that *independent* wage-push is not the cause of inflation and so an incomes policy must eventually be frustrated because it does not tackle the root cause of the problem. This leads to the second point which is that while an incomes policy can have no long-run effect, it will work in holding down wages in some areas, and so there will be distortions introduced in the allocation of labour. The economy will thus be less efficient. Finally, and perhaps strongest of all, is the point that it has proved extremely difficult to demonstrate that incomes policies have had any significant effect at all in the United Kingdom in the last twenty-five years. Parkin, Sumner and Jones (1972), for example, in their survey of the evidence on this subject, conclude that:

> On the basis of our present knowledge, it is possible to say that, with the exception of the immediate post-war experiment, incomes policy apparently has little effect either on the wage determination process or on the average rate of wage inflation. (p. 13)

> The existing evidence indicates that incomes policies have had no identifiable effect on the price equation. (p. 25)

How then might an incomes policy work in the context of the model in Figure 7.7? It should be clear that the long-run position of the economy depends only upon the long-run budget constraint and upon the natural rate of unemployment or NAIRU. The long-run budget constraint depends entirely upon the policy-determined growth of monetary demand. So incomes policy could not influence the long-run inflation rate in this model. However, it could influence the short-run course of the economy if it succeeded in lowering inflationary expectations. In this case the short-run Phillips curve would shift down to the left. For a given short-run budget constraint inflation would be lower and employment would be higher than otherwise. If this could be achieved, then, even if the long-run inflation rate was unchanged, a higher average level of output and lower average unemployment could be attained. This would undoubtedly be preferable to the situation in which there was no incomes policy.

The problem with an incomes policy is that even if the initial effect is favourable, the belief that the policy is ending can have an equally adverse effect or even worse. The expectation of the collapse of an incomes policy would shift the short-run Phillips curve up to the right, thus making inflation and unemployment worse. Many economists believe that this is exactly what happens. A short-run benefit is fairly quickly offset by an equal deterioration. Henry and Ormerod (1978), for example, conclude that:

> Whilst some incomes policies have reduced the rate of wage inflation during the period in which they operated, this reduction has only been temporary. Wage increases in the period immediately following the ending of the policies were higher than they would otherwise have been, and these increases match losses incurred during the operation of the incomes policy. (p. 39)

Thus while it is logically possible that incomes policies could improve the dynamic path towards any long-run inflation rate, there is no evidence that they have done so in the recent past. Any short-run benefit in terms of higher employment and lower inflation is subsequently offset by higher inflation and lower employment as the policy breaks down.

There are two possible stories about this breakdown. The first is the catching up of expectations that has been mentioned above. The second gives a critical role to the public sector. It is argued that incomes policies have their greatest impact on public sector wages since the government is in effect itself the employer, whereas private sector employers can get around the policy if market conditions demand. As time passes the public sector employees notice that their wages are falling behind comparable private sector groups and demand 'pay comparability'. This leads to substantial public sector 'catch up' awards which effectively herald the end of the incomes policy. In 1979 the Labour Government even went so far as to set up a Public Sector Comparability Commission to deal with the multiplicity of public sector groups who felt that they had suffered under successive phases of incomes policies.

This points to the existence of two separate problems in this area. The first is how to make incomes policies more widely effective and other than in the short run. The answer to this is that it is probably not worth trying, since the administrative and distortionary costs would seem to be prohibitive in peacetime. The second problem is how to determine public sector wages. The larger is the public sector share of employment the more inappropriate it becomes to set public sector wages by comparison with the private sector. In the end there could be just one person left in the private sector whose wages determine those for the rest of the economy! A more coherent public sector wages policy is required which is made consistent with other aspects of policy such as employment and public expenditure targets and bears a sensible relationship to the underlying growth pattern of the real economy. Neither the adoption nor the abandonment of incomes policies obviates the need for a sensible policy towards public sector pay.

In one sense, the failure of past incomes policies is that they impose a *regulatory* solution to a market failure. The market failure in this case is essentially one of coordination. In terms of the Phillips curve, all parties in the economy would like to be at the natural rate with zero inflation. The aim of an incomes policy is to move us straight to this 'bliss' point. On the face of it, an external, legislative policy can be seen as a perfect example of a pre-commitment, which, as we saw in Chapter 4, is one means of achieving otherwise unattainable positions. However, regulatory solutions to macro-economic problems carry with them the baggage of microeconomic inefficiencies, and this dilutes the credibility of the commitment. What would be preferred, therefore, is some solution that would make the best interests of each party – crudely, firms and unions – to voluntarily *choose* the optimum level of inflation and employment. Two proposals have been made along these lines: tax-based incomes policies, and a reform of the collective bargaining system.

Tax-based incomes policies were introduced into the UK policy debate by Jackman and Layard (1982, 1986, 1990). The basic idea is to tax excessive wage increases. This increases the incentive for firms to resist rises, and makes higher wages more costly for unions (in terms of lost jobs from higher wage costs). So wage (and subsequently price) inflation is reduced. But proponents of the scheme go further and argue that the NAIRU itself will be reduced. In terms of the bargaining approach to the Phillips curve discussed above, it reduces the target real wage as the marginal trade-off between wages and unemployment is worsened. In effect, the NAIRU is reduced; in terms of Figure 7.7, the long-run Phillips curve shifts to the left. It may seem paradoxical that a *rise* in labour taxes should lead to a *fall* in unemployment. However, the fiscal impact is designed to be neutral – a blanket subsidy is given to all firms financed by the wage inflation tax – while the incentive effects remain in place. Thus the tax-based incomes policy substitutes private incentives for the regulatory enforcement problem.

The main problem with the policy is that it fails to distinguish productivity-based increases in wages and inflationary ones. The former are efficient, in the sense that they reward higher productivity; indeed, efficient allocation of resources requires price signals of this kind. It is hard to assess how large a distortion this will create. In some sectors at some times, it could be very large. It would have the effect of precisely targeting fast-growing areas with higher taxes; for example, computer software design would have been singled out in the late 1980s. This is a peculiar industrial policy. It is also unclear how robust the theoretical results are when the labour market model is extended to richer characterisations than the right-to-manage model. For these reasons, the case for a permanent policy of this type may be weaker than its proponents suggest although the distortions it engenders are likely to be less than those observed under the conventional type of policy.

Reform of the wage bargaining system has also been advocated in the United Kingdom. Most observers agree that there is a serious problem of wage rigidity in the UK labour market. Wages adjust only slowly to demand and supply shocks, exacerbating the resulting problems of slow growth and high unemployment. Countries with highly decentralised bargaining systems and low union power seem to be more responsive than the United Kingdom. Japan is the prime example of this, although there are other factors at work there. There is clear evidence that wages respond more to aggregate shocks, and employment less, in Japan. So the anti-union policies pursued in the 1980s in the United Kingdom can be seen as anti-inflationary but their effect seems to have been remarkably small. After three years of continuous falls in non-oil GDP, UK real wages were still rising at about 4 per cent per annum in April 1993; this does not look like strong evidence for a weak labour force. Recall the discussion earlier in the chapter relating to insiders and outsiders.

Nevertheless, there do exist alternative ways to organise wage-bargaining that seem to offer equivalent benefits to full competition. In Scandinavia and Austria powerful unions bargain centrally with national employers' organisations in a coordinated bargaining process. To some extent, this happens in the Japanese Shunto, or 'spring offensive' on wages. From an economic point of view, the advantage is that an external cost (inflation) is internalised. The problem with decentralised uncoordinated bargaining is that, in effect, competitive unions and firms bid wages up against each other. The aggregate effect of a given wage increase over the underlying increase in productivity is (roughly) to simply increase prices by that amount. So collectively it makes sense to restrict wage increases. For an *individual* union the effect of its own wage increase on the aggregate price level is vanishingly small, so there is no incentive to take account of the aggregate effect. As all unions are in this position, and similarly all firms willing to accede to wage demands without taking account of the aggregate effect, the result is high inflation. By contrast, if unions and firms are able to act collectively, then a mutually beneficial outcome is attainable, with (say) the same real wage outcome, but at lower inflation. If such institutions had existed in the United Kingdom, then perhaps the unemployment explosions of the early and late 1980s could have been avoided.

What is needed to make this kind of outcome work is unclear. Several elements may be required.

First, national union and employers' organisations are needed. Furthermore, these organisations must be able to enforce agreements. As usual in game-theoretic problems like this, there is a free-rider problem. If national negotiators achieve low inflation, then any local bargain over the national norm constitutes a real increase. So there is a strong incentive for individual unions to bid for higher wages. In the absence of a legislative framework or tough penalties on miscreants, a degree of social cohesion is required to make the process work. This does seem to exist in some of the Social Democratic North European countries and in Japan; it is less clear if it will work in the Anglo-Saxon countries,[13] and especially in Britain.

Second, a national forum for debate has to exist. This (probably) involves explicit tripartite talks between government, unions and employers. It also requires a national debate to take place in order to help establish a consensus view of the state of the economy, informed by recognised and independent bodies. In the United Kingdom such independent bodies do exist, in the form of the independent forecasting teams, notably the National Institute for Social and Economic Research and the Centre for Economic Forecasting at the London Business School, and also the Institute for Fiscal Studies. The City also has a role to play here. What is absent is a forum within which the three concerned parties can meet and negotiate. Indeed, the closest thing to such an institution, the National Economic Development Office (NEDO), has recently been dismantled by the government. A third precondition is that the wage bargaining timetable probably needs to be compressed into a short period, essentially to aid coordination and to avoid news being used as a device for justifying divergence from the norm.

If these preconditions were met, there is a strong chance that inflation would be lower and wages more responsive to shocks. However, it is not at all clear that the social structure of the United Kingdom is consistent with this kind of institution.

Summary

Britain is a small economy in a big world. Some of its economic history is explained by world developments alone. However, the inflation of the mid-1970s and the unemployment of the early 1980s were both worse than could be blamed upon developments in the world economy. The former is largely explained by the excessive fiscal and monetary expansion of the 1971–73 period. The latter results from an over-appreciation of sterling caused by a combination of North Sea oil and tight monetary policies. There is also the extreme persistence of unemployment and the rise in real wages to explain, the causes of which are still uncertain, although we have offered possible explanations. As we will see in Chapter 8 on financial deregulation, the most recent rise in unemployment (between 1990 and 1993) was largely due to the slump in consumers' expenditure caused by the collapse of the mid-1980s credit boom, itself caused at least in part by a fundamental deregulation of the UK financial system. Thus although we cannot hope to understand changes in unemployment by ignoring factors that affect the equilibrium rate of unemployment, the 'natural rate' framework for the analysis of unemployment gives only a part of the answer.

Notes

1. UK unemployment figures are among the least consistent of all economic series. Since 1979 there have been 29 changes to the way unemployment is measured. Remarkably, only one of these had the effect of increasing the recorded figure. All figures are on the new basis. The actual number reported at the time was higher, about 2.6 per cent.

2. There is a potential confusion of notation here. It is conventional to use $\dot{p} = dp/dt$. The rate of inflation should therefore be $\dot{p}/p$. However, $\dot{p}$ is used for convenience.

3. Usually we think of unions, rather than individual workers, as the bargainers, but this does not have to be the case. Unorganised individuals may still have bargaining power, as they have idiosyncratic, firm-specific human capital that employers will lose if they quit.

4. The term 'natural' was first applied by Friedman in the context of unemployment; we examine the idea more closely below.

5. Clearly, the long-run Phillips curve is intimately related to the long-run aggregate supply curve of the New Classicists, introduced in Chapter 4. Indeed, the two relations are often used interchangeably if the context allows: see Note 7 below.

6. Labour supply is drawn with a negative slope: equally, it could be vertical at the natural rate of unemployment without materially altering the analysis.

7. Although we have interpreted (7.6) in a Phillips curve framework, we could as easily invert the equation to yield an expression determining unemployment in terms of the expectational error and z. If we then relate output to unemployment via the production function, (7.6) becomes a bargaining version of the surprise supply function of the New Classicists.

8. Both these figures are on the 'old' basis, which scores unemployment rather higher than the current official statistics.

9. However, mismatch is defined in a rather unusual way here. It is the absolute change in industrial employment, which, as employment fell more or less continuously in this sector, amounts to an index of falling industrial demand. Other, more intuitive, measures of mismatch tend not to show any trend, nor to work econometrically.

10. As we might expect, the table shows that an increase in union militancy is not a major part of the explanation of the rise in unemployment during the Thatcher years.

11. See Price (1992b) for a theoretical model that explores this issue.

12. These changes were partially reversed in the late 1980s under a number of government initiatives; some argue – notably, Professor Patrick Minford – that the NAIRU may consequently have fallen to perhaps as low as one million in the early 1990s.

13. Australia has recently attempted to move to such corporatist bargaining structures; its success, or otherwise, has yet to be established.

8

Financial regulation and monetary rules

It is impossible to give a balanced explanation of the behaviour of the British economy in the last two decades without discussing important changes in the regulatory environment. In particular, the changing structure of financial regulation has produced implications for the behaviour of the economy as a whole which are still fully to be worked out. Indeed, while the 1980s were characterised by domestic liberalisation (and re-regulation) in the United Kingdom, the 1990s are likely to be dominated by supranational regulation associated in part with the EC Single Market Programme but also with global banking and securities regulation.

We have already mentioned, in Chapter 3, how financial innovation undermined the stability of key monetary relationships and made the conduct of monetary policy much harder to judge. However, the impact of changes in the financial system is much more pervasive. It has affected the financial behaviour of every part of the private sector. As a result, the most recent boom and recession were rather different than previous ones (in the post-war period). We will look at the nature of the 1985-93 cycle before discussing financial innovations.

Boom and bust: 1985–93

The characteristics of the latest boom and bust cycle of the UK economy are easy to describe in terms of the traditional indicators of inflation and unemployment. Figure 8.1 shows that in 1985–86 unemployment was at a post-war record high, over 11 per cent – not far short of 3.5 million, and inflation was around 5 per cent. There followed a boom which lowered unemployment to around 5.5 per cent or 1.5 million by 1989–90 but at the

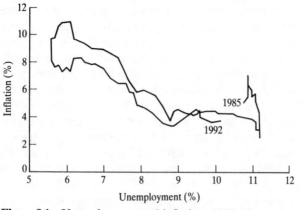

Figure 8.1 Unemployment and inflation: 1985–92.

same time pushed up inflation to 10 per cent. The boom started to burst in some sectors (especially housing) in 1988 but the economy entered serious recession in 1990. Inflation fell to under 2 per cent by early 1993, while at the same time unemployment headed back to the region of 3 million or over 10 per cent. The pattern of unemployment and inflation changes over this period looked like it was tracing out a classic Phillips Curve (see Chapter 7). However, the level of unemployment associated with low inflation in the 1980s (and 1990s) seems to be much higher than was apparent in the previous decades. We do not entirely explain this significant upward shift in unemployment. However, it is one of the dominant facts which is going to be important for the foreseeable future.

The 1985-93 cycle was different in origin from its predecessors (the 1971–73 Barber Boom period has the most similarity, but this was complicated by the oil price shock and was worked out in a quite different environment). It has its origins in a sustained period of economic recovery after the 1980 recession. This growth was healthy (in the sense of stable inflation) up to about 1985 but from then on it became artificially stimulated by lax monetary and fiscal policy, and the cumulative effects of financial liberalisation. The evolution of this scenario requires a more detailed exposition of the changing policy environment.

The changing policy environment

The 1950s and 1960s were characterised by the continued existence of (wartime) quantitative controls. The dominant macro policy constraint was the commitment to peg the exchange rate to the US dollar (from 1949 to 1967 at the rate of $2.8 to the pound, and from November 1967 to August

1971 at $2.4). There were tight foreign exchange controls, controls on consumer credit and quantitative ceilings on the expansion of bank lending. Shortage of international reserves, which were required to maintain the exchange rate peg, meant that domestic demand had to be kept closely under control. Any move to expand demand in the economy led fairly quickly to balance of payments problems. Contractionary demand policies soon followed. This was known as the 'Stop–Go' policy environment.

The financial system was characterised by segmentation and rationing. Segmentation involved financial institutions concentrating on particular product areas and not diversifying to compete with other types of institution. This segmentation was preserved by a combination of regulation, convention and restrictive practice. There was little incentive to break out of these constraints because of the aggregate quantitative restrictions on the growth of business imposed by the government. (The main exception to this rule was the 'Secondary Banks' which borrowed money in the wholesale markets and lent largely to property companies. They were not subject to quantitative ceilings. Collapses in this sector in 1974 were a major stimulus to reform of bank regulation.)

The external environment within which the UK economy operated changed significantly at the end of the 1960s. The dollar shortage of early post-war years turned into dollar glut. The United States was involved in a war against poverty at home and against the Viet Cong in Vietnam. The United Kingdom found itself with a relatively healthy balance of payments position and a more or less balanced government budget.

In 1971, the Conservative government of Edward Heath decided to remove the quantitative ceilings on banking and to introduce more competition into the monetary system. Their reform package, introduced in September 1971, was known as Competition and Credit Control (see Hall, 1983). This was the first major attempt to liberalise the UK financial system in the post-war period. Two years of rapid expansion of bank intermediation followed. Also a rapid increase in the supply of mortgage finance led to a house price boom. Indeed, the inflationary consequences of this rapid monetary expansion were felt right through the decade – inflation peaked in 1975 at around 26 per cent.

This attempt to liberalise the financial system was abandoned in December 1973. Inflation was picking up sharply in the United Kingdom. Added to this came the first 'Oil Shock' which involved a quadrupling of the price of oil. The government returned to the use of quantitative ceilings. They took the form of a maximum rate of growth of banks' interest-bearing liabilities. This had the effect of stopping banks from competing for deposits (interest-bearing) and thereby reducing the forces of competition in intermediation in general. The credit squeeze of 1973–74 had a similar effect on the housing and commercial property market as occurred in the recent cycle (1990–92). There were collapses of developers and severe strain on individuals who had geared up (borrowed) to buy property. However, high inflation helped to ease the debt burden before too long. (In the 1990s, low inflation means that debt is harder to redeem.)

The 'Corset', as the controls introduced in 1973 were known, remained in place (with a couple of breaks) until June 1980. It is for this reason that the 1980s is such an unusual decade in post-war British monetary history. It is the decade in which all these remnants of wartime direct controls were swept away and a more competitive environment was established. The regulatory regime had also to be updated to keep up with developments in the finance industry.

The liberalisation of the UK financial system was probably not the result of a clear and conscious decision by policy-makers, though the 'free-market' ideology of the Thatcher Government certainly helped. Rather, it was the result of a combination of external forces and piecemeal decisions (which led to unanticipated implications in many cases).

The primary trigger for a directional change came from the strength of sterling in the late 1970s. (The source of this strength is still controversial, but North Sea oil had some part to play. See the discussion of exchange rates in Chapter 6 and supply shocks in Chapter 12.) In October 1979 exchange controls were swept away *in toto*. The abolition of exchange controls meant that it became impossible to maintain the Corset. This was abolished in June 1980. The reason the Corset had to go was that banks would be free to intermediate offshore even though they were restricted in the domestic market, hence the restrictions could easily have been bypassed. Ceilings which can be avoided simply create distortions and serve no useful purpose.

The removal of the Corset did not lead immediately to a dramatic surge in bank lending (as removal of restrictions in 1971 had done), though the removal of distortions did produce a noticeable growth in M3 (as some business was brought back on the balance sheet). Rather, 1980 was a year of severe recession, especially in the manufacturing sector. Hence banks initially were fairly cautious in seeking out new lending opportunities. One area they deliberately expanded into was the mortgage market. This was relatively safe and profitable at the time.

Building societies responded to this encroachment on their traditional patch by competing more aggressively for deposit business and lobbying for greater freedom to take the banks on in other areas. The building societies expanded their payments services through credit cards, automated teller machines (ATMs) and cheque books while paying competitive interest on cheque accounts. Banks were forced to respond by paying interest on current accounts and offering a more attractive range of savings accounts.

The 1986 Building Society Act gave building societies more freedom to offer unsecured loans and to resort to wholesale funding (at first up to 20 per cent, later increased to 40 per cent). It also gave them the right to convert from mutual to PLC status. To date, Abbey National has been the only one to take up this option, thereby becoming a 'bank'.

The significance of all these changes for the macroeconomic environment was that they created competition, not just for deposits but also for loans. The scramble to maintain market share in deposit markets was matched by a scramble to maintain market share in the loan market. This facilitated a boom in borrowing. Much of this borrowing was housing related, either through primary mortgages or through lending secured on the net worth in a house. A house price boom fed both the illusion of wealth and the panic of those afraid to be left behind. Figure 8.2 shows the real price of houses as measured by the ratio of house prices to average incomes. Figure 10.5 below also shows the financial surplus/deficit of the UK personal sector. Normally, the personal sector is a net accumulator of financial assets. However, in the second half of the 1980s it went into substantial deficit. This was all due to a surge in borrowing and not at all to a decline in gross saving (see Chrystal, 1992). The high level of debt built up at this time added to the depth of the subsequent recession which was associated with high interest rates and a collapse in the housing market.

Developments in the UK financial system did not happen independently of the external world. The abolition of exchange controls (not just in the United Kingdom but almost simultaneously in Japan, and later in other countries – the United States had no significant controls and Germany had liberalised in the 1960s) led to the emergence of 'global' financial markets, at least in wholesale funds. This meant that there were international competitive pressures as well as domestic ones. The reforms of the UK securities markets, known as 'Big Bang', in 1986 also increased the

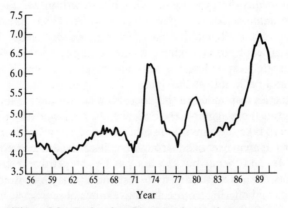

Figure 8.2 Ratio of real house prices to income.

potential foothold of foreign firms in the UK domestic financial system and reduced the segmentation within the financial system.

The Third World Debt Crisis of 1982 forced the major UK banks to reexamine their global ambitions and probably made them even more determined to maintain their share of the domestic market – their extensive customer base being their main competitive advantage. British banks had been keen to expand their overseas business in the 1970s (as had US banks for different reasons) because they had no possibility of expanding their liabilities significantly at home. However, severe losses in international lending combined with narrowing of margins on wholesale business led the major UK banks to redirect their business strategy towards the home market.

In short, the developments of the 1980s converted the domestic sector of the UK financial system from a protected, segmented and uncompetitive financial system into an open and 'contested' sector. (It should be emphasised that the 'Eurodollar' banking sector in London was already competitive and highly efficient in the 1960s and 1970s. This was untouched by the regulations which affected the domestic sterling sector. When exchange controls were eliminated some of this segmentation disappeared. However, the implementation of the Basle Agreement, which imposed capital requirements on banks based on their global business, completed the integration of 'offshore' and 'onshore' banking. The presence of large numbers of foreign banks in London (originally because of the Euro markets) created a much greater potential competitive threat in the United Kingdom than in some other liberalising economies.)

The housing market

The UK housing market played a central role in the boom of the late 1980s and the subsequent recession. The connection between financial innovation and housing made for an unusual coincidence of circumstances which is unlikely to recur this century.

Over the long term, UK house prices tend to rise in line with average earnings. The ratio of average house prices to earnings tends to return to a little over four (Figure 8.2). In 1972–73 there was a dramatic house price boom following the financial liberalisation of 1971. House prices stagnated for a while after 1973, but they did not fall in money terms. Rather, inflation in money wages (and other prices) restored normal relativities after a few years.

The 1988 house price boom had more fundamental significance for the economy because it affected more people and its effects were worked out in a more damaging way. This was not a short sharp boom like 1972–73. On the contrary, the build-up started in about 1982–83 and the effects were still being felt ten years later.

The origins of the boom lay in the steady and sustained recovery of the economy from the 1980–81 recession combined with financial liberalisation. The former provided growing confidence and employment while the latter made available finance on competitive terms. There was nothing abnormal in the cycle until about 1985. Then some extra features combined to turn a normal recovery into a speculative 'bubble'. First, the UK monetary authorities abandoned the targeting of broad money just as it was about to contain useful information about impending inflation (see Chapter 3). Second, the bidding for securities firms and staff in London, associated with the Big Bang, created a temporary and unrealistic perception of wealth in the London area. Third, banks started to make it easier to borrow against the net worth in housing. Fourth, interest rates were allowed to drop to low levels – particularly after October 1987 when the stock market crash made many commentators afraid of recession (see Figure 8.3). Fifth, there were tax-cutting budgets in the springs of both 1987 and 1988. The former may have been expected by a politically cynical population, coming as it did in the run up to an election; but the second, post-election, budget signalled an apparent determination to reduce taxes significantly over the medium to long term. Finally, the Chancellor of the Exchequer, Nigel Lawson, announced a reform of housing tax relief such that unmarried couples would only be able to claim two sets of tax relief if their mortgage were set up by August 1988. This gave several months lead time to the change and added to the existing panic to complete house purchases.

The anatomy of a speculative bubble is easy to explain. Individual behaviour in the 1980s boom was particularly rational *ex ante*. House prices had never fallen in the United Kingdom in living memory. Many people had friends or relatives who had done well by buying a house and watching its value rise. As prices were seen to be rising in the 1980s it seemed sensible to get into the market, and to buy as big a house as possible with as big a mortgage as possible. The more valuable the house was, the bigger the potential capital gain. For a while the strategy paid off, so more people tried it.

For the first-time buyer the problem was that prices were getting out of reach. With low interest rates it was a case of buy now or miss out forever . . . or so it seemed. Lax lending terms and competition for market share by lenders enabled people to take out mortgages well above normal income multiples. (The traditional maximum mortgage was two and a half times income. In 1988 multiples of three times income or higher were not uncommon.)

The housing market boom was paralleled by a boom in consumer spending – housing turnover is often closely related to certain kinds of consumer durable purchases such as carpets, furniture and white goods.

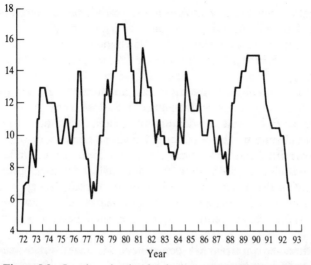

Figure 8.3 London clearing banks base rates 1972–93. Source: Datastream.

The booms in housing and the High Street fed off each other.

The boom peaked out in the summer of 1988. The turnaround in the housing market was triggered by the end of double taxation relief for unmarried couples in August and the raising of interest rates in September. The tightening of monetary policy continued for some time. Indeed, it only started to loosen noticeably in 1990, by which time the economy was well into the longest recession since the war. House prices continued to fall through 1992 (and perhaps longer).

The worst effects of the recession were on those who lost their jobs or lost their houses through repossessions. Large numbers found their budgets squeezed by high interest rates and by early 1993 there were 2 million people with negative net worth in their houses – the mortgage debt was greater than the value of the house. This debt trap is likely to slow the return of consumer confidence and the pick-up of the housing market. It has made the current cycle much harder to forecast than previously. The British economy has not been in a similar situation before. Those who geared up (took on large mortgages) were bailed out in the 1970s by rapid inflation. That is not likely to happen in the 1990s. Hence many households face a severe debt burden for several years to come.

Consumption and saving

One of the tasks which is going to occupy macroeconomists for some time to come is the explanation of consumption and saving behaviour in the context of the new financial environment. Traditional consumption theory which relies upon permanent income or life-cycle approaches did not perform well in forecasting either the 1988 boom or the 1990–92 recession. Indeed, this failure was at the centre of the policy failure of macro management.

At least one well known study which attempted to explain the falling savings ratio in the 1980s (Muellbauer and Murphy, 1989) found it necessary to include an *ad hoc* dummy variable to capture the effects of financial innovation. This was despite having a complex model including detailed wealth terms (both liquid and non-liquid assets), inflation and interest rates. A similar need for financial innovation proxies was discovered in the demand for money study of Hall, Henry and Wilcox (1989). Such arbitrary variables are really a measure of our ignorance. They are saying that the conventional terms are inadequate to explain what is going on.

Whether the unexplained component of behaviour is caused by confidence factors, by a speculative belief in rising house prices or perhaps by an end to credit rationing (or some combination of these and other things) is hard to say without a great deal more research. What is sure, however, is that the new financial environment with, for example, its high level of personal debt and uncertain employment prospects, is no easier to forecast than it was in the last cycle. Despite fifty years or so of consumption research, in a very real sense, things are different now.

Monetary policy failure

The 1980s boom and bust is testament to a massive failure of UK monetary policy. It is particularly ironic that this occurred during the incumbency of a government that had been widely labelled 'Monetarist'. Certainly, the goal of low and stable inflation had been given explicit priority (in words if not deeds) and monetary targeting had at first been a central part of the policy strategy. (Targeting was actually introduced by the Labour Chancellor Denis Healey in 1976, but he had the extra weapon of the Corset.) To say that monetary policy was a failure is not to say that it was obvious what should have been done, even with the benefit of hindsight. However, it is easier to identify the factors which contributed to the problem.

From the Second World War until 1972, UK monetary policy was dominated by the commitment to maintain convertibility of sterling into the dollar at a fixed price. (Indeed, the fixing of sterling against gold (and silver) from the early 1700s until 1931 – with a break for the Napoleonic Wars – had provided the United Kingdom with an unparalleled record for long-term price stability.) The maintenance of external convertibility is a monetary policy, since it implies that domestic money balances are demand-determined and the inflation rate will be closely related to that of the currency to which pegging is done. If excess domestic credit is supplied, the central bank has to buy back sterling with reserves. If excess sterling is demanded, the central bank has to sell sterling and buy foreign currency (reserves). (See the discussion of the monetary approach to balance of payments in Chapter 6.)

Whatever the pros and cons of maintaining a fixed exchange rate, at least it gives a clear and immediate signal for the monetary authorities. A loss of reserves signals policy-tightening and gains of reserves signal policy-loosening (ignoring day-to-day fluctuations).

The problem of UK monetary policy in the last two decades is that we have never found a clear set of guiding principles for operating in the absence of an external convertibility constraint. In the twenty years or so since floating in June 1972 the United Kingdom has suffered a more than five-fold increase in its price level. This has not been compensated by any increase in trend real growth, indeed, the costs of removing inflation have probably wiped out any benefit achieved in boom times.

When floating was first introduced, UK monetary policy had already been relaxed under the Competition and Credit Control reforms. The temporary float of the dollar in August 1971 helped to make this possible. At first the rapid growth of broad money – measured by £M3 – had been justified as a temporary phenomenon which would settle down once the banking system had adjusted to the new regime. Once it became clear (even to the authorities) that the money supply was growing too fast and inflation was picking up significantly, quantitative ceilings were reimposed on the banking system. Target rates of growth of £M3 were explicitly announced from 1976 in order to attempt to establish a counter-inflationary credibility.

The Thatcher Government, elected in 1979, made a big deal about using monetary targets in order to control inflation. However, in practice their targets were only slightly tighter than those inherited from the previous Labour government and they came nowhere near to hitting them after the summer of 1980. This failure of monetary targeting was not necessarily due to lack of will, but also owes a lot to the changing environment.

The key external event was the strength of sterling. This appreciated in both real and nominal terms from 1976 until 1981 (see Figure 6.5). Labour Chancellor, Denis Healey, intervened massively in 1978 to stop the pound rising, but gave up after becoming worried about the implications for domestic monetary growth. Thus, when the Thatcher Government came to power it was already accepted in official circles that direct intervention in foreign exchange markets was not the solution. The only major Tory response was the abolition of exchange controls – and the then inevitable abolition of the Corset. The latter led to a sharp increase in the growth rate of £M3 after mid-1980. At this time the economy was in the deepest recession since the Second World War, manufacturing output fell nearly 20 per cent in one year and unemployment was rising.

The proximate cause of the recession was clearly the strength of sterling. However, many concluded that the strength of sterling was indicative of tight monetary policy. They continued to believe this despite the rapid growth of £M3. A famous but unpublished report by Niehans (1981) supported the conclusion that monetary policy was too tight on the evidence of slow growth in M0 – though it is more likely in the British context that slow M0 growth is effect rather than cause. Buiter and Miller (1981a) argued for 'overshooting' due to tight monetary policy, but later (1983) admitted that the interest rate evidence did not support the monetary tightness hypothesis. (They shifted the blame to fiscal policy, even though fiscal policy tightening did not come until 1982, well after the exchange rate had peaked.)

North Sea oil was the main alternative to monetary policy as an explanation of sterling's strength. (See Chrystal (1984) for a review of the controversy.) All that matters for present purposes is that rapid growth of £M3 took place in the early 1980s while the economy was in recession and inflation was falling. This led observers to doubt the significance of broad money measures as a guide to monetary policy stance. The 'temporary adjustment' argument could be used for a while but other causes of distortion soon followed. The payment of interest on current accounts created a further fall in velocity just as it had done in the United States. The monetarist-leaning economists, like Tim Congdon, who warned about the dangers of rapid growth of broad money had to wait an uncomfortably long time for their predictions of inflation to be borne out. Rapid growth of £M3 started in 1980 but it was 1988 before a significant pick-up of inflation was observed. (Indeed, the money measures themselves were changed several times. By the end of the decade M4, which included building society deposits, was the standard measure of broad money.)

The main reason why monetary growth in the early 1980s did not (for a while) indicate inflationary pressure was that the growing deposits in banks and building societies were being held for savings rather than transactions purposes. Monetary expansion which leads to spending tends to create inflation. However, monetary expansion associated with accumulation of savings deposits may have no inflationary significance. Competition by deposit-takers to attract savings led to higher interest being paid. Hence banks were able to attract savings that might otherwise have gone into, say, national savings. In other words, there was a shift in money demand associated with the changing characteristics of deposits. (See Chapter 3 for a discussion of the Divisia method of measuring money services which endogenises substitution effects resulting from interest rate changes on components of 'money'.)

By the time broad money growth really was indicating inflationary conditions (perhaps because velocity had stabilised or financial innovation had slowed down), the authorities had given up taking the figures seriously (even if they ever had). It was only inflation itself that convinced everyone that policy had to tighten. By then it was too late. Inflation rose to around 10 per cent by 1988 and a very tight monetary policy was introduced in the autumn to control it.

Nigel Lawson (1992) has admitted that, as Chancellor of the Exchequer, he wanted to give up on monetary targeting as early as 1984, because of his lack of confidence in the monetary aggregates as a guide to policy. His preferred alternative was an exchange rate target which was available in the form of UK entry into the Exchange Rate Mechanism of the EMS. This option was vetoed for many years by Mrs Thatcher. There resulted a period of very confused monetary policy in which serious errors built up. (See Pepper (1990) for a detailed discussion of these monetary policy mistakes.) Lawson implicitly targeted the Deutschmark for a while and as a result allowed UK interest rates to go too low for too long in 1988. These mistakes made the 1988 credit boom much worse than it needed to be.

Nigel Lawson eventually resigned over his disagreements with Mrs Thatcher (and her advisor Sir Alan Walters). His successor John Major took the United Kingdom into the ERM in October 1990. Whatever the merits of the policy, the timing appears unfortunate (and not just with the benefit of hindsight). Monetary policy had already been tight for two years. Inflation had started to fall. Germany by contrast was still growing and was about to encounter the massive restructuring costs of reunification. These were widely predicted to be about to lead to a period of DM strength. The UK economy probably needed falling interest rates and a lower real exchange rate. Instead it got a high real exchange rate and sustained high interest rates. Fortunately perhaps, the United Kingdom was forced out of the ERM in September 1992 by a bout of speculative pressure, which had already led to the departure of the lira. The case in favour of ERM entry was that it would create 'credibility' for monetary policy-makers in the United Kingdom (see Chapter 4). This credibility would enable inflation to be brought down with a lower cost in terms of unemployment. Certainly, inflation was brought down to low levels by 1993, though it is far from clear that the unemployment cost was any lower than it might have been outside ERM.

The UK departure from the ERM meant that by the autumn of 1992, the United Kingdom was again without an anchor for monetary policy. The Chancellor, Norman Lamont, in his Autumn Statement for 1992 reintroduced a target for the growth rate of M4, though this did not carry much conviction, in the light of the recent history of broad money targets.[1] The longer term goal was to return to the ERM, but this was not likely to happen in a hurry if ever.

Monetary policy was intended to bring low inflation and stable growth. Low inflation has been achieved for the time being, but at what cost? Far from creating a stable environment, swings in monetary policy stance have almost certainly exacerbated the business cycle.

Policy options

The difficulties of monetary policy in the United Kingdom in the 1980s illustrate the potential conflict between micro liberalisation and macro control. The innovations in the financial system changed the underlying behavioural relationships and loosened links between 'money' and the economy. This made reliance on traditional monetary aggregates dangerous. Unfortunately, it also created the false conclusion that money could be ignored. There has to be some guiding principle for monetary policy, however difficult a changing system may be to monitor. The long-term policy structure is particularly difficult to predict at present given the possibility of a European Central Bank and a single currency, if the Maastricht Treaty is implemented (see Chapter 9). The main options are as follows:

1. *Base control.* In 1980–81 there was a debate about the appropriate conduct of monetary policy. The advocates of base control lost (see Pepper, 1990) but the argument has continued, especially in the light of the success of countries like Switzerland and Germany. The principle of base control is that the Bank of England should fix the rate of growth of M0 (cash held by the public and the banks' reserves with the Bank of England). This, it is claimed, would guarantee that broader monetary aggregates do not grow too fast to be consistent with price stability. Critics of base control claim that it would introduce too much interest rate volatility and that the desired growth rates of broader monetary aggregates can be achieved by other means.

2. *Judgement.* The policy of the early 1980s was supposed to be based on broad money targets achieved by manipulation of interest rates. In practice, judgement was continually used to overrule the signals that deviations from targets were giving. In the early 1980s this was probably the sensible thing to do given the pace of financial innovation; however, by the time inflation picks up it is far too late to react. Monetary judgements based upon policy makers trying to choose the 'correct' nominal interest rate have

always been subject to large error (see Friedman, 1953). The whole point of Monetarism was that monetary policy changes acted with long and variable lags. Hence, it was inappropriate to try to use monetary policy in a discretionary countercyclical way. Such policies were likely to exaggerate the cycle rather than smooth it. This has been the recent UK experience.

3. *Exchange rate peg.* The problems of getting monetary policy right and the pressures for European Monetary Union (EMU) may lead the United Kingdom to return to an exchange rate link with the other members of the EMS. This may merely be as a transition to full monetary union. Certainly ERM-type arrangements, as with Bretton Woods arrangements before them, are more difficult to maintain than either free floating or a single currency. Freely floating exchange rates adjust in line with market forces, while within a single currency area money flows freely between regions without putting pressure on exchange markets. Pegged regimes are the most difficult to maintain because they require recurrent intervention by monetary authorities with reserves they may not have. When speculators are convinced that rates have to change (as in September 1992) the authorities may not be prepared to intervene sufficiently heavily or raise short-term interest rates high enough to avoid caving in. This is why an ERM-type arrangement may not be the sensible transition towards a single currency as stability and convergence may never be achieved. Rather, a jump to a single currency (as was done in uniting Germany) may be preferable as it cannot be thrown off course by destabilising speculation.

4. *Single EC currency.* The adoption of a single EC currency would not solve the monetary policy problem. However, it would move it to a new arena. The United Kingdom would no longer have its own monetary policy, rather the monetary policy for Europe (or all of it that joined in) would be determined by the European Central Bank (ECB). It is intended that the ECB would be considerably independent of politicians and that its primary objective should be price stability. The ECB would still have to determine exactly how to implement monetary policy, but the discussion of targeting will be at the EC level.

5. *Independent Bank of England.* One proposal for improving UK monetary policy outside the ERM or EMU is to give independence to the Bank of England. This would take monetary policy out of the control of elected politicians (along the lines of the Bundesbank or the Federal Reserve Board). Even if this were to happen it is not clear that UK monetary policy would improve. It has after all been Bank of England officials who were most resistant to base control and rigid monetary targets. Their faith in their own judgement remains undimmed. Independence without better tools does not promise improved performance. It takes time

to establish 'credibility' in the conduct of monetary policy (see Chapters 4 and 9). Independence alone gives no guarantee of credibility. Bank of England independence is only likely to be extended in the context of the development of the European Central Banking System. Indeed, independence in the monetary control function may well raise issues about separation of other key duties currently performed by the Bank, such as bank regulation and broker to the government.

6. *New measures of policy stance.* A final policy option is to base policy on a more sophisticated set of monetary policy indicators which are not subject to the obvious distortions which afflict traditional simple sum aggregates. Obvious candidates include the Divisia-weighted aggregate proposed by Barnett (1980, 1982) or the Currency Equivalent aggregate of Rotemberg (1991) (see Chapter 3).

It seems likely, on the basis of past behaviour, that the UK authorities will attempt to muddle through by judgemental methods unless forced to integrate with Europe by overwhelming political pressures. Despite more than five-fold price increases over two decades and three major recessions (all of which involved significant monetary policy errors), the UK authorities are unlikely to admit that they are just not very good at monetary policy.

Summary

Financial innovation has been a fact of life in the UK economy over the last decade or so. It has many beneficial effects associated with greater competition in the market for financial services. This has increased the choice available and reduced the cost of financial services to consumers (as measured, for example, by spreads between deposit and loan rates). One effect of these innovations, however, has been the shift of behavioural relationships which underpin aggregate monetary policy. The intended monetary policy of the 1980s – to reduce inflation by means of monetary targets – was never fully implemented in practice (and rightly so) because of the behavioural shifts introduced, first by abolition of the Corset and later by greater competition in banking. By the time targets for the growth rate of money were formally abandoned they were probably starting to give a correct warning of accelerating inflation. A classic credit squeeze was then needed to get back to the levels of inflation which had been targeted all along.

It is easy with the benefit of hindsight to say that things should have been done differently. However, policy-makers can only use the information available at the time. The monetary policy problem remains. It cannot be assumed that financial innovation is over (technological and regulatory changes are still happening and likely to continue into the future). There has to be *some* guiding principle for monetary policy if similar costly mistakes are to be avoided in the future.

The solution may involve the move to a more explicit base control system, or it may involve greater reliance on Divisia-style index numbers of monetary services. An alternative possibility is that the European Community will adopt a single currency and the problem will be shifted out of the hands of the UK authorities. Some believe, on the basis of the recent track record, that this may be no bad thing!

Note

1. The policy was to specify a target range for inflation and to state a monitoring range for M0 and M4. Research was also initiated into the usefulness of other indicators including Divisia money measures.

9

International macro policy coordination

Since the mid-1980s there has been an explicit attempt by the major industrial countries of the world to develop an agreed strategy for coordination of policies to stabilise the global economy. This started in a big way (though there were earlier examples) with the Plaza Agreement of September 1985, continued with the Louvre Accord of February 1987 and has carried on through each G7 summit since. Accompanying the political rhetoric has been a torrent of academic research, most of which has been supportive of the endeavour.

The purpose of this chapter is to review this academic literature, critically to assess the theoretical case for coordination, to discuss what coordination might mean in practice and to consider what directions policy-makers might usefully take in future. An international perspective is essential to complete the understanding of the forces affecting macro policy. International influences have become at least as important as traditional domestic targets in determining policy outcomes. In the UK case, membership of the ERM had a particularly strong impact on the course of policy and the economy and the plans for a single currency set out in the Maastricht Treaty will eventually integrate monetary policy for the entire European Community (assuming the plans go ahead).

It is to be emphasised that we are not concerned here with those aspects of international cooperation which involve the setting and policing of the rules by which commerce takes place – examples of which include the General Agreement on Tariffs and Trade (GATT) which regulates international trade and the Basle Agreement which concerns global bank regulation. Rather, the concern is with interactions between macroeconomic policy-makers which lead to monetary and/or fiscal policies different from those which would be set by individual authorities acting alone.

The gains from cooperation

It is easy to establish in theory that policy coordination should be beneficial. All that is required is for countries involved to be sufficiently large to influence the economic environment of each other. In such circumstances, how well one country can do is not independent of what everybody else is doing. If countries simply react to what other countries have already done this would lead to some set of economic outcomes. It is common to argue that this 'non-cooperative' outcome will normally be dominated by a cooperative solution which would be preferred by all.

The analytical demonstration of this (in this context) is due to Hamada (1976) and is drawn from the microeconomic theory of the firm. In effect it is the same analysis as that which shows that collusion by oligopolistic firms dominates the non-cooperative (Nash) equilibrium. This is illustrated in Figure 9.1.

Each country is presumed to have choice over one policy instrument, P_1 for Country 1, and P_2 for Country 2. Each country has an optimal outcome for itself which is represented by points O_1 and O_2 respectively. If policy outcomes were independent of each other, Country 1 would have a set of vertical indifference curves with the 'best' being the one that passes through O_1 and lower levels of preference being achieved the further one goes left or right. Country 2's indifference curves would be horizontal with the most preferred passing through O_2. However, as it is assumed that the two countries are interdependent, the indifference curves are concave, in this case reflecting the fact that one country's welfare is not independent of the

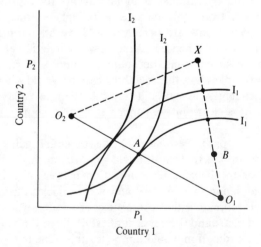

Figure 9.1 Gains from policy coordination.

other's actions. These indifference curves map out a surface which peaks at O_1 for Country 1 and at O_2 for Country 2.

The Pareto efficient set of policy outcomes is the tangency points of the indifference curves of the two countries. This is illustrated by the line connecting O_1 and O_2. Once a point on this line has been achieved, it is possible for one country to gain only at the expense of the other. If policy-makers simply react to each other's policies as if they were given constants, this is likely to lead to outcomes on points where indifference curves are horizontal and vertical respectively. Such non-cooperative reactions will lead to an outcome such as point X which is the Nash equilibrium. The outcome at X is definitely worse for both countries than at any point such as A on the Pareto efficient locus.

There are two reasons to be cautious about the conclusion that cooperation dominates non-cooperation. The first is that at cooperative solutions like point A there is an incentive for both parties to cheat on the agreement. For example, if Country 1 knows that Country 2 is going to set its instrument at the level required to achieve that outcome then it can do better for itself by changing its own instrument to take it to point B. This is a better outcome for Country 1, but worse for Country 2. Hence, cooperation without monitoring and enforcement may fail.

The second reason for caution is that the real world is not a two-player game. It is well known in game theory that when only some of the players cooperate the outcome may be worse than when there is no cooperation at all. Indeed, even if all governments cooperate, Rogoff (1985) has shown that including private agents as actors in the game may make government cooperation counterproductive. His argument is that if government cooperation is perceived by rational economic agents to improve the inflation–unemployment trade this may lead to higher money wage bargains (because governments are perceived to have an incentive to introduce money surprises) and hence make for a worse inflation environment. It is, of course, possible to construct counter-examples. Carraro and Giavazzi (1991) for example, show that in a three-country world where one country leads independently, it may still pay the other two players to cooperate. However, it is clear that we cannot assert that cooperation is always a good thing.

One well known empirical estimate of the potential gains from cooperation also raises doubts that efforts might be worth much. Oudiz and Sachs (1984) consider the benefits of cooperation between the United States, Germany and Japan in monetary and fiscal policies during the period 1984–86. Their estimate is that complete coordination would only have produced a gain of around 0.5 per cent of GDP. Even this is on the high side, as perfect coordination would not be feasible. One reason why perfect coordination might not be achieved is that governments may not agree about how the world works – they may have different models in mind. Frankel and Rockett (1988) investigate the importance of this issue by calibrating all the possible outcomes where the United States and the rest of the world can subscribe to any of six different models, while the 'truth' may be any of the other models. In about 60 per cent of cases policy coordination is beneficial. However, in nearly one-third of cases coordination makes at least one party worse off than otherwise.

Holtham and Hughes Hallett (1987) confirm the finding that 'optimal cooperative policies according to one model frequently lead to lower welfare compared to the Nash equilibrium when those policies are evaluated on other models. This means risk-averse policy makers have little incentive to cooperate.' (p. 163). However, they point out that if cooperation only involves 'strong' bargains, which offer prospective gains to both parties according to both views of the world, the prospects for gain are greatly increased.

The problem of model uncertainty was turned around to favour cooperation in an important paper by Ghosh and Masson (1988). They pointed out that policy-makers should take account of model uncertainty before setting their own policy. Indeed, consultations about the state of the world between different governments may represent the most valuable of all the gains from cooperation, since they improve knowledge about alternative perceptions and give a clearer view about what others are likely to do, while making it less likely that any individual government can maintain an idiosyncratic view of the world. Hence, even if the scope for cooperative action were small, the benefits of information exchange may be significant.

An important line of investigation which responds to the Rogoff demonstration of the possibility of counter-productive cooperation is that followed by Currie, Levine and Vidalis (1987). The conclusion they reach is, perhaps, one of the most important in the entire cooperation literature. The Rogoff problem arises from the 'time-inconsistency' of policy in many circumstances, associated with the work of Kydland and Prescott (1977). Governments that have achieved low inflation may have an incentive to induce a temporary boom, notwithstanding the fact that they forswore such actions in order to get inflation down in the first place. Thus a government which found it appropriate to promise low inflation at one point in time may later find it beneficial to renege on its promises. The fact that there is a benefit (at the later time) for reneging is what earns the label 'time inconsistent'. The alternatives to such time-inconsistent policies are 'reputational' policies which involve governments being committed to their promises and being generally accepted to be so.

Currie, Levine and Vidalis show that potentially harmful effects of cooperation (the Rogoff result) are eliminated with high probability so long as both partners to cooperation follow reputational policies. Gains from cooperation are small or negative if reputational policies are not followed. Even more importantly, however, they also show that reputational policies alone (that is, without simultaneous cooperation) may also be harmful in the sense that they produce potential instability in the international system.

This is a very significant result because it is counterintuitive and it disproves one of the main criticisms of cooperation. Such cooperation, it is sometimes argued, would be unnecessary if all governments followed sensible and stable policies. On the contrary, this evidence shows that such policies may produce a very poor outcome for the world economy unless cooperation makes for consistency of such policies. In the absence of such consistency large real distortions, such as real exchange rate changes, may build up over time. We shall discuss the practical significance of this further below.

It may be worth summarising the main points to emerge from this review of the academic literature.

1. There is a potential gain from international policy coordination, though this may be small, or even negative.
2. One of the benefits from cooperation may result from the information exchange which is involved, in so far as this widens the perspective of policy-makers and alerts them to alternative views about the state of the world.
3. Beneficial cooperation requires reputation on the part of policy makers, but reputation also requires cooperation. Cooperation without reputation may be harmful, as may reputation without cooperation.

Rules versus discretion

The debate about policy coordination is an extension of a debate about macroeconomic policy that has been going on since (at least) the 1960s. Lines which were drawn in earlier rounds between Monetarists and Keynesians are still relevant, though the international dimension adds some interesting new twists. Broadly speaking, Keynesians favoured using monetary and fiscal policy to 'fine tune' the economy, the goal being to minimise fluctuations of real activity around the long-term growth trend. Monetarists, in contrast, focused on the potential destabilising potential of mistimed policy interventions. For them the preferred policy stance was rule-bound – monetary growth being set in line with trend real GDP growth and fiscal policy being bound by a balanced budget (on average).

International policy coordination seems naturally to be an extension of the Keynesian approach to policy. The goal, after all, is to fine tune the world economy, rather than domestic economies in isolation (though the cooperation literature has taken on board rational expectations and, thus, is discussed in the context of the kind of policy games mentioned in Chapter 4). It is, thus, common for those with a Monetarist attitude to domestic policy to react negatively to the idea of international policy cooperation. Implicitly, it is presumed that the Monetarist prescription applied to individual countries would be sufficient to generate the ideal outcome for the world. However, the analyses summarised above add a new twist to this debate. Reputational policies followed by governments independently may actually produce a ˜ rse outcome than cooperative Keynesian or time-inconsistent p⁻˙ ˙ e reason for this is that inconsistent reputational policies can lι ˙ve swings in real exchange rates. Kenen (1989) makes this po˙ vhen he argues that coordination is more necessary under ˙ nge rate regime than it is under a fixed rate regime. However, ˙gime is clearly part of the story of what form coordination ˙gimes impose rules which limit freedom of action. Hence we ι 'y discuss policy coordination without also discussing altern˙ thin which it may take place.

Before moving on tι es it is worth pointing out why it is that policy coordination em attractive to some governments some of the time. This is ι ˙ may be the most likely way of rescuing policy-makers who have ˙ιen following non-reputational policies and currently find themselves with a balance of payments deficit (combined perhaps with a budget deficit). Domestic fiscal tightening may be the 'correct' policy response but policy makers would prefer an external balance improvement to come from an external demand boost rather than domestic deflation – they want to neither cut government spending nor raise taxes. Hence, if they can persuade a big neighbour to stimulate demand that may help solve the domestic problem.

Of course, if the other country is following reputational low inflation policies it will be reluctant to go along with this suggestion because it will have to be more inflationary than it otherwise would. This is one of the reasons why Monetarists are suspicious of policy coordination – it puts pressure on low inflation countries to inflate.

This is not a reason for giving up on coordination entirely, for the reasons outlined above. However, it is a reason for being very careful about examining the real effects of coordination in specific cases and not recommending coordination blindly. It also suggests that we examine the regime within which policy operates in order to ensure that it does not introduce an inflationary bias.

Regimes

The present international monetary system has been described as a 'non-system' because it emerged by default after the collapse of the Bretton Woods System in 1973. For some time it was thought that perhaps a floating exchange rate regime would be an adequate arrangement. However, the big swings in real exchange rates – especially those associated with the dollar – which were observed in the 1980s are what has persuaded many observers to contemplate a coordinated attempt to provide greater stability. What is not clear is whether the way forward consists of *ad hoc* bouts of concerted action (such as Plaza and Louvre) or whether there is any realistic possibility of creating a new regime. However, it is worth recalling the principal features of the three major regimes which have existed over the past century before proceeding to outline some proposals for change. The three major regimes are the gold standard, the Bretton Woods System and floating blocs. In the absence of global reform there has also been a trend toward 'sub-systems' which involve a subset of countries of the world creating their own mutual arrangements. The European Monetary System (EMS) is the most obvious example of this.

Most of the coordination literature reviewed above assumes a floating regime, though it is as well to recall that that has not always been the context, and the way forward may lie with a regime change rather than cooperation within the current regime.

Gold standard

Millennia of monetary history produced what was believed by most to be the natural order of financial affairs – currency based upon precious metals, especially gold. The evolution of gold and bimetallic standards need not concern us. Important for present purposes is the fact that the existence of what we shall refer to as the gold standard provided not just an internal monetary mechanism but also an international monetary regime with implicit rules resulting from the nature of the constraints imposed.

The gold standard only operated as a genuine global system for a few decades at the end of the nineteenth and into the early twentieth centuries. However, the dominant influence of commodity standards lasted much longer. Apart from a break around the Napoleonic Wars and the end of the First World War, Britain was on a gold (and sometime silver) standard from 1700 until 1931. (Its price level was approximately the same at the end of that over-two-century period as at the beginning.) Gold continued to have some explicit role in the international monetary system until as recently as 1971.

Even under the pure gold standard, gold coin and bullion were not the only money tokens in circulation. Rather, deposit notes and later deposits themselves circulated as part of the means of payment. The critical factor was that notes and deposits were convertible into gold at a fixed price on demand. Hence gold underpinned the acceptability of paper – it was 'as good as gold'.

There were three important characteristics of the gold standard so far as international policy is concerned. First, as all currencies were convertible into gold at a fixed price, it was a fixed exchange rate regime. This meant that no disruptive real exchange rate swings could arise from nominal exchange rate volatility (except, of course, when countries went off gold). Second, there was no direct role for 'government' as the gold convertibility was achieved by the private banking system. Gold was the ultimate backing for the note issue and for deposit liabilities. Third, external balance adjustment was automatic (or at least was perceived to be so by classical economists since Hume) through the 'price-specie flow' mechanism. A country with balance of payments surplus received an inflow of gold. This expanded the money supply (both directly and through a money multiplier) which in turn led to higher prices. Higher domestic prices eventually cause expenditure switching which eliminated the balance of payments surplus. Balance of payments deficits were associated with gold outflows and reductions in domestic money supply and prices.

In many people's eyes the gold standard was an ideal system. It provided a low inflation environment on average and it required the minimum of policy activism. However, it was not immune from severe cycles and it was constrained arbitrarily by cumulative gold production. Whatever its merits or demerits, it did not survive. It is notable, however, that Europe before World War I had a single currency, no barriers to free trade or movement of people and a highly integrated transport system – a situation it is trying to recreate by moves towards EMU.

Bretton Woods

The Bretton Woods System was established by an agreement signed in a town called Bretton Woods, New Hampshire in July 1944. It was designed to provide a stable international monetary regime which would avoid the economic instabilities of the 1930s that followed the general abandonment of the gold standard. The 1930s were characterised by a major financial collapse in the United States, competitive devaluations and a growth of protectionism. The intention was to provide a stable monetary regime which would facilitate a liberal trade regime and a growing world economy. The key features of this system were as follows:

1. Countries were to peg their exchange rates to the dollar at an explicit 'par' value (plus or minus 1 per cent). Currency devaluation was to be available only to correct a 'fundamental disequilibrium'.
2. The dollar was pegged to gold at $35 per ounce.
3. The International Monetary Fund (IMF) was established to monitor the system.
4. Each member subscribed funds to the IMF and in return received a borrowing facility to aid balance of payments adjustment.

There are a number of innovations resulting from the Bretton Woods Agreement which are worthy of comment. First, it required governments to have explicit control over international reserves and it thereby politicised the issue of the balance of payments. Second, it introduced for the first time a supranational organisation responsible for some form of coordination. Third, it produced an adjustment system in which there was some degree of asymmetry. Deficit countries were placed under considerable pressure to correct their imbalance – especially if they resorted to borrowing from the IMF. Surplus countries were under no such pressure. The direct link between balance of payments surpluses and high-powered money increases was broken by the general adoption of sterilisation policies. (The effectiveness of sterilisation has been extensively debated. It was likely to have been most successful in those many countries which retained capital controls. The idea of sterilisation is that the authorities sell long-term debt, or non-reserve assets, to mop up the money created by buying reserves.)

The Bretton Woods System worked well for a time. It provided a stable international monetary environment during the 1950s and 1960s. Certainly, most countries (except the United States) had fairly rigid capital controls for much of this time and there was plenty of grumbling in the 1960s about the endemic surpluses of West Germany and Japan. However, there was rapid growth in the world economy, low inflation and no major recessions. The asymmetry of the system, however, proved its ultimate undoing. In the late 1960s the dollar became one of the weaker currencies (partly as a result of Vietnam War expenditures and the US domestic War on Poverty). Convertibility of dollars into gold for all but other central banks was suspended in March 1968 and the official 'gold window' was closed in August 1971. From the latter date currencies floated against the dollar. There was a temporary repegging at new parities arranged in December 1971 but this only lasted until the spring of 1973 when the major currencies were floated (sterling floated from June 1972).

The current concern with policy coordination is really an extension of discussions which started after the collapse of Bretton Woods about how to run the system in the absence of pegged exchange rates. The Committee of Twenty was set up within the IMF to develop a blueprint (see Williamson,

1977) but the only two things agreed were that the world should return to pegged exchange rates and that the newly invented Special Drawing Right (SDR) should be the principle reserve asset. Neither of these has come to pass.

Floating

The system which came into being in 1973 has generally been described as a floating exchange rate regime. However, it is worth bearing in mind that only about a dozen of the well over one hundred currencies have floated freely. Most small countries peg their currency either to a large neighbour or to a basket of currencies. There is little alternative for those countries which would have very thin and, therefore, unstable exchange markets.

Floating had long been advocated as a sensible policy by some economists (Friedman, 1953) as it provided the possibility for each country to run its monetary policy independently of others. It was anticipated that there may be some exchange rate volatility in the early days, though it was presumed that this would settle down as speculators learned to smooth markets. Implicitly it was presumed that real exchange rates would be fairly stable. The fact that these expectations were not fulfilled is why we are discussing policy coordination today. It is in the context of a floating regime that most of the literature surveyed in this chapter poses the problem.

The European Monetary System (EMS)

In the absence of a global return to a pegged exchange rate regime, the countries of the European Community have determined that they wish to limit the range of mutual fluctuations of member currencies. Indeed, the ultimate goal goes well beyond this to the establishment of a single currency.

Attempts to limit exchange rate fluctuations within Europe predate the EMS. The 'Snake in the Tunnel' was first set up in April 1972. European currencies were at that time pegged to the dollar at Smithsonian parities. The mutual fluctuations between member currencies were to be kept within narrower bounds than those permitted under the Smithsonian agreement, hence the snake was a narrow band within a broader tunnel. Britain left the snake after only six weeks. The tunnel was abandoned in the spring of 1973 when member currencies floated against the dollar. Other members, including France, departed later. So by 1976 the snake just involved a few small countries pegged to the Deutschmark.

In 1979 there was a renewed attempt to create a 'zone of monetary stability' in Europe with the establishment of the EMS. All of the then members of the European Community joined the EMS. There was some pooling of reserves to create the European Monetary Cooperation Fund (EMCF) and the European Currency Unit (ECU) was established as an accounting unit for EC business. (The ECU is defined as a weighted basket of member currencies.) The key feature of the EMS was the exchange rate mechanism (ERM) which involved maximum fluctuation bands between the highest and lowest currencies. Most countries adopted a 2.25 per cent band while Italy adopted 6 per cent to accommodate its higher inflation rate. Britain joined the EMS from the beginning but stayed out of the ERM until October 1990 when it entered with a 6 per cent band. New EC members, Spain and Portugal also joined the ERM with 6 per cent bands, but Greece, which joined the European Community in 1982, remained out of the ERM. Britain and Italy were forced to leave the ERM in September 1992 as a result of massive speculative pressure, though both are committed to returning at some stage in the future.[1]

The Delors Report of 1989 called for a three-stage process of convergence to full economic and monetary union (EMU) within the European Community, with full ERM membership leading through rigidly fixed exchange rates to the adoption of a single currency. The Maastricht Treaty of February 1992 called for the establishment of a European Monetary Institute[2] in 1994 and the adoption of a single currency by 1999. It also established convergence criteria which members would have to meet to qualify for the single currency club. These included fiscal deficits no greater than 3 per cent of GDP, public debt no greater than 60 per cent of GDP and inflation no greater than 2 per cent above the average of the lowest three. While these criteria could be viewed as a local attempt at policy coordination they are really more than this as the goal is to achieve full monetary (and to some extent fiscal) integration. None the less, the presence of these criteria does affect the context in which policy coordination takes place in the rest of the world. They place limits on what EC countries can do over the next decade. Given that few countries currently meet all of these limits, there is likely to be a deflationary bias to monetary and fiscal policies within the European Community for the foreseeable future.

There is another implication of developments in the EC when viewed in the context of world trade. This is that the world economy could be sorting itself into three major trade blocs – North America, Europe and the Asian Pacific Basin. If these three trade blocs do solidify and they also become areas of currency pacts of some kind, then the global policy problem becomes that of coordination between a dollar zone, a DM zone and a Yen zone. Certainly if coordination were adequate between the United States, Germany and Japan, much else would fall into place.

Reform proposals

The generally perceived failure of the floating exchange rate system is that it has created instability in the world economy which has been greater than would otherwise have been necessary. The symptoms of this greater instability have been wide swings in real exchange rates and episodes of boom and recession greater than were experienced under Bretton Woods.

Ronald McKinnon (1984) argues that the instability of the world economy has been exacerbated by inappropriate monetary policy strategies on the part of the leading nations. He identifies the United States, Germany and Japan as the three key players. Monetary policy strategies have been based upon narrow domestic targets, without sufficient regard for the international situation. Money supplies in the leading nations tend to move together, thereby exaggerating the world cycle. Policy should be conducted so as to stabilise the world money stock, much as under the gold standard – when Germany's money grows US money should shrink. In addition to monitoring the aggregate world money supply, the authorities should act to avoid extreme currency fluctuations, thereby avoiding the wide swings in real exchange rates which have disrupted the international economy in the last decade or so.

John Williamson and Marcus Miller (1987) share McKinnon's concern about real exchange rate volatility. However, they propose to achieve greater world economic stability by means of a system of targets and indicators for all of the world's major countries (G7). Central to their scheme is the identification of 'Fundamental Equilibrium Real Exchange Rates' FEERS (first discussed in Williamson, 1983). This is the real exchange consistent with a current account balance on average. In particular the G7 countries would agree to the pursuit of the following two intermediate targets:

1. A rate of growth of domestic demand in each country calculated according to a formula designed to promote the fastest growth of output consistent with gradual reduction of inflation to an acceptable level and agreed adjustment of the current account of the balance of payments.
2. A real effective exchange rate that will not deviate by more than [10] percent from an internationally agreed estimate of the 'fundamental equilibrium exchange rate', the rate estimated to be consistent with simultaneous internal and external balance in the medium term.
   To that end, the participants agree that they will modify their monetary and fiscal policies according to the following principles:
   A. The average level of world (real) short-term interest rates should be revised up (down) if aggregate growth of nominal income is threatened to exceed (fall short of) the sum of the target growth of nominal demand for the participating countries.

B. Differences in short-term interest rates among countries should be revised when necessary to supplement intervention in the exchange markets to prevent the deviation of currencies from their target ranges.

C. National fiscal policies should be revised with a view to achieving national target rates of growth of domestic demand.

The rules A to C should be constrained by the medium term objectives of maintaining the real interest rate in its historically normal range and of avoiding an increasing of excessive ratio of public debt to GNP. (Williamson, 1983, p. 2)

Such rules would have the effect of providing an automatic response on the part of policy-makers once clear deviations of real exchange rate from some normal parity are identified. They would also put constraints on governments in terms of inflation targets and public debt not dissimilar from those envisaged in the Maastricht Treaty for EC members.

An alternative proposal is that due to Artis and Ostry (1986). They recognise the political difficulty of delivering and sticking to a set of policy rules which would be binding on all the major nations. However, they also recognise the potential costs of non-cooperation. Their solution is to organise coordination around a regular summit process. This would provide for a global economic assessment and a forum for the cooperative determination of policies that appeared to be required at the time. This is not very different from what happens at present except that the current system leads to action only for crisis management purposes while the ideal system would adjust policy in advance so that crises do not arise.

Costs and benefits of a single currency

In the absence of a new global monetary order, the European Community is going it alone. In this section we discuss some of the costs and benefits of moving to a single currency. It does not matter what this currency is called, though 'ECU' is likely. However, it would be a different ECU from the current one as it could not be defined as a weighted basket of other currencies which cease to exist. The single currency could have different names and notes in each country (just as the Scots still have their own banknotes today) but each local currency must exchange at a fixed price for each other at round numbers and with no transaction cost. The political problems associated with creating a European Central Bank may be significant but we shall concentrate on the economics of the issue.

The dominant beneficial effect of a single currency is that, by eliminating exchange rate risk and lowering transactions costs, it greatly increases the efficiency of the market mechanism in the allocation of resources. It could be argued that foreign exchange transactions are cheap, especially for wholesale deals, and that risk can be hedged through very efficient derivatives (forward, futures, options, swaps) markets. However, the potential gain is not just the reduced transaction cost of existing patterns of trade. It involves an element of trade creation, associated with greater efficiency of industrial organisation. These are the same kind of gains as result from trade creation in the customs union literature. In this respect, the single currency enhances the benefits of the Single Market. Indeed, in the financial services industry, complete integration of markets is unlikely to be achieved without a single currency. Of course, the European currency is likely to be floating against the rest of the world, so there will still be exchange risk and transactions costs associated with extra-European trade.

The dominant negative effect of having a common currency is that it removes the use of devaluation as a tool for correcting a loss of competitiveness in the United Kingdom relative to our European partners. UK monetary policy is targeted on UK economic conditions alone; in this respect we retain monetary sovereignty. Notice, however, that such sovereignty is only of benefit if it is used wisely. In reality, monetary policy since floating (June 1972 to October 1990 and since September 1992) has been a source of major disruption to the UK economy. From 1972 to date we have had nearly 600 per cent inflation, three major recessions and a rising trend in unemployment. Under the gold standard prices were stable for two hundred years. External convertibility constraints are the norm in British history, not the exception.

The potential benefit from being able to devalue, of course, creates only a short-run gain. In the long run, real market forces should work to restore appropriate relative prices. The freedom to 'print money' (i.e. expand the money supply) can never make a country permanently richer, but it can provide a tool for stabilising the business cycle around the long-run trend. The significance of this was illustrated dramatically by the problems of British membership of the ERM in 1990–92. High interest rates were needed in Germany because of the problems of reunification. High interest rates in Britain exacerbated a serious recession. Only by leaving the ERM could Britain pursue independent monetary policy. In a single currency system the exit option is permanently removed and monetary policy is centralised with the European Central Bank (ECB).

The only scenario under which monetary policy freedom is unambiguously beneficial in the long run is where the single currency itself is debauched by inflationary monetary policies. Only if the common currency can be guaranteed to be of stable value would it necessarily dominate on efficiency grounds. Hence, the single goal which has been specified in the draft constitution of the European Central Bank – price stability. This is why some economists have advocated competition among currencies. High inflation currencies would be driven out by low inflation ones. However, the costs of this transition may be very high. This route, along with the parallel currency option, no longer seems to be on the European agenda so it will not be discussed further.

The single currency could be harmful to the City of London, especially if the operating arm of the European Central Bank were established outside London, as seems likely. (The damage could be even greater if Britain were not a member of the single currency system.) The London Discount Market is most unlikely to survive a single currency as it is unlikely that the ECB would retain this peculiarly British buffer between the central bank and the main money markets. There would also be some loss of foreign exchange business in respect of cross-markets between EC currencies but there would be massive markets between the ECU and the US dollar and Japanese Yen, much of which could pass through London. What is less clear is the extent to which other aspects of London's role are threatened. After all, London grew in the 1960s and 1970s on the basis of the Eurodollar market. This was essentially 'offshore' to the whole of Europe, including the United Kingdom. Further back in history London was seriously damaged as a financial centre by the First World War – if it can survive that it can survive anything! The combination of commercial and financial skills in London is unique in Europe, and will continue to be so, irrespective of the currency structure.

An alternative way of looking at the single currency debate is through the perspective of the 'Optimal Currency Area' literature. Nation states have universally 'nationalised' the right to print money, but nation states differ radically in economic structure. Supposing we could design the currency structure of the world for economic efficiency, what would it look like? Would there be one world currency, or would there be more than one currency in some existing single currency areas? The founder of the modern literature on this subject was Robert Mundell (1961).

Mundell argued that currency areas should be small and economically homogeneous, so that devaluations could compensate for demand shifts, where real market forces had failed to do so. It is a very 'Keynesian' way of looking at the problem since it assumes that devaluations can correct appropriately for misalignments which cannot be worked out through the market. Implicitly, real wage changes can be achieved by devaluation which would not happen automatically (or at least not quickly). This way of looking at the problem has caused people to test for internal labour mobility as indicative of a potential optimal currency area. On this basis the United States passes, but the European Community may fail – the unemployed in Newcastle are not thought likely to move to Marseille to find work.

A contrary approach to that of Mundell was suggested by Ronald McKinnon (1963). He pointed out that Mundell's logic was for small areas with a single industry having their own currency, but this does not make sense from a monetary theoretic point of view. An individual industry could not sustain its own currency because a very specialised economy is very 'open' – a high proportion of its trades are with external neighbours. The value of a medium of exchange is that it is widely accepted in diverse trades. A successful currency area must have a high proportion of trade internal to that area – otherwise people will just use the external currency and the internal currency will go out of use. Even worse, if devaluation is used to stimulate demand for domestic output, residents will substitute into external currency because it is a more stable store of value. The monetary function of money suggests that the optimal currency area is large and diverse, possibly as large as the world. In this sense, the best you can do for monetary arrangements is to have a stable-valued currency traded over the widest possible domain.

Curiously, one of the main problems relating to the EC single currency is the design of fiscal policy arrangements. The Maastricht Treaty puts restrictions on fiscal policy through limiting the size of budget deficits and accumulated debt. However, there is a powerful case for arguing that divergent fiscal policies will be needed. Monetary policy will not permit regional variation so fiscal policy is the only tool left. There is no reason in principle why a government should not be able to resort to deficit financing if it wants to. It cannot utilise the inflation tax. The constraint is whether the markets will buy the debt – not whether someone in Brussels likes the policy. Only if fiscal excesses had to be bailed out by other countries would this inevitably be problematic. However, this is more of a problem of transition (a country may be tempted to print money in the run up to currency conversion knowing that it would soon become a Community debt).

The view that fiscal policy will have to be used to compensate for regional differences will certainly be persuasive to those who are Keynesian in their attitude to economic policy. However, even if one accepts the need for regional fiscal policy this does not establish that it cannot be coordinated from the centre. Indeed, interregional transfers are presumably more powerful than local deficit financing which has to be repaid out of local taxes. At present the regional adjustment funds of the European Community are relatively small (less than 1 per cent of Community GDP). Some feel that this fiscal compensation will have to grow if a single currency area is going to appear equitable. However, this is clearly a potential source of future conflict.

Even if we could agree the ultimate structure there are still serious problems of transition. The current strategy of a gradual convergence via a narrowing ERM may not work. Convergence may not arrive and shocks may force departures from the transitional arrangements, as occurred in September 1992 when Italy and Britain were forced to leave the ERM. It may be that a subset of countries (such as France, Germany, Belgium, Holland and Luxembourg) will join their currencies up first, while other countries join later when they are ready. If this happened it would be hard for Britain to stay out, since it would lose a primary role in the financial market arrangements. An alternative might be a float towards pre-announced conversion at known prices. This could accommodate slow adjustment. However, an alternative is a 'Big Bang' approach which simply announces a currency conversion, closing the banks over a weekend and opening on Monday with a new currency. The Big Bang has its dangers but the alternative of slow convergence may never reach the target. Certainly the problems of maintaining the transition mechanism in the form of ERM do not prove either way whether the single currency would be beneficial once introduced. What is sure is that the single currency for Europe is a bold adventure which involves a high degree of policy coordination. There are many dangers but there are also many potential rewards. Only time will tell how this all works out. The stakes are high.

Conclusion

Policy coordination continues to be an active issue because of the continued swings in real exchange rate and the continued belief in some quarters that a more cooperative approach to global macroeconomic policy may produce a better outcome. The academic literature has demonstrated that 'reputational' policies on the part of major governments acting alone may not be sufficient to guarantee an optimal policy outcome. Equally it has demonstrated that policy coordination in the absence of reputation may be worse than the non-cooperative outcome.

Even if a theoretical ideal could be identified (which is unlikely) the chances of elected politicians being able to commit themselves and their successors to specific policy rules and being able to deliver on those commitments seems unlikely. The alternative might be a return to a regime with specific convertibility commitments (such as those under Bretton Woods or the gold standard), though at the present time no such proposals seem to be on the table. In the absence of a global consensus about a regime change two forces seem to be at work. First, subgroups of countries, such as the European Community, are actively designing their own local integrative arrangements. Second, the world economy stumbles from cycle to cycle with policy cooperation at the global level only being effective (if at all) when real exchange rates get so out of line that radical action seems necessary. These periodic bouts of policy activism may be the worst of all possible outcomes because the unpredictable nature of the policy interventions may add more instability than they take away. In any event it should be clear that the issues discussed above continue to be of ongoing importance.

Notes

1. Most remaining members of the ERM went to a 15 per cent band in the summer of 1993 as a result of speculative pressure on the French Franc, and continued high interest rates in Germany.
2. It has been agreed that formation of the European Monetary Institute will go ahead on time and that it will be located in Frankfurt.

10

Taxing and spending

One of the central tenets of the new conservative macroeconomics is that the excessive growth of 'government' has been harmful to economic performance. The public sector is alleged to utilise resources inefficiently, and the taxes necessary to pay for public services are claimed to be a disincentive to productive effort. The purpose of this chapter is to discuss some of the macroeconomic aspects of this issue. The broader question of government versus the market is surveyed in Alt and Chrystal (1983).

The chapter considers two aspects of this controversy. We begin by analysing the question of 'crowding out', where government spending squeezes out the private sector. Then we examine the public finance aspects of government spending. This has risen to particular prominence with the seemingly inexorable rise of the US government deficit. In the United Kingdom, there has been an extraordinary turnaround from the budget surpluses of the mid-1980s to the near double-digit deficit (expressed as a percentage of GDP) in the early 1990s; this motivated a considerable fiscal squeeze announced for the financial years 1994–95 and 1995–96 in the 1993 April Budget, despite the fact that Britain was still gripped in a severe recession at that time.

Crowding out

The traditional macroeconomic case against government spending is that it squeezes or 'crowds out' private sector expenditure. Crowding out can be said to occur when an increase in government expenditure of say, £100m leads to an increase in national income of less than £100m. In this case, where total private expenditure falls, crowding out is associated with the existence of a multiplier effect of less than unity. Super-crowding out arises when the multiplier is negative.

Within the Keynesian paradigm, an increase in government expenditure would increase the level of national income by some multiple of the initial expenditure, through the multiplier process. Some resources would thus be acquired by the public sector, but the resulting income of the private sector would be greater than it was before: so fiscal expansion is a free lunch. Of course, even in this favourable case, some private sector expenditures (notably investment) could fall (partial crowding out). This picture may be correct in a deep depression, but it would not seem to characterise the behaviour of modern economies closer to the full employment level of output; although it is important to realise that an antipathetic attitude to state intervention is not new. Rather, it is as old as economics itself. The Keynesian view is the misfit, though this does not make it wrong. Spencer and Yohe (1970), for example, point out that even Adam Smith believed that government spending financed by borrowing involved 'the destruction of some capital which had before existed in the country, by the perversion of some portion of the annual produce which had before been destined for the maintenance of productive labour, towards that of unproductive labour' (*Wealth of Nations*, 1937 edn, p. 878). Spencer and Yohe (1970, p. 15) also refer to Hawtrey's evidence to the Macmillan Committee in 1930: 'Hawtrey stated that whether the spending came out of taxes or loans from savings, the increased governmental expenditures would merely replace private expenditures.'

The resurgence of a belief in crowding out was clearly associated with the Monetarist critique, but it did not flow directly from the work of Friedman himself.[1] Rather, the main impetus came from the work of Anderson and Jordan (1968). They ran a reduced-form regression of money national income on current and lagged values of government expenditure and current and lagged values of the money stock. The results indicated that while the impact effect of expenditure was positive this was soon offset by negative effects, so that, 'A change in Federal spending financed by either borrowing or taxes has only a negligible effect on GNP over a period of about a year' (Carlson and Spencer, 1975, p. 3). Monetary expansion, on the other hand, had a positive cumulative effect. For more recent estimates of the 'St Louis equation' see Batten and Hafer (1983).

The Anderson and Jordan result has been widely discredited. This is partly due to the failure of their equation on more recent data. More important is the theoretical argument of Goldfeld and Blinder (1972) who point to the inaccuracy of reduced-form techniques when the government reacts systematically to the state of the economy. An intuitive explanation of the Goldfeld–Blinder point is presented by Chrystal and Alt (1979). Basically, if fiscal stabilisation policy is designed to offset the effects of fluctuations in an exogenous variable, there need be no correlation between income and the budget deficit even if fiscal policy is working *perfectly* as a stabiliser.[2]

A further important point to be aware of before proceeding is that the crowding-out issue is often regarded as being identical to the question of the effects of the government budget constraint. The latter arises because if the government runs a budget deficit, this must be financed by either printing money, borrowing or raising taxes. This restriction has often been ignored in the past, as indeed it is in all three textbook models above. We shall see below that crowding out could occur even without a government budget constraint but that, once the government's financing requirement is taken into account, crowding out becomes so much more likely as to be highly probable, except when there is considerable slack in the economy.

The IS–LM Classical case

It was seen in Chapter 3 that one common interpretation of both the Monetarist and the Classical case arises if the demand for money is strictly proportional to income. The effect of this in terms of Model II is that the LM curve becomes vertical. This is illustrated in Figure 10.1 where LM_0 is the relevant curve. A shift of the IS curve from IS_1 to IS_2 caused by an increase in government expenditure in Model I (the Keynesian expenditure system) would have caused an increase in income from Y_0 to Y_1; but with a vertical LM curve there can be no increase in income. Rather, the interest rate rises to r_2 until there has been a reduction in private investment equal to the initial rise in government expenditure. Even if the LM curve were upward sloping, as it clearly is in reality, there would still be *some* partial

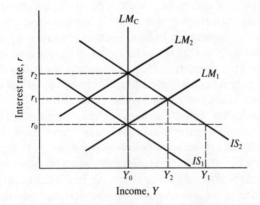

Figure 10.1 Crowding out in the Classical IS–LM model.

crowding out of private investment, say, on LM_1 at an interest rate of r_1. However, the rise in income from Y_0 to Y_2 *could* represent a multiplier in excess of unity.

Other Model II possibilities

A number of other cases are listed by Carlson and Spencer (1975) and we present these among others, though some of them would seem a bit unlikely.

The first is the 'Expectations Effect'. At one point in the 'General Theory' Keynes himself suggested that a government expenditure programme could, in 'the confused psychology which often prevails', have an adverse effect on confidence. This could cause either an offsetting reduction in private investment or an upward shift in the LM curve. Both could cause crowding out with respect to income, and the latter would involve a higher interest rate. This case seems unlikely to be of general importance, though it may apply in certain unusual circumstances. Another remote possibility is the horizontal IS curve. If investment were perfectly elastic with respect to the interest rate, the IS curve would be horizontal and fiscal policy would not shift it. Since national income is fixed by the LM curve, a rise in government expenditure would be exactly offset by a reduction in private expenditures. Despite frequent appearances in textbooks, this is a pathological case which can be immediately dismissed as unreasonable. There may also be microeconomic direct substitution effects. There are some areas in which government expenditures provide services which the private sector would otherwise buy for themselves. Thus it is possible that there is some direct substitutability between state and private expenditures; but it is not very likely that this substitutability is of major significance at the margin.

A much more significant effect comes in near full employment, via the price level. It should go without saying that if the initial position of the economy is at full employment, say at $r_0 Y_0$ in Figure 10.1, there can be no increase in income. A shift in the IS curve to IS_2 will lead to a price-level rise which will shift the LM curve to LM_2. Government expenditure will necessarily have a multiplier effect of zero, and again it will lead to an equal reduction in private investment.

There may also be financing effects, operating via the budget constraint. The case which has been emphasised by Friedman relies upon the fact that sales of debt by the government will reinforce the negative feedback already noted in Model II. Consider the initial position in Figure 10.1 at $r_0 Y_0$ on IS_1 and LM_1. An increase in government expenditure shifts the IS curve to IS_2 and the economy to $r_1 Y_2$. This rise in the interest rate is due to the increased transactions demand for money coupled with a fixed money supply. The rise in the budget deficit will have to be financed by sales of government debt which will put further upward pressure on interest rates. This upward pressure will be cumulative, so long as the deficit persists, whereas the initial multiplier is of a once-and-for-all nature. Thus any positive initial effect on income will eventually be offset by the negative cumulative effect of debt sales on private investment expenditures.[3] We consider the budget constraint further below.

Finally, we note that even in Model I, if an increase in government expenditure is financed by raising income taxes, the so-called balanced budget multiplier would be equal to unity. In Model II, however, since there is some rise in income with a fixed money supply, interest rates will have to rise. There will be some reduction in private investment and so the balanced budget multiplier becomes less than unity. Thus an increase in government expenditure financed by raising taxes will almost certainly involve some crowding out.

Crowding out in Model III

It should be clear that if we add a supply side to the model, crowding out will be even more likely to occur. Consider, for example, the version of Model III outlined in Chapter 7. This is pictured in Figure 10.2. The short-run aggregate supply curve AS_s is upward sloping because labour supply depends upon expected prices, whereas demand for labour depends upon actual prices. There is a rise in output in the short run because expectations lag behind actuality and so there is a temporary fall in the real wage. More labour is employed and more output produced.

An initial increase in government expenditure would move the economy

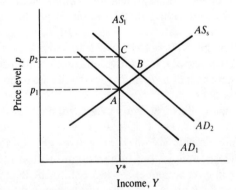

Figure 10.2 Crowding out in the Classical AD–AS model.

from *A* to *B* (ignoring the government budget constraint). However, over time price expectations will catch up with reality and, as they do, the short-run aggregate supply curve will shift up to the left. Eventually the economy will settle again at *C* where output is on the long-run aggregate supply curve. The increase in government expenditure will have crowded out private expenditures of an equal amount. It will be largely private investment that is crowded out, since the fall in the real money stock will raise interest rates. Thus the story we are left with from this model is that crowding out is quite likely in the long run but there may be a short period during which government expenditure leads to income increases through the multiplier process. Only if the economy could be shown to start off well to the left of the AS_1 curve, and not to be there because of an inflation cycle, could we argue that there was a chance that there would be no long-run crowding out.

An additional factor which could increase the likelihood of *short-run* crowding out would be if price expectations are formed 'rationally', in the sense defined in Chapter 4. It has implicitly been assumed above that price expectations are formed adaptively, as a revision from the prediction error made last time. If, however, all actors understand the model and realise that the expansion of government expenditure is going to raise prices, it could be that there will be no short-run output gain at all. Rather, the AS_s curve will shift up rapidly and the economy will go straight from *A* to *C*. This is the source of the argument that only unanticipated policy changes will have any real effects.

The remaining question concerns the position of the long-run supply curve. It has been argued that this will be positioned at the level of output corresponding to the NAIRU – the natural rate of output. This is basically determined from year to year by the underlying growth trend of the economy. It would seem from the above analysis that the only chance of long-run crowding out *not* occurring is if rises in government expenditure can increase the underlying growth potential of the economy. This is certainly possible; we examine this question in more detail at the end of this chapter. Nevertheless, the most vociferous commentators on this issue believe that exactly the opposite will occur. Brunner and Meltzer (1976, p. 769), for example, argue that:

> Reduction in the output of the private sector could, in principle, be offset by the increased output of the public sector . . .. It does not happen. Instead, there are loans or subsidies to enterprises that earn no profit or suffer large losses. Private saving is directed, in this case, toward enterprises that often do not earn rates of return equal to the interest on the bonds issued to finance the government budget deficit. Or, investment is used to increase 'prestige' as in the case of Concorde, national airlines, steamship lines and other enterprises that operate at negative rates of return. These enterprises direct material, skilled labour, and capital toward less productive uses than

the private output that is crowded out. The list of such enterprises can be expanded by every knowledgeable reader.

Absorption of labour by the government does not substitute public output for private output of equivalent value. Much public employment has the opposite effect. Complex rules and regulations absorb the time of civil servants and create demands in the private sector for lawyers, accountants, negotiators and clerks to keep abreast of the rules, to fill out the forms and hopefully to obtain more favourable interpretations than competitors have obtained.

Employment is generated by this process, but much of the output produced by the employees has little value to society. More efficient output is crowded out, replaced by records, completed forms and administrative decrees that in the aggregate subtract more than they add to wealth and to welfare.

Crowding out in macroeconometric models

One way of testing for the presence of crowding out is to use estimated econometric forecasting models to simulate the effects of various policy changes. The Macroeconomic Modelling Bureau based at Warwick University regularly undertakes comparative simulations of the major UK models. Church and Whitley (1991) present the results of simulations on the Treasury and Bank of England (and other) models (as of June 1991). As a cautionary preamble, it is worth recalling the criticisms of this procedure made by Robert Lucas (see Chapter 4 in this book). Such exercises require the structural model of the economy to be policy invariant. There is no reason to believe that this is so. As a result, the safest conclusion is that these simulations tell us a lot about the properties of the model in question but, perhaps, not very much about the properties of the economy itself.

Table 10.1 reports the effects produced in the Treasury and Bank of England models of a rise in government spending under two different assumptions. The first simulation is for a rise of government consumption of £2bn, holding interest rates fixed, while the second fixes the exchange rate. The simulations allow the full range of supply and demand effects to work through. The long-run multiplier implied by the models for both taxes and government spending is about one, although the effects on other variables like inflation and the balance of payments differ between the two cases; for example, a cut in income tax tends to reduce pressure on wages so inflation is lower than when government spending rises. The effect on the balance of trade is the reverse, but as the table shows, the results are very sensitive to the assumption about the exchange rate. If the exchange rate is fixed, then the consequences of a rise in government spending are quite different; output falls, and the multiplier is *negative*. If nothing else, this

Table 10.1 Percentage effect on real GDP of a £2 billion rise in government spending (1990 prices) and equivalent fall in income tax.

Year	Bank			HMT		
	1	3	5	1	3	5
G:(i)	0.40	0.53	0.56	0.43	0.50	0.46
G:(ii)	0.36	−0.20	−1.10	0.39	0.15	−0.36
T:(i)	0.13	0.40	0.59	0.11	0.34	0.52

Notes: (i) fixed interest rate; (ii) fixed exchange rate.

example serves as a salutary lesson about the relationship between simple economic theory and actual economies. In theory, a boost to government spending raises interest rates which leads to upward pressure on the pound; the government is forced to respond by expanding the money supply and reducing interest rates, thus expanding the economy. In the 'real' model, the worsening current account leads to a potential depreciation, forcing higher interest rates in defence of the exchange rate, reducing aggregate demand.

Government as producer

In the debate about crowding out, deficits and taxation, it is sometimes easy to forget that some government spending is actually useful. The macroeconomic debate is usually about the effect of a given deficit or fiscal stance on output and other macroeconomic variables. However, the components of G are not theoretical quantities, but real doctors and teachers, and roads that private individuals drive along. Nevertheless, a Martian visitor reading the macroeconomic literature[4] and listening to British government rhetoric during the Thatcher years might be hard pressed to understand why politicians are elected with any mandate to spend anything.

A particular version of the crowding-out thesis that took this view of government spending – namely, it is entirely unproductive – had a great deal of attention in the United Kingdom, through the publication of a series of articles in *The Sunday Times* in the 1970s. The argument was developed by Bacon and Eltis (1976), in a book entitled *Britain's Economic Problem: Too Few Producers*. The title makes the central idea very clear. Their basic point was the same as that made by Adam Smith exactly two centuries earlier, which is that, by the expansion of the public sector, there has been a 'perversion of some portion of the annual produce which had before been destined for the maintenance of productive labour, towards that of unproductive labour'.

Bacon and Eltis pursue their argument by dividing the economy into two sectors, defined by whether or not they produce a 'marketed' output.

The economy's market sector must produce all exports . . . all investment and all the goods and services that workers buy. It is to be noted that the market sector will include the nationalised industries in so far as these cover their costs through sales of output, as well as the private sectors of modern economies. It will exclude public services which are provided free of charge. (Bacon and Eltis, 1976, p. 123)

By definition, only marketed goods can go into exports, investment and towards satisfying personal consumption expenditure. The 'surplus' of the marketed sector is equal to its total output less what is consumed by the workers in the market sector themselves. This surplus of goods can either be reinvested in the market sector, exported or used up in the non-market sector in the form of consumption and investment. The basic Bacon and Eltis thesis is that Britain's growth and balance of payments problems can be substantially explained by the fact that non-market sector absorption of market sector surplus has crowded out market sector investment and exports.

It is a small step now to identify the non-market sector with the non-industrial public sector, including all those supported by social services such as old-age pensioners. In these terms the argument is that expenditure and especially employment in the public sector is too great for the 'health' of the economy. This diagnosis is supported by a casual glance at productivity trends which show that productivity rises in the market sector whereas it is static in the public sector. Diversion of resources into the public sector thus reduces the average productivity growth for the economy as a whole. This is a dangerous argument, however, because public sector output is typically *measured* by its labour input. So there is no way productivity in the public sector can rise – by definition.

The Bacon and Eltis taxonomy provided an interesting framework within which to view the economy. However, their methodology at best established correlations but not causation. They did not establish that growth in the marketed sector, which would otherwise have happened, was prevented by the employment of resources, especially labour, in the public sector. The upward trend in unemployment over the last two decades would testify to that. Indeed, the argument could just as easily be reversed. Because of the slow output growth in the industrial sector coupled with a continued productivity growth, there has been a decline in the demand for labour in industry. As a result it is essential to expand other forms of employment. This argument has become even stronger in recent years.

Another problem for Bacon and Eltis, however, was the breakdown of the categories of public sector employment. The biggest growth in employment between 1961 and 1974 seems to be in medical services and education. It is hard to believe that nurses and schoolteachers could just as easily have been employed as car workers. Furthermore, it is abundantly clear that in many other economies, health services and education are marketed products. It is quite possible that, if these services had been sold and priced through the market, employment in them would have grown even faster, though the significance of such an expansion would be far from clear.

The important point to notice here is that many of the services provided by the public sector such as health, education, police and leisure services may well be luxury goods. In other words, demand for them would rise more than in proportion to real income growth. There can be no presumption about the 'correct' size of the public sector without some analysis of the underlying demand for the goods involved. Even if these publicly produced goods were to be a constant proportion of total national output, the underlying production functions would lead to a growing proportion of all employment being in the public sector. Public sector services, being labour intensive, require a bigger growth of labour input for any given growth of output than do manufacturing industries.

While it would not be surprising to find a growth of government consumption more than in proportion to the growth in national income, particularly when health services and education are provided by the state, it is not at all clear that this has happened to any significant degree in the United Kingdom. Chrystal and Alt (1979), for example, find that the elasticity of government consumption with respect to GDP is not significantly different from unity over the period 1955–74. They also find that British experience is not at all out of line with other countries. Figure 10.3 shows the ratio of current government expenditure on goods and services[5] to GDP since 1955. Although the ratio is higher in 1992 than in 1955, the graph mainly reflects the steep rise in government spending that occurred around the end of the 1960s and early 1970s. By the mid-1970s, the

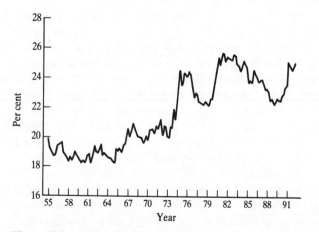

Figure 10.3 Ratio of nominal government expenditure to GDP.

Labour Prime Minister James Callaghan announced to local authorities (who were largely responsible for the rise in total government expenditure) that 'the party's over': cash limits on government spending categories (to replace rather elastic real spending targets) were introduced as a means of control. After 1974, the graph is pretty flat. Much of the variation comes from fluctuating GDP, rather than government spending.

A more detailed analysis of the causes of government growth as well as evidence from Britain and a number of other countries is available in Alt and Chrystal (1983, Chapters 8–10). Their general conclusion is that what has to be explained is not the excessive growth or variability of government but, rather, its remarkable stability in relation to national income both in Britain and in many other countries. Government behaviour is characterised by 'inertia' more than it is by any other simple hypothesis.

The knockdown argument against Bacon and Eltis must be that from the perspective of the post-1979 era (characterised by a decline in manufacturing employment and consistently high unemployment). It now seems absurd to suggest that the growth of manufacturing industry has been constrained by excessive public sector employment.

Optimal government spending

Even if one does not adopt an extreme anti-government spending stance, it is quite legitimate – even desirable – to ask how many goods and services the government should ideally provide. In other words, what is the optimal level of government expenditure? To consider this properly, we need to distinguish current expenditure on goods and services from capital formation.

As we observed above, goods and services provided by the government are directly useful to the extent that they are consumed by the public; however, the provision may be inefficiently high or low. There are standard arguments that justify the provision of some goods by the government. This is not the place to rehearse those arguments, but clearly it is entirely appropriate for the government to provide goods with a 'public good' component – for example, defence. In other cases, the argument may not be so clear cut. For example, many countries provide their health services privately, but in this case and others, there are grounds for thinking that public provision may be more efficient. The issues are partly to do with efficiencies stemming from economies of scale (e.g. centralised drug purchases), but there are also more subtle arguments. For example, there is a profound information asymmetry between doctors and patients; the doctors know more about the causes of and cures for illnesses than patients. In a private system there may be an incentive for doctors to exploit this asymmetry by over-providing medical services – especially if the insurance company picks up the tab. Education may be another case in point. The usual argument to justify free education for all is a distributional one; we (society) judge that citizens should not be deprived of an education because they lack the means to pay for it. However, there is a case to be made that one of the great unsung determinants of economic growth is human capital – provided, in large measure, by education.[6] If education does have this beneficial, external, effect on growth, then education is not simply useful in itself (is valued by consumers), but is also an input to the national productive process. If so, as is always the case in the presence of an externality, left to itself the private sector would demand and provide too little education, and growth would be inefficiently low.

This last argument revolving around externalities affecting growth has a wider application in the other field of government spending: capital formation. There is now a mounting pile of evidence to support the idea that government capital is productive – and indeed, may be highly productive. More motorways help industry produce more. This plausible idea was formalised in terms of modern theory by Barro (1990). He derived a condition for the optimal provision of public infrastructure capital, and provided some tentative estimates suggesting that internationally, the level of provision may be fairly close to the optimum. Lynde and Richmond (1993) look at the UK evidence for manufacturing and find that public capital expenditure is about as productive as private expenditure; this means that public capital formation is potentially very important. The bad news is shown in Figure 10.4. Figure 10.3 showed that if we allow for the effects of the cycle, government *current* expenditure has been largely flat since the mid-1970s; but this is not true for *capital* expenditure, which has been the target of cuts in planned government expenditure since the squeeze of the mid-1970s. Furthermore, the effect matters; the low level of public investment may well have involved substantial losses in output. Lynde and Richmond estimate that the annual effect of the contraction in public capital formation may be worth about $\frac{1}{2}$ per cent of GDP *per annum* in recent years. If true, this is a depressing statistic.

The government budget constraint

We now return to the financial implications of government fiscal policy. In the 1987 Autumn Statement the Chancellor did not refer to the UK public sector borrowing requirement (PSBR). Instead, they reported the public sector debt repayment (PSDR).[7] This quite properly reflected the fact that the PSBR had been progressively reduced during the 1980s to the point where debt was being repaid on a massive scale. Indeed, Mrs Thatcher

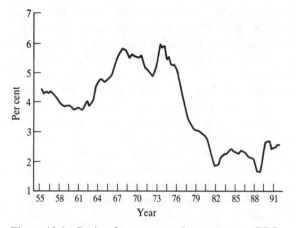

Figure 10.4 Ratio of government investment to GDP.

famously asked in Cabinet how long it would take to repay the entire national debt at the current rate: the answer was a mere 17 years. It soon became clear that these surpluses were to some extent illusory, caused largely by the rise in tax receipts following the unsustainable deregulatory boom stoked up by the policies of the Conservative Chancellor, Nigel Lawson. At the time of writing the official forecast for the 1993–94 PSBR is £50b,[8] or about 8 per cent of GDP. Inflation erodes the value of debt, but at the current rate of inflation a deficit of this size would lead to a national debt about 50 per cent larger than total GDP in seventeen years! With interest rates of 7 per cent, 11 per cent of GDP would have to go on interest payments alone. Deficits of this size are unsustainable.[9]

Like any other institution or person, the government faces a budget constraint. Throughout most of this book, as is common in much of macro, we are happy to ignore this. To the extent that we are concerned with short-term issues, this makes sense. A government deficit changes the *stock* of debt, but not by very much in any one year. However, as our example above showed, for medium- and long-term analysis, this partial approach will just not do. The first economists to spell out fully the government budget constraint were Blinder and Solow (1973), ironically in the context of a very Keynesian model. In any period, the government must finance its current spending together with the interest bill on the outstanding stock of bonds. It can do this by taxing, issuing more bonds or printing money. This last possibility is known as *seignorage*. The government, having a monopoly over the issue of money, is in a unique position to exploit this privilege; as we shall see, this may be an important matter. Assume for simplicity that all bonds are perpetuities. The government budget constraint may then be written[10] as

$$G_t + rB_{t-1} = T_t + \Delta B_t + \Delta M_t \qquad (10.1)$$

Government spending on goods and services, G, plus the interest bill on the outstanding stock of bonds, rB, are financed by taxation, T, new issues of bonds, ΔB, and increases in the monetary base, ΔM.

where Δ is the first difference operator. The government deficit is simply defined as

$$D_t = \Delta B_t = G_t + rB_{t-1} - T_t - \Delta M_t \qquad (10.2)$$

Notice that this differs from the UK PSBR. The PSBR includes asset sales on the 'wrong side' of (10.2) as negative government spending (a meaningless concept in this context). A proper accounting treatment would include asset sales as a form of finance, precisely analogous to a bond issue. Thus privatisation receipts, land sales and council house disposals should not affect the measured government deficit; they are merely alternative means of financing it.

We should also consider how the deficit changes over the economic cycle. There are essentially two issues to consider: distortions induced by the business cycle, and the effects of inflation.

The former arises from the well-known 'automatic stabilisers'. In a downturn, tax revenues fall (after a lag), while government spending, especially on transfers to the unemployed, tends to rise. So given an unchanged policy stance (for example with respect to government investment plans and tax rates), the deficit will tend to rise. Quantifying these effects is problematic, and requires the use of an explicit model of taxation and expenditure. Forecasting deficits is notoriously difficult, as the quantity in question is the relatively small difference between two very large numbers. Government revenue itself is very hard to model, but attempts have been made; see Buiter (1987) and Miller (1985) for a wider discussion. It does seem that these cyclical effects can be large: the second column of Table 10.2 gives some estimates for various years in the 1970s and 1980s. Notice that the apparent deficit in the infamous tax-increasing recession year of 1981 is transformed into a surplus after cyclical adjustment.[11]

Table 10.2 Cyclical and inflation adjustments to the general government deficit

Year	Deficit (% of GDP)		
	Raw	Cyclically adjusted	Inflation adjusted
1975	4.5	3.2	−7.6
1981	2.8	−1.8	−6.4
1984	2.8	−2.0	−4.2

Note: − indicates a surplus.
Source: Miller (1985).

The additional inflation adjustment also reported in the table is a little more subtle, but is nevertheless a simple idea. Government debt is denominated in nominal terms – so many millions of pounds. When the price level rises, the real value of the debt falls by an exactly proportional amount. Another way of looking at this is that when there is positive inflation, the nominal interest rate exceeds the real by the rate of expected inflation: the Fisher Effect. Thus, the real rate of interest is given by the following expression:

$$r_t = i_t + \dot{p}^e_{t+1} \tag{10.3}$$

The nominal rate of interest r is equal to the real rate of interest i plus the expected rate of inflation $\dot{p}^e_{t+1}$.

What this implies is that inflation forces debtors to repay a part of the principal, equal to the value of debt multiplied by the rate of inflation. Unlike the cyclical adjustment, which gives us information on the discretionary part of government fiscal policy, the inflation adjustment does matter when we wish to assess the tightness of policy. A 10 per cent public sector deficit at zero inflation is not at all the same as the same nominal deficit at 20 per cent inflation.

To conclude, (10.1) tells us the apparently obvious point that government spending not covered by taxes will lead to either a rise in the stock of debt, or a rise in the money supply. These simple observations turn out to have profound implications. We will take each in turn, beginning with debt.

Ricardian equivalence

The government budget constraint tells us nothing about the ultimate constraint on national debt, but it is clear there must be one. The extreme case is when the interest burden of the national debt exceeds GDP.[12] It is unlikely we would reach this point; well before then the government would find itself unable to borrow. The implication is that the government *eventually* has to repay its debt, albeit possibly at a very distant date. So current budget deficits increase future tax liabilities. This insight is due to the nineteenth century economist David Ricardo, but it was Robert Barro who reintroduced the idea in modern terms.

To see more concretely how the mechanism operates, suppose the government lowers taxes by £100m, financed by an increase in borrowing, keeping government spending constant. The aim is to see what the implications are of a shift from taxation to deficit finance. Assume for simplicity that the borrowing is done by issuing a perpetuity with a 10 per cent yield (equal to the rate of interest). Again for simplicity, assume that the government will raise taxes to pay the interest on these bonds (although the principal is never repaid). This assumption is not crucial; the government could Ponzi finance for a while; all that matters is that it *eventually* has to raise taxes. Clearly, in each future year taxes rise by 10 per cent of £100m, or £10m. Rational taxpayers will appreciate this, and will presumably adjust their lifetime spending plans to take account of the higher future tax burden. If they could, they would like to set aside a lump sum to cover the present value of this future burden. What is this sum? By the standard rule, the present value of the future increase in the tax burden (PV) in millions of pounds is given by:

$$PV = £10m/(1 + r) + £10m/(1 + r)^2 + £10m/(1 + r)^3$$
$$+ £10m/(1 + r)^4 + \ldots \tag{10.4}$$

which turns out to be worth

$$PV = £10m/r$$
$$= £100m \tag{10.5}$$

In other words, the rise in the future tax burden *exactly* offsets the tax giveaway in the current year; taxpayers are neither better nor worse off. The remarkable conclusion is that the method of finance is irrelevant. Whether the government taxes or borrows, the effect is the same. Hence the name for this effect: Ricardian *equivalence*. So there is no need to worry about the government deficit! This conclusion may seem perverse, coming as it does from a conservative macroeconomist, but Barro writes

> In recent years there has been a lot of discussion about U.S. deficits. Many economists and other observers have viewed these deficits as harmful to the U.S. and world economies. The supposed harmful effects, predicted by theories of the life-cycle type, include high real interest rates, low saving, low rates of economic growth, large current-account deficits in the United States and other countries with large budget deficits, and either a high or low dollar (depending apparently on the time period). On the other hand, this crisis scenario has been hard to maintain along with the robust performance of the U.S. economy since late 1982. This performance features high average growth rates of real GNP, declining unemployment, much lower inflation than before, a sharp decrease in nominal interest rates and some decline in expected real interest rates, high values of real investment expenditures, and (until October 1987) a dramatic boom in the stock market.' (Barro, 1987)

The big objection to Ricardian equivalence is that the future tax burden may lie very far in the future, and individuals do not usually live for ever. Barro's major contribution was to show that under some circumstances this objection has no force. All we need is that individuals care about future generations enough to want to make bequests, no matter how small, and the theorem goes through. The idea is that those leaving bequests are able to make offsetting adjustments to the amount they intend to leave that will exactly compensate for the changing tax burden. Of course, they will not be able to do this if their optimal bequest is *negative*; but individuals typically do leave bequests. Even where individuals do want to make negative bequests, the argument will still stand if children support their parents in old age, as many do. However, even if everyone were selfish and childless so that perfect Ricardian equivalence does not hold, there should still be *some* effects; and anyway, not everyone falls into those categories. There are other arguments for and against Ricardian equivalence; see Bernheim (1987) for a survey, and Barro (1987) for a spirited defence.

In the end, as usual, the case must be resolved by empirical evidence. Unfortunately, the econometric evidence on the issue is not very tight, although Bernheim concludes that the weight of the evidence is finally against Ricardian equivalence. However, there is one piece of evidence for the United Kingdom that is at least mildly persuasive. Figure 10.5 plots quarterly data on the UK public and personal sector financial deficits. The financial surplus of the personal sector is not quite the same as saving. Rather, it is equal to saving *minus* gross capital formation; in other words, the net acquisition of financial rather than all assets.

If Ricardian equivalence were correct, we would expect these two deficits to be inversely related. And indeed, what is most striking is that the series are near mirror images of each other. The growing personal sector surplus of the 1970s matches the public sector deficit. The dramatic lurch into deficit by the personal sector after 1985 is paralleled by a surge into public surplus. After 1988 both turn round.

Of course, one should not be too eager to interpret this pattern as

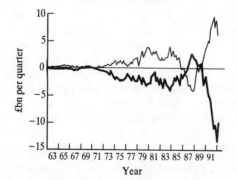

Figure 10.5 Financial balance of personal and public and sector: ———— public sector financial deficit, ———— personal sector financial deficit. Source: Datastream.

evidence for Ricardian equivalence. There may be alternative explanations. For example, the rise in inflation in the 1970s reduced the real value of government debt, making it rational to allow larger deficits. By the same token, the value of personal sector financial assets fell, encouraging households to acquire more financial assets to compensate. Furthermore, there is the issue of the underlying accounting identity. In a closed economy (or with balance of payments equilibrium) and no corporate sector, the personal sector surplus must be identically equal to the government budget deficit. And finally, anecdotal and macroeconometric evidence suggests that tax cuts unmatched by spending cuts are not all saved; some do leak into spending, *contra* Ricardian equivalence.

Seignorage and Monetarist arithmetic

If governments will not tax or borrow, they can always print money. The problem with this is that, *ceteris paribus*, money growth produces proportional inflation. This is costly, as it erodes the value of existing stocks of money and other nominal assets. Nominal interest rates will be higher, but this cannot compensate for the erosion of the non-interest-bearing monetary base. So money finance can be thought of as the levying of an inflation tax. This phenomenon is a serious problem in countries with small tax bases and unable to issue debt; for example, many Latin American countries have suffered from very high levels of inflation generated in just this way, as has post-Soviet Russia. A similar, albeit less serious, problem exists in Italy, where the large black economy is outside the tax base. This helps to explain why Italy has resorted to more money and deficit finance than other European countries, with correspondingly higher inflation.

The effects set out above are well known. However, Sargent and Wallace (1975) pointed out a surprising consequence. Clearly, if money growth increases inflation is likely to rise. So, all things being equal, one might expect that a shift from money to debt finance would lower inflation. Sargent and Wallace point out that *if* taxes and spending are fixed institutionally, as they may well be in practice in the United States where successive presidents have signally failed to reduce the government deficit, then deficit finance ultimately leads to the national debt knocking against a practical ceiling, as discussed above. At this point, if taxes and spending are fixed, there must be a move to money finance, and therefore more inflation. So far so obvious. The twist in the tale, however, is that the higher inflation anticipated in the period before this point is reached causes agents to shift out of money, so long as they have rational expectations. A reduction in money demand has much the same effect as a rise in money supply; consequently, inflation rises in the period before money finance takes over.

However, as this process can be anticipated, agents see *this* bout of inflation and shift out of money, causing inflation the previous period ... and so on. This backward chain of causation, characteristic of forward-looking rational expectation models, may even lead to higher inflation in the *current* period (given the right parameters). So, paradoxically, the apparently anti-inflationary shift towards deficit finance away from seignorage may turn out to be inflationary. However, the practical significance of this is debatable.

Summary

The conclusion reached in this chapter is that, while crowding out must realistically be accepted as a property of reasonable macroeconomic models, it is far from an established truth that over-expansion of government expenditure has actually been responsible for any significant crowding out of the private sector in the United Kingdom in the last twenty-five years. Indeed, there is some evidence that UK growth has been held back by inadequate public investment. A similar argument may be made for education. As regards the long-run implications of deficit finance, the consequences of expanding the national debt are clearly taken seriously by the Major government.[13] Lax fiscal policies may lead to higher inflation in the future (and possibly now), and cannot ultimately stave off the day of reckoning. The basic insight we have gained over the last twenty years is that there is no such thing as a fiscal free lunch. Deficits have a habit of (eventually) coming home to roost.

Notes

1. Apart from any influence *Capitalism* and *Freedom* may have had.
2. What the St Louis result really amounts to is that prices are proportional to the money stock and real government expenditure is a stable proportion of real GDP.
3. However, Blinder and Solow (1973) pointed out that if government bonds are considered to be net wealth (which is not obvious, as they have to be repaid out of taxes, a point to which we return below), then consumer spending may rise, boosting demand and tax revenues. This *may* restore a long-run positive effect.
4. The quote from Brunner and Meltzer given above is a good example of the extreme view.
5. That is, excluding capital investment.
6. We return to this issue in Chapter 12 when we consider the long-run determinants of growth.
7. Sad to say, this development proved temporary, as the budget deficit returned with renewed vigour after only a brief absence.

8. This figure understates the true deficit, as the PSBR is reduced by nearly £6b of privatisation receipts, raising the deficit to around 9 per cent of GDP, an extraordinarily high figure at a time of low inflation. It also appears that the forecast may turn out to be an underestimate.
9. High inflation will change this conclusion, as we see below.
10. This identity is somewhat simplified. It ignores the effect of changing interest rates, which alter bond prices.
11. It should, however, be borne in mind that the automatic stabilisers do deliver a stimulus; we should not conclude that the 1981 fiscal stance was 'really' in surplus.
12. There is one other possibility, that the government could borrow further to repay interest on its debt. This 'chain letter' case, also known as Ponzi finance after the 19th century fraudster who built a pyramid of bonds using this method, is usually ruled out *a priori*. We also know from the experience with Third World debt in the 1980s that in practice there comes a point when lenders will no longer support this kind of scheme, even when the borrowers are sovereign states.
13. The 1993 April budget proposed legislation to substantially increase the tax burden in future years. This stands in marked contrast to the situation in the United States, where politicians are long on anti-deficit rhetoric but are astonishingly short on action to correct it.

11

Business cycles: Causes and control

Many leading economists who worked in the first half of the twentieth century regarded the explanation of the recurrent cycles in the economy as a high priority. Interest in this area died down somewhat in the 1950s and 1960s, both because cycles had ceased to be a major problem, and because the theoretical focus of Keynesian economics was on the determination of the level of income at a specific point in time. Such dynamic theory as there was, was more concerned with the characteristics of stable growth paths than with cycles about such paths. This is not to say that there was no concern with cycles, merely that the dominant view was that the new Keynesian policy tools ensured that cycles need no longer be a problem. This view was reinforced by the apparently self-evident absence of major cycles, which was interpreted by many to mean that these policy tools were highly effective. There is, of course, another interpretation of these events, as we shall see.

An understanding of the nature and causes of business cycles is at the heart of policy controversy between Keynesians and Monetarists. A different explanation was offered by New Classical economists, notably Robert Lucas, which, as we have already seen, is even more damaging to the case for active stabilisation policy than the Monetarist arguments. At the centre of the problem is the question of whether the private sector of the economy is basically stable, and whether government intervention makes it more stable or less stable. This distinction was emphasised by Modigliani (1977) in his presidential address to the American Economic Association:

> In reality, the distinguishing feature of the Monetarist school and the real issue of disagreement with non-Monetarists is not Monetarism, but rather the role that should probably be assigned to stabilisation policies.

Non-Monetarists accept what I regard to be the fundamental practical message of the General Theory: that a private enterprise economy using an intangible money needs to be stabilised, can be stabilised and therefore should be stabilised by appropriate monetary and fiscal policies. Monetarists, by contrast, take the view that there is no serious need to stabilise the economy; that even if there were a need, it could not be done, for stabilisation policies would be more likely to increase than to decrease instability, and, at least some Monetarists would, I believe, go so far as to hold that, even in the unlikely event that stabilisation policies could on balance prove beneficial, the government should not be trusted with the necessary power. (p. 1)

These issues are now of urgent importance. Most countries have been through two major depressions in the last twenty years (1974–75 and 1981–83, though the precise timing differs from country to country) more serious than any since the 1930s, and the United Kingdom through a third (1990–93). As a result of this it should be no surprise that there has been a revival of interest in business cycle theory.

Theory of business cycles

One of the most famous students of the business cycle, Joseph Schumpeter (1939), identified three different amplitudes of cycle in the previous 150 years. These he named after writers who had noticed them previously. There was a sixty-year wave (Kondratieff), a ten-year cycle (Juglar) and a forty-month cycle (Kitchin). It is the shortest of these which is the one most economists refer to as the business or trade cycle. Subsequent empirical research, particularly that in the United States associated with the National Bureau of Economic Research (NBER), has concluded that business cycles cannot be accurately characterised by periodicity. The time profile is in fact irregular. What does characterise these cycles, however, is a remarkably common pattern of co-movements of aggregate economic series.

The principal among these are the following:

(i) Output movements across broadly defined sectors move together. (In Mitchell's [1941] terminology they exhibit high conformity, in modern time series language they have high coherence.)
(ii) Production of producer and consumer durables exhibits much greater amplitude than does the production of non-durables.
(iii) Production and prices of agricultural goods and natural resources have lower than average conformity.
(iv) Business profits show high conformity and much greater amplitude than other series.
(v) Prices generally are procyclical.

(vi) Short-term interest rates are procyclical, long-term rates slightly so.
(vii) Monetary aggregates and velocity measures are procyclical.
(Lucas, 1977, p. 9)

Keynesian approach

While the literature contains large numbers of attempts to explain cycles
(see, for example, R. A. Gordon, 1961, Chapters 12 and 13), attention here
is restricted to the main differences between the macro contenders.

Keynesian economics would appear to have no serious difficulty in
accounting for these stylised facts. The initial event would be a change in
exogenous expenditures such as exports or investment. This would be
transmitted through the economy by a combination of the multiplier effect
and the accelerator (Samuelson, 1939). The latter reflects the induced effect
on investment of the change in output. Upswings or downswings may be
explosive but constrained by ceilings (resource constraints) and floors (net
investment cannot be negative) as, for example, in Hicks (1950). Alternatively the dynamics of the economy may themselves be cyclical (Matthews,
1959) – possibly damped cycles, possibly explosive. To illustrate this let us
consider a specific case set out by Matthews (1959, p. 23).

The accelerator derives from the fact that a given capital stock is
required to produce a constant level of output. This means net investment
(increases in capital – depreciation is ignored) must be associated with
growing output. Assume that there is a lag between changes in output and
investment so

$$I_t = v(Y_{t-1} - Y_{t-2}) \tag{11.1}$$

The consumption function is the familiar one

$$C_t = \alpha + \beta Y_t \tag{11.2}$$

The solution for current income when (11.1) and (11.2) are substituted into
$Y = C + I$ is

$$Y_t = [v/(1 - \beta)](Y_{t-1} - Y_{t-2}) + \alpha/(1 - \beta) \tag{11.3}$$

This is a second-order difference equation, the course of which will depend
on the precise values of the parameters (v and β in this case) but it is quite
likely[1] that a once-and-for-all change in exogenous expenditures (α) will
lead to *cycles* in Y. Consider Matthews' numerical example which is set out
in Table 11.1. Take the values of v and β as 3/5 and 1/2 respectively. Set the
initial values of variables as follows: Income (Y) = 100, Capital (K) = 60,
Investment (I) = 0, Autonomous Consumption (α) = 50. Then in the third
period, α increases to 75 and stays at the new higher level. The immediate
impact is a multiplier effect on income of 50 ($1/(1 - \beta) = 2$).

Table 11.1 A multiplier/accelerator model

Period	α	I	Y	C	K (beginning of period)
1	50	0	100	100	60
2	50	0	100	100	60
3	75	0	150	150	60
4	75	30	210	180	60
5	75	36	222	186	90
6	75	7	164	157	126
7	75	−35	81	115	133
8	75	−50	50	100	99
9	75	−19	113	131	49
10	75	38	225	188	30
11	75	68	285	218	68
12	75	36	222	186	135

In the next period investment starts to rise because income rose the period before. The investment has a further upward multiplier effect on income, so the next period investment is a bit higher, though only a little. So the rate of increase in income slows down, and this leads to a reduction of investment which itself leads to a downturn of income, etc.

The central elements of this mechanism still seem highly plausible. The model is, of course, highly simplified and would in reality have to include many other structural constraints. None the less, in an IS–LM type framework augmented by a simple Phillips curve this model could account for all the stylised facts set out above. Seen as caused by a shifting IS curve, the cycle would evidence positive correlations between output and all of prices, profits, interest rates and velocity. The accelerator is also a very convincing reason why cycles in capital goods industries are of much greater amplitude than in consumer goods industries. However, the analysis also carries the strong implication that government behaviour could change all this. In the above example, if government expenditure had been included in the analysis, a reduction of G by 25 in Period 3 would have left income stable. Similarly, a government reaction function of the form $G = -v(Y_{t-1} - Y_{t-2})$ would eliminate the cycle by offsetting the accelerator.

Monetarist approach

The Monetarist approach to the business cycle is rather different from this and is most clearly evident in the work of Milton Friedman and Anna Schwartz (1963a, b). It cannot be claimed that monetary factors were ignored in Keynesian-style explanations – they were not (see Hicks, 1950, Chapter 11; Harrod, 1936, Chapter 3; Matthews, 1959, Chapter 8). Indeed, the trade cycle had been described by one of Keynes' contemporaries, R. G.

Hawtrey, as 'a purely monetary phenomenon' (though Hawtrey could hardly be described as a Keynesian). What was different about the work of Friedman and Schwartz (apart from the detailed empirical evidence they produced to support their case) was the emphatic insistence on the importance of the money stock, rather than on credit conditions and interest rates in general. Most stories would have tightening credit associated with the slowdown and easy credit associated with the upturn. Friedman and Schwartz argued that changes in money were the dominant cause of cycles and that these changes were predominantly exogenous. The following statements are the main findings of Friedman and Schwartz (1963a):

> There is unquestionably a close relation between the variability of the stock of money and the variability of income. This relation has persisted over some nine decades and appears no different at the end of the period than at the beginning. (p. 43)

> There is a one-to-one relation between monetary changes and changes in money income and prices. Changes in money income and prices have, in every case, been accompanied by a change in the rate of growth of the money stock, in the same direction and of appreciable magnitude, and there are no comparable disturbances in the rate of growth of the money stock unaccompanied by changes in money income and prices.
>   The changes in the stock of money cannot consistently be explained by the contemporary changes in money income and prices. The changes in the stock of money can generally be attributed to specific historical circumstances that are not in turn attributable to contemporary changes in money income and prices. Hence, if the consistent relation between money and income is not pure coincidence it must reflect an influence running from money to business. (p. 50)

> Our survey of experience leads us to conjecture that longer-period changes in money income produced by a changed secular rate of growth of the money stock are reflected mainly in different price behaviour rather than in different rates of growth of output; whereas the shorter-period changes in the rate of growth of the money stock are capable of exerting a sizable influence on the rate of growth of output as well. (p. 53)

Even if the above statements are accepted, we still do not have a reason to believe that a step change in the rate of growth of the money stock will generate anything but an (ultimate) step change in the rate of inflation and a one-off temporary effect on the level of real output. How does this provide the basis for a theory of business cycles? The answer provided by Friedman and Schwartz is that the transmission mechanism contains forces that will produce overshooting. The principal of these is associated with the fact that the demand for real money balances depends upon the rate of inflation (this is the opportunity cost of holding money relative to goods). Suppose there is a step increase in the rate of growth of money. In equilibrium there will be a similar step increase in the rate of inflation. However, as a result of the higher inflation, demand for real money balances will fall. This means that the price *level* must be higher relative to the *nominal* money stock than it was initially. Therefore, during the transition to the new equilibrium, the rate of inflation must overshoot its steady-state value. This temporary overshooting of inflation will lead people to run down their real money balances too far. As they build them up again the inflation rate must be below its equilibrium level, etc. The rundown of money balances phase will, of course, be associated with upturns in business activity and *vice versa* for the build-up of money balances.

In purely mechanical terms there are obvious similarities between this explanation of cycles and the accelerator mechanism. In one case the dynamics result from the fact that the stock demand for one variable (money) depends upon the rate of change of another (prices). In the other case, a flow demand (investment – itself the change in the stock of capital) depends on the rate of change of another variable (income). In both cases the time paths of endogenous variables may be described by difference or differential equations which, depending upon the parameters of the system, may generate cycles once disturbed. In terms of their implications for policy, however, the Keynesian and Monetarist explanations are very different.

The main policy difference derives from a disagreement over the source of disturbances. For Keynesians the shocks come from changes in autonomous expenditures, such as exports, or shifts in private expenditures, such as investment. This reflects intrinsic instabilities of the market economy and it is the job of government to try to spot these movements and offset them by changes in its own behaviour. For Monetarists the shocks are primarily changes in the rate of growth of money and, at least in the modern world, control of the money stock is the responsibility of central monetary authorities. The shocks, therefore, are primarily due to control failures on the part of government or governmental agencies. Hence, the conclusion that the discretionary powers of these authorities should be reduced and they should be made to adhere to a more or less rigid growth rule for the money stock.

Even if shocks are identified as being from other sources, monetary policy should not be used as a tool of stabilisation policy because it is too clumsy. In Friedman's well worn phrase, the impact of monetary policy is subject to 'long and variable lags'. As a result, a policy which is intended to be stabilising may, in reality, be destabilising. A stimulus, for example, intended to help the economy out of a depression may add fuel to a subsequent boom because its effects are felt with a lag. The variability of such lags makes the stabilisation role of monetary policy severely limited.

New Classical approach

The New Classical approach to business cycles contains elements of both the accelerator mechanism (as, indeed, could the Monetarist story, though it is not emphasised) and monetary shocks. However, in one respect the New Classical economists have made a major break with the post-World War Two macroeconomic tradition. This is their insistence on developing an *equilibrium theory* of the business cycle. The reason for this insistence is the problem posed by the Lucas Critique (discussed in Chapter 4) rather than the inability of earlier theories to explain the general pattern of past cycles.

> The ability of a model to imitate actual behaviour ... has almost nothing to do with its ability to make accurate *conditional* forecasts, to answer questions of the form: how *would* behaviour have differed had certain policies been different in specified ways? . . . Any disequilibrium model, constructed by simply codifying the decision rules which agents have found it useful to use over some previous sample period, without explaining why these rules were used, will be of no use in predicting the consequences of non trivial policy changes. (Lucas, 1977, p. 12)

> Before the 1930s economists did not recognise a need for a special branch of economics, with its own special postulates, designed to explain the business cycle. Keynes founded that sub-discipline called 'macroeconomics', because he thought explaining the characteristics of business cycles was impossible within the discipline imposed by classical economic theory, a discipline imposed by its insistence on adherence to the two postulates (a) that markets clear and (b) that agents act in their own self-interest. The outstanding facts that seemed impossible to reconcile with these two postulates were the length and severity of business depressions and the large-scale unemployment they entailed . . .
> . . . The research line being pursued by some of us involves the attempt to discover a particular econometrically testable equilibrium theory of the business cycle, one that can serve as the foundation for quantitative analysis of macroeconomic policy. There is no denying that this approach is counter-revolutionary, for it presupposes that Keynes and his followers were wrong to give up on the possibility that an equilibrium theory could account for the business cycle. (Lucas and Sargent, 1981b, pp. 304–6).

It should be immediately obvious that to have an *equilibrium* theory of cycles requires a different concept of equilibrium from that normally used in textbook economics. Equilibrium is not, in this sense, a state of rest. Rather, it means that at each point of time actors respond optimally to the prices they perceive (which are being perpetually disturbed) and that markets should clear, given the supply and demand responses by actors to their perceptions of prices. In other words, the economy will be describable by a stable statistical process, rather than by displaying constant values of all variables. The idea of optimising individuals should not be alien to economists. However, the statement that markets perpetually clear at first sight seems outrageous. We shall see that it is not so outrageous and amounts to little more than an analytical device. It should not be interpreted as a statement about the real world, though unfortunately it often is. For example, it does not deny the existence of registered unemployed.

The central mechanism that generates the cycle is the (surprise) supply relationship that was described in Chapter 4. When applied to the explanation of business cycles (Lucas, 1975, 1977), the story contains elements of both speculative supply behaviour (Lucas and Rapping, 1969) and signal extraction (Lucas 1972, 1973). Consider an individual self-employed producer. The producer has to decide each period how much to work and therefore produce, as well as deciding how much to invest (that is, increase the capital stock). Both these decisions are made on the basis of one piece of current information – the price of the output. They learn about everything else going on in the economy with a lag except that, as before, they do know the probability distribution of real and nominal shocks.

Let us suppose that our actor observes a rise in the current price of the output. How should she react? As before, it depends on the extent to which this is regarded to be a shift of (real) relative prices in her favour, as opposed to a rise in the general price level. To the extent that this is perceived as real, one also has to decide whether it is temporary or permanent. If it is temporary, the actor should work harder now and take leisure later when the return to effort will be lower. If it is permanent, it will pay to increase capacity by investing. The claim is that since all these decisions have to be made on the basis of a single price signal, the optimal response will be a weighted average. The weights depend on the relative variances of real and nominal shocks as before. The price rise will be associated with both a higher current output and higher level of investment. This relation between output and investment can be thought of as an accelerator, though it will be damped as compared to the Keynesian accelerator. Investment will only respond to output changes perceived to be permanent. We return to this idea – of *intertemporal substitution* – below.

Two important problems remain. Why do random shocks generate cycles of considerable duration? Why are the cycles evident in the aggregate rather than simply averaging out across the economy? For the New Classical business cyclist persistence is a serious problem, but not insuperable. There is no necessary inconsistency between the randomness of shocks and the fact that output and employment changes are auto-correlated. Two factors in combination are used by Lucas (1975) to explain the duration of cycles. One is the lag in receipt of information; the other is the durability of capital goods. The role of lagged information has been discussed above. Obviously, the longer the information lag the longer will be the full-adjustment period. This would not matter so much if decisions were costlessly reversible. However, once changes are made in the capital stock this is no longer true because capital formation is assumed to be irreversible. Mistakes made in one period will continue to affect output in future periods – hence the persistence of effects resulting from a random shock.

Why, then, is there a tendency for all sectors to expand and contract together? Lucas' answer is that the nature of the shock cannot be a random shift between markets or, indeed, any kind of disturbance that will wash out in the aggregate. Nor can it be an aggregate supply shock because this would lead to a negative correlation between price and output, which is not the typical pattern of business cycles. The strongest candidate is an aggregate monetary disturbance since this is the most likely to affect the price signals in all markets simultaneously. It should go without saying that this monetary disturbance has to be unanticipated.

However, even a fully anticipated change in the rate of monetary expansion will have real effects if prices are not perfectly flexible for the same reasons as there is overshooting in the Monetarist business cycle. If there is a step increase in the rate of monetary growth this will lead to a corresponding step increase in the inflation rate. Demand for real money balances will fall. This can only be achieved at a higher relative price level. If the increased growth rate of money is *fully anticipated*, the price level will jump up at the initial point in time. Similarly, an anticipated lowering of the rate of monetary growth will both lower the inflation rate and cause an immediate downward jump in the price level. Friedman and Schwartz implicitly assume that prices are sticky so that some of the adjustment pressure is felt on output. It is hard to believe that prices are so flexible that there would not be real effects in any realistic economy. However flexible prices are, it is hard to believe that the price level could jump downwards overnight in immediate response to the announcement of a tighter monetary policy. This, of course, reinforces the case for monetary causes of business cycles, but it would not meet with the approval of New Classical economists because of the arbitrary presumption in favour of price stickiness. However, the assumption of a jump in prices is also problematic because at the point in time at which the jump takes place the return to nominal assets is either plus infinity or minus infinity. If this jump is anticipated, the model will be explosive. New Classical economists handle this problem by assuming it away. The economy is simply assumed to jump to the new stable (saddle) path. Whether a real world economy could jump in this way depends on what price we are discussing. While it does not seem sensible to construct models where, say, the aggregate price level jumps, it is not at all implausible in financial markets.

It is this assumption that prices adjust continuously to clear markets that has been the cause of the most serious misgivings about New Classical economics among economists. While markets do exist in which prices are determined to clear the market at the time (such as commodity markets and foreign exchange markets), most goods and services are traded in what Hicks (1974) calls 'fix-price markets' and Okun (1981) calls 'customer markets'. Certainly, the rhetoric of New Classical economics is inconsistent with arbitrary stickiness in prices. However, in reality the disagreement is more apparent than real. It is an issue of semantics rather than economics. This is because as we have just seen New Classical economists have to introduce *imperfections and rigidities of some kind* in order to explain real world data. The effect of this is to introduce auto-correlation into activity series (such as GDP) so that the series becomes describable by a difference or differential equation as above. Once in this form, the theory is *observationally equivalent* (Sargent, 1976) to a large number of other theories including versions of the ones outlined above. There may be no way of discriminating between them from the data alone.

In behavioural terms this has an obvious interpretation. The price-stickiness view of markets has some actors at the *market place* frustrated because they cannot buy or sell at the going price. The price does not adjust immediately to reflect this excess demand or supply. We would commonly say that the market does not clear. In the New Classical set-up the price does clear the market made up of the actors who actually express the demands or supplies actively at a point in time at the *market place*, but it does not reflect the demands and supplies of actors who are delayed in their response because of poor information or being locked into the wrong location or equipment because of past mistakes. In the first view, for example, the unemployed worker is knocking at the factory gate, yet the employer does not reduce wages immediately to make it profitable to employ him. In the second view, there are no workers left outside the factory gate today. All who turned up today struck a wage bargain with the employer such that all get employed today. However, there are other workers who would work at that wage agreed today. It is just that they will not get there until after they hear about it and then have time to move house and arrange transport, etc. Either way there is slow adjustment and it is surely a matter of taste which way the problem is specified. The former conforms to many of our (perhaps Keynesian) prejudices whereas the latter may well offer methodological advantages. These are that the reasons for the slow adjustment have to be explicitly stated and, as a result, can be formally modelled. It does, however, seem unnecessarily narrow to rule out, *a priori*, some form of price stickiness which might be justified by optimising models such as that discussed in the implicit contracts literature; but see Chapter 5 for more discussion on this.

The implications of the New Classical approach are, of course, even more cautionary for stabilisation policy than was the Monetarist approach. Here, though, the strictures are much stronger. It is not the problem of long and varied lags. Rather, it is the fact that *any* systematic policy will come to be anticipated by actors. This argument is set out in detail in Chapter 4. Stabilisation policy would be beneficial if the authorities had superior information or were able to react quicker than private actors.

Real business cycles

As we have seen, the New Classical economists broke with a forty year tradition shared by both Keynesians and Monetarists, in which both saw business cycles as being in some sense *disequilibrium* phenomena. To the extent this was true, the business cycle could (at least in theory) be smoothed by appropriate government policy. The New Classical vision, by contrast, is one of *equilibrium business cycles*. Random shocks bounce the economy into booms and recessions which (because of adjustment costs, say) tend to persist. However, agents are always optimising – we are always in equilibrium. This was a radical departure; but what the new school kept from the old world-view is the notion that demand shocks are the driving force behind the business cycle. However, to some economists this presented a number of puzzles.

The first puzzle is about where the surprises are supposed to come from. In Chapter 4 we looked at three views of the model underlying the surprise supply function. Each of these seemed problematic. The most basic problem is that in the modern world there are a great many individuals who are paid large sums of money either to generate economic information – for example, government statisticians or city economists – or to disseminate it – TV and other journalists, for example. A lack of information about prices drives the surprise models, but aggregate price inflation figures are routinely given prominence on national television immediately they are published, with a relatively small lag after the period they refer to. Indeed, the retail price index is one of the most accurately known and speedily published of all the economic statistics. Ironically, perhaps only the money supply is published with a shorter lag.

Another puzzle is an empirical one, to do with the movement of real wages over the business cycle. An omission from Lucas' list of business cycle characteristics is any discussion of the real wage. This is convenient for Lucas, because it turns out that the real wage presents the biggest challenge for all demand-side stories of the business cycle. All demand-driven explanations of the business cycle – be they Keynesian or New Classical – predict a countercyclical relationship between real wages and output. For example, in the asymmetric information version of the New Classical story, as prices rise the workers' *perceived* real wage rises (due to higher nominal wages), while in fact the real wage *falls*. So employers demand more labour and output rises. Unfortunately for the model, there is very little evidence for such a relationship. Indeed, if anything the evidence is for a procyclical relationship – real wages tend to rise in booms.

A third puzzle is perhaps less worrying outside the economics profession. Realistic New Classical models must have some persistence in output, as discussed above. The explanations put forward (information lags, irreversible investment and adjustment costs) deal with this very satisfactorily. Nevertheless, some economists feel uncomfortable with these *ad hoc* explanations.

One solution to all these puzzles was found in the 'real business cycle' approach. These models cut through the misperception problem (Puzzle 1) by arguing that it is not *demand* shocks that drive the business cycle, but ('real') *supply* shocks. These can be 'taste' shocks (changing consumer preferences), price shocks (like the fluctuations in the price of oil observed since 1973) or productivity shocks. Most models concentrate on the latter. Although the details can be complicated, the basic ideas are simple.

Firms use capital and labour to produce output, which can be either consumed or kept as a capital (investment) good for next period. To keep things simple, pretend that households can be identified with firms – are self-employed producers, like farmers – so we can put the labour market to one side. Suppose there is a positive productivity shock. Households are now richer. Unsurprisingly, the optimal choice is to increase utility now by producing more output for consumption purposes, *and* simultaneously to hold back some extra output to use as investment, thus increasing the size of the capital stock. What this second decision does is to spread the benefits of the one-off improvement in productivity over time, just as consumers will save some or most of 'transitory' increases in income in the permanent income model of consumers' behaviour. This 'smoothing' effect means that random shocks will induce long-lasting changes in output, exactly what is required. This will be true even if productivity shocks are uncorrelated over time, as the capital stock lasts beyond the current period. Thus we have a perfectly consistent, optimal explanation of persistence. The theory also explains the procyclical movement in wages, as labour is paid its marginal product. It is also easy to explain the common output movements across sectors (point (i) made by Lucas on page 195 above) without appealing to economy-wide shocks, by noting that capital inputs come from other industries, providing a transmission mechanism through the economy.

What is missing from this story is a convincing explanation of *employment* fluctuations, which are clearly procyclical. This is true also for the New Classicists. The main idea to recognise is that for equilibrium business cycle theorists, fluctuations in employment reflect labour supply decisions, so that the rise in unemployment when employment falls is a purely institutional phenomenon. The unemployed are voluntarily registering for longer periods because they wish to work less. Given this argument, which convinces economists in the United States rather more than in Europe, the focus moves to the elasticity of labour supply with respect to wages. In booms, as productivity rises, wages rise and more people want to work for longer hours. The awkward fact, unfortunately, is that (for men at least) the long-run elasticity is rather small; the supply curve for labour is pretty close to vertical.

One way to rescue the model is to appeal to intertemporal substitution in labour supply. The idea here is closely related to the permanent income hypothesis. Lucas and Rapping (1969) originally introduced the idea in the context of a natural rate explanation of the Phillips curve. When wages are temporarily high, workers will take advantage of this by substituting leisure across time periods and working more. So even if the long-run labour supply curve is vertical, there may be a positive short-run relationship. The problem with this explanation is that all the microeconomic evidence suggests that intertemporal effects are very weak indeed. An alternative approach is to allow interest rates to affect labour supply – workers work more when interest rates are higher, which boosts the return to saving (recall that interest rates are procyclical: point (vi) on page 196). Here also, the microeconomic evidence is against this hypothesis. Kydland and Prescott (1982) use a utility function which allows more possibilities for substitution, thus generating the required result. However, the evidence also rejects this approach.

This failure to explain the unemployment facts is a major problem with the theory. However, Lucas argues that the 'work of "equilibrium" macroeconomists is often criticized as though it was a failed attempt to explain unemployment (which it surely fails to do) instead of as an attempt to explain something else' (1981, p. 48). This defence may not convince everyone, but if we accept the claim it implies we concentrate on the implications for output. The obvious way to assess the empirical adequacy of a theory is to set out its implications, construct an empirically tractable specification, and test the predictions of the theory against the data by standard econometric techniques. This has not been the preferred methodology for testing real business cycles, as essentially, they fail. Instead, models are constructed using plausible benchmark values for parameters, and are then simulated to see if the results are comparable to the real data. This method has two major problems, one to do with statistical theory, and one more conceptual in nature. First, there can be no formal tests of statistical significance with this approach. Second, the whole process is driven by inherently unobservable productivity shocks. Originally, the variance of these shocks was chosen to generate an output variance equal to the actual data. It is obvious that this has a strong smell of circularity about it. However, there is no cast-iron alternative, although Prescott (1986) does try to estimate the shocks from a production function. Other empirical tests are available, though. One such is to look for *permanent* responses to *temporary* shocks, an idea which while not necessarily implied by real business cycle theory, is certainly consistent with it. Technically, this follows if output can be shown to have a 'unit root'. To understand this, take a simple example where the time series of output is given by:

$$Y_t = \alpha + \beta Y_{t-1} + \varepsilon_t \quad 0 \le \beta \le 1$$

where ε_t is a random error and β is a parameter lying between 0 and 1. Begin with the case where $\beta < 1$. In the 'long run' Y will settle down to a steady state value, say Y^*. So if the 'long run' value of ε_t is zero,

$$Y^* = \alpha + \beta Y^*$$

$$= \alpha/(1 - \beta)$$

A positive shock to Y_t ($\varepsilon_t > 0$) will have a short-run effect on Y which will persist, but in the end, the long run is unaltered. If $\beta = 1$, the whole picture changes dramatically. In this case,

$$Y_t = \alpha + Y_{t-1} + \varepsilon_t$$

or

$$Y_t - Y_{t-1} = \alpha + \varepsilon_t$$

and the long run is simply not defined – there is *no* single long-run value towards which Y is tending. In this case, Y_t is said to be 'non-stationary', or to have a 'unit root'. What happens if $\varepsilon_t > 0$ is that the effects of the shock persist forever. A 1 per cent shock will raise output by a permanent 1 per cent.

A technically complex debate began with the paper by Nelson and Plosser (1982), who argued there is a unit root in US output. Much of the problem is that in practice it can be extremely difficult to distinguish between a unit root and stationary processes *close* to but not actually at a unit root. The jury is still out and is fiercely arguing about this issue. In the end, with regard to real business cycles, it may not be conclusive either way. Other models may also lead to unit roots – for example the insider–outsider model of Blanchard and Summers (1986) where employed 'insiders' act via their unions to maximise only their own welfare, ignoring the unemployed (see Chapter 5 for more discussion). This leads to the phenomenon known as 'hysteresis' where output or unemployment is determined by its own history (see Cross, 1988b). Finally, many other models may generate behaviour very close to and statistically indistinguishable from a unit root; for example, the overlapping contract model discussed on pages 68, 78 and 79.

The final piece of evidence does not rely on arcane econometric techniques or arguments about the predictions with respect to unemployment, or any other variable. Instead, it is the simple observation that while there may well be something in real business cycle theory, it seems very unlikely that it can be the major explanation of the three most recent recessions, beginning in 1974, 1979 and 1989. We have argued that two of these were affected by supply shocks, but these are not the stochastic draws of the real business cyclists; rather, they were massive blows from exogenous clubs. The effects were compounded by inept demand management. We would be quite incapable of explaining these episodes with real business cycle tools alone.

Political business cycles

A popular cause of economic cycles arises from the fact that economic policy is made by elected politicians. Such policy may reflect the political objectives of the government. For example, to the extent that popularity is influenced by the state of the economy, a government may hope to improve its re-election chances by generating boom conditions just before a general election. A slump would presumably follow after the election. Such a pattern where booms coincide with elections is known as a political business cycle. One American author (Tufte, 1978) has gone so far as to argue that the cycles in the US economy are, more or less, *all* election-related. His evidence, however, is unconvincing, except for the case of the 1972 presidential election. Then, there was a substantial rise in Federal transfer payments (Veterans' benefits etc.) just a week before the election.

The most explicit theoretical case for a political business cycle relies upon the government riding the short-term Phillips curve. This argument is explicitly set out in Nordhaus (1975) and provides the basis of his claim that democracy causes inflation. Consider Figure 11.1.

The curves labelled P are short-run Phillips curves, higher numbers reflecting higher levels of expected inflation. The curves labelled U are social indifference curves, the points along which will generate the same vote for the government – lower numbers reflect higher utility and a higher

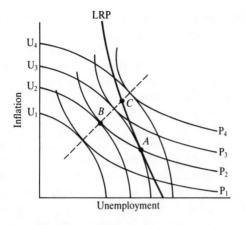

Figure 11.1 The Nordhaus model of the political business cycle.

vote. The curve LRP is the long-run Phillips curve (Nordhaus takes it to be non-vertical, though this is not important so long as it is steeper than the P curves).

Each government finds itself on a particular P curve such as P_2. The vote-maximising strategy will be to run the economy at point *B*, which yields the highest possible vote. During the next period, however, since *B* is to the left of the long-run Phillips curve, the economy will be on a higher P curve like P_3. This process will converge to a point like *C* which is on the LRP curve and, therefore, stable. This is sub-optimal because point *A* is the point of highest sustainable social welfare. The political process has generated higher inflation and lower unemployment than would be preferred. Readers may recognise this story; it is very similar to the inflation policy game set out in Chapter 4. In fact, much of the discussion there applies to the political business cycle.

As long as we are prepared to disregard the implications of rational expectations, it is easy to tell a story about cycles in this framework. Governments simply ride up the P curve to the highest U curve at election time. Then, after the election they depress the economy – to the right of LRP – so that they find the economy on the lowest possible P curve by the time of the next election. They then generate a boom again in time to be re-elected.

Plausible as this account may be, the evidence for it is remarkably weak. Even the proponents of this kind of 'political' view of policy (Frey, 1978) seemed to give up looking for electoral cycles in the *targets* of economic policy such as inflation and unemployment. Also, the evidence concerning the influence of the state of the economy on political popularity and voting is not at all clear cut. It is certainly true that popularity can be significantly related to economic variables for some historical time period. The problem is that the results have tended to be heavily sample-dependent. For other time periods they are often substantially different. Particularly strong swings in coefficients are discovered when the results for the 1960s are extended into the 1970s. However, recent work by Price and Sanders (1993), who explicitly looked for structural change over the post-war period, revealed a stable relationship explaining popularity.

An alternative, and highly revealing, way of looking at the question is to ask whether the electorate can be fooled in the short run, and whether the government acts as if they can. Asking the question this way focuses attention on the electorate's expectations, as well as upon the current state of affairs. If electors are fully rational they will anticipate the post-election deflation and so there will be no benefit for the incumbent party in running a pre-election boom. Macrae (1977) incorporates expectations explicitly by distinguishing between a myopic and a strategic electorate. A myopic electorate only considers the current state of the economy whereas strategic voters have a longer time horizon. Macrae's results for the United States appear to show that the government assumed myopia from 1960–68 but strategic voting before and after. Applying Macrae's model to the United Kingdom, Chrystal and Alt (1981) conclude that 'the myopic hypothesis never significantly outperforms the strategic hypothesis'. And they are thus led to conclude that while on some occasions the government may indeed have manipulated unemployment with a vote loss or social welfare function in mind, there is no evidence that the desire to win the next election, as distinct from remaining in office as long as possible, was the motivation. Thus we must conclude that the evidence for a simple political business cycle in Britain is negative. There can be no presumption that the government manipulates the economy on the assumption of a short-sighted electorate.

What appears to be a more sophisticated attempt to incorporate political goals into economic policy analysis is provided by Frey and Schneider (1978). They develop what they call a 'politico-economic' model of the United Kingdom. There are two elements to this. First, government popularity depends upon certain economic variables. Second, various components of government expenditure are shown to be altered as a result of popularity, the time before elections and the political make-up of the incumbent party. Chrystal and Alt (1981) show that if government expenditure and revenue are related to trend GDP virtually all the political factors drop out. The only significant political factor to remain is that transfers are higher under Labour than Conservative governments, as might be expected. We must, therefore, conclude that electoral-cyclical and politico-economic explanations of budgetary policy in the United Kingdom are not well founded. A fuller discussion of these issues is available in Alt and Chrystal (1983).

Recently, however, political business cycles have made something of a comeback. As we observed above, the big problem with the earlier vintage described above was the implicit assumption that the electorate can be fooled – that the government is smarter than voters. This is inconsistent with rational expectations.[2] However, it is possible to generate limited business cycles even with the RE assumption.

There are two strands in this 'rational political business cycles' literature. The first is one of opportunistic parties introduced by Rogoff and Sibert (1988). Political parties differ only in their competence. Competent parties get re-elected. The problem is that it is difficult to tell whether parties are competent. The electorate rely on 'signals'. One such could be the ability to deliver goods and services at low tax revenues. So a government may 'cheat' by lowering taxes in an election year to fool voters into believing they are competent. Eventually, voters find out the truth: but by then the election is past. The twist is that not cheating has a payoff, as the government can acquire a reputation for playing with a straight bat, which it can then cash in by cheating at the most advantageous time. It should be clear that this theory cannot explain regular business cycles, although it may well help us understand particular episodes in history.

The alternative is a 'partisan' model, where parties differ in their preferences. In particular, parties of the right are presumed to care more about inflation than parties of the left. This is public knowledge. In its original incarnation, as in Hibbs (1987), voters are irrational, and outcomes are determined by which party is in power, but in Alesina (1987) voters are rational. What drives the cycle here is that the result of elections is unknown before they occur. After an election, left parties will allow higher inflation than right parties, *ceteris paribus*. However, in a world of overlapping contracts, wages must be set prior to the election, and are done so on the rational expectation of inflation after the election, which will be an average of the left and right inflation rates, weighted by the expected probability of each party forming a government. In this set-up, we would expect recessions after the election of right-wing governments (price expectations were too high) and booms after left elections. Alesina (1989) has found there is evidence for this in post-World War II United States. However, this can by no means be the whole story – the timing of the Bush and Major recessions in the United States and United Kingdom were entirely wrong in the 1988–92 period. When the model was tested for the United Kingdom by Alogoskoufis *et al.* (1992) there was only a little evidence for the model in the pre-Thatcher era, and that hedged with qualifications.

Assessment

How then do these broad approaches to business cycles stand up to the facts? This is not the place to discuss the evidence in detail, but it is worth considering how we should explain the obvious contrast of experience between the 1950s and 1960s on the one hand and the inter-war and post-1970 periods on the other. Keynesians would presumably argue that the 1950s and 1960s were the example, *par excellence*, of what can be achieved by the successful application of Keynesian principles. Against this a strong case can be made for the contrary point of view on the grounds that the 1950s and 1960s were, above all, a period of *monetary stability*. The United States was following (until the mid-1960s) conservative policies and the rest of the world pegged their currencies to the dollar. It was the attempt by the United States to follow Keynesian expansionist policies that caused the system to break down. Subsequent events are to be explained by big swings in monetary policy (accompanied by exchange rate instability) which have been responsible for the depressions of the last two decades. At least in the UK case, it is hard to believe that the poor performance of the UK economy since 1970 did not have something to do with monetary shocks – notably the excessive stimuli of 1971–73 and 1987–88, and the excessive tightening of 1973–74, 1979–81 and 1989–91. The mechanism for the transmission of these effects is discussed in Chapter 6.

Summary

Business cycles and their study have staged a revival. Keynesian business cycles relied on multiplier and accelerator interaction in response to exogenous expenditure changes. Monetarists emphasised changes in monetary growth as the source of cycles. The New Classical analysis also relies on exogenous monetary disturbances but has the novel feature of an equilibrium methodology. The real business cycle view is also that cycles are equilibrium phenomena, but it is supply rather than demand disturbances that drive the cycle. While these approaches may generate models which are observationally equivalent, they have very different implications for the role of government. In the Keynesian view, governments could and should attempt to stabilise the economy. For the Monetarists (and to some extent the New Classicists), governments are the major source of disturbances. Their discretion should therefore be limited. For Real Business Cyclists, government is largely irrelevant. There may be cycles, but as they are due to a succession of supply shocks, there is really very little point in the government attempt to smooth output with changes in *demand*.

Notes

1. In this case the model is explosive if $v/(1 - \beta)$ is greater than one and cycles if it is less than four.
2. Having said this, the evidence for rational expectations among the electorate is not overwhelming. Price and Sanders (1992) reject the hypothesis on UK data.

12

The supply side: Shocks and growth

Macroeconomics was developed as a framework for analysing the transmission of aggregate demand changes through the economy. This framework has proved inadequate for handling disturbances which originate on the supply side. Traditional macroeconomic models have a production sector which has a single homogeneous output made for the most part with a single variable input; technological progress is essentially ignored. This framework is unhelpful when we need to analyse changes such as a major price rise in one of several variable inputs, or the emergence of a major new extractive industry; both these examples are highly relevant to understanding the United Kingdom over the past two decades. It is also unhelpful if we wish to understand the determinants of economic growth over the medium to long term, as opposed to short-run fluctuations in the growth rate over the business cycle. Even the real business cycle theorists (discussed in Chapter 11), who rely on 'real' technological and taste shocks to drive the business cycle, are not able to address these major stuctural and long-term issues. With real business cycles, technological progress may be random, but it is still exogenous and unchanging (in the statistical sense of stationarity).

The oil price rises of 1973 and 1979, the expansion of North Sea oil production and the worldwide productivity slowdown of the 1970s were too important to be ignored. For example, in Chapter 7 we gave evidence that the dramatic decline in manufacturing employment in the United Kingdom since 1979 may not be unrelated to North Sea oil production. It is beyond the scope of this book to present a formal structural analysis of the UK economy. However, it is important to realise that such an analysis is necessary if the policy implications of these changes are to be fully understood. Aggregate demand policies have a place, but this may not be it.

In this chapter, we examine the two large supply shocks that have hit the United Kingdom since the end of World War Two, consider the evidence for a productivity growth miracle in the 1980s, and examine the long-run causes of growth.

The 1973 oil price rise

It is instructive to recall the way in which the 1973 oil price rise was analysed by various commentators on the UK economy. The analysis of this section draws on Miller (1976). Remember that the problem at that time was the quadrupling of the oil price. Virtually all oil was imported.

The principal way in which the policy-makers in the United Kingdom looked at the problem seems to be through orthodox Keynesian eyes. In the context of Model I, imports are a leakage from the circular flow system so they affect the economy just like a massive increase in indirect taxes. The tax revenue, however, accrues to foreigners. A typical figure quoted for the size of this increased import bill was £1500m. A clear example of how a Keynesian should see this problem is provided by G. D. N. Worswick, the Director of the National Institute, in his evidence to the Public Expenditure Committee (1974):

> If nothing is done about the substantial rise in the price of oil, that figure of £1500m will be taken out of the system. There will be that much less spent in the following period and there will be a contraction of demand and a contraction of output in due course together with a contraction of employment. In this case the rise in the price of oil has a profound contractionary effect on all countries. (p. 42)

> When the government is making up its balance of the budget over the year as a whole it must allow for the fact that real consumption will be less than it would be if the price of oil had not risen . . .. The present Chancellor has said that he wishes to have a new look at the situation later in the year. As I see it now, he would need to be expansionary. (p. 43)

The effect of a rise in the value of imports can easily be analysed in the context of Model I. The initial position in Figure 12.1 is with the aggregate expenditure line $C + I + G + X - P_0$. This gives an initial level of income equal to Y_0. An increase in the value of imports represents a greater 'leakage' of expenditure from the circular flow, so the aggregate expenditure line falls to $C + I + G + X - P_1$. This will lead, through the downward multiplier effect, to a lower level of income Y_1. We would normally expect this downward fall in income to be accompanied by an increase in unemployment. This is why the Keynesian response to the oil crisis was to point to the dangers of a depression and to propose a reflation.

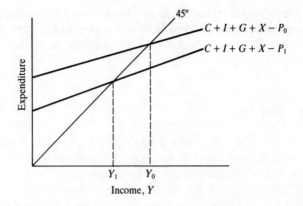

Figure 12.1 The Keynesian analysis of the oil price rise.

Offsetting policies on the part of the government would simply involve either increasing expenditure or reducing taxes so that aggregate expenditure shifts back towards its original position. The balance of payments deficit is thus reinforced.

The problem, of course, is not really as simple as that. For one thing we have said nothing at all about inflation. More importantly in the present context, however, the concept of income is ambiguous. The simplest way to see this is to ask what would have happened if the elasticity of demand for oil had been unity. The import bill would have remained constant following the oil price rise. Does this mean that domestic income would have been unchanged? The answer is clearly no. Although there is no direct change in real GDP because physical output and the GDP deflator are unchanged, since the value of the things we produce has fallen relative to the things we buy from abroad, domestic income has unambiguously fallen in a real and more general way. What this means is that, even if there was no impact effect on unemployment, the possibilities for domestic absorption have fallen. There has to be a fall in domestic real income.

While domestic income has to fall owing to this terms-of-trade loss, it does not necessarily follow that some reflation should not be applied. Miller argues that the view at the time was that the required fall in income was less than the fall from Y_0 to Y_1 in Figure 12.1 and this is why expansionary measures were advocated. The problem with this approach, of course, is that even if it were successful in avoiding unemployment in the short run, it certainly increases inflation, which many would argue would increase unemployment even more in the long run. The outcome would appear to be consistent with this latter view. Unemployment did not rise as rapidly in the United Kingdom through 1974 and 1975 as it did in many other countries, whereas the inflationary experience was considerably worse in the United

Kingdom. Unemployment in the United Kingdom, however, continued to rise subsequently, though in many countries it started to fall after 1976.

Miller concludes that while Keynesians were not unaware that there would be 'imported inflation', they believed that a gradual return to full employment should be possible through 'expansionary fiscal policy and permissive monetary policy'. In strict contrast to this Miller believes that 'the Monetarist logic predicted no inflation or recession as a consequence of the change in the terms of trade so long as fiscal and monetary policy were unchanged' (Miller, 1976, p. 509). Miller bases his analysis of the Monetarist position upon the summary of the evidence presented by Laidler to the Expenditure Committee (Laidler, 1974). However, this summary was written either by the Committee members themselves or by the Civil Service. Laidler's own evidence does not bear the interpretation Miller puts upon it (nor, in reality, does the summary).

The first point to notice about Laidler's evidence is that he is absolutely clear that 'If oil prices have gone up and the terms of trade have moved against this country, we are poorer, and it is impossible for people to protect their standards of living against that' (p. 55). Second, he answers the question about the price level by reference to an earlier point about the net effect of a decrease in indirect taxes financed by higher direct taxes, at a given level of national income. There he says, 'If there were no net decrease in purchasing power, I cannot see how *ultimately* the price level would be different' (p. 51). In contrast, the Director of the National Institute was reported to have argued, by analogy to an increase in indirect taxes, that inflation would rise because people would ask for and obtain higher wages to compensate for the higher oil price. Indirect taxes rising would be inflationary and more inflationary than income taxes of equal yield. To this Laidler replied:

> If it is the case that people notice that indirect taxes have changed the purchasing power of their gross incomes before they notice that direct ones have done so, I cannot believe that this is any more than a very *short-run* phenomenon. It is one thing, in any case, to ask for a wage increase and another thing to have it granted. (p. 55)

The overwhelming impression that emerges from Laidler's evidence, in its entirety, can be expressed as two main points. First, the impact effects of the oil price rise should be clearly distinguished from the ultimate or long-run effects. Second, a clear distinction must be drawn between relative price changes and sustained inflation of the general price level. The oil price rise is a relative price change and, although it will undoubtedly raise the price index in the short run, it will only lead to a *long-run* rise in the price level if it is followed by monetary expansion. An appropriate framework for expounding the Monetarist analysis might be Model III.

Consider the initial position at *A* in Figure 12.2. The short-run aggregate supply curve can be thought of as depending on the expected price level. What then is the effect of a rise in the price of imports? First notice that, although the *physical* production possibilities of the economy are unchanged, since the relative price of domestic output has fallen, we should regard long-run aggregate supply as having fallen from Y_0 to Y_1. This is the terms-of-trade loss. There are two other effects. First, there is a leftward shift of the short-run aggregate supply curve from AS_{s0} to AS_{s1}. This is due to the direct effect of import prices on the domestic price level plus any immediate effect on price expectations. The second effect is the Keynesian one. Aggregate *domestic* demand will move from AD_0 to AD_1 due to the rise in the import bill. Both Monetarists and Keynesians should accept the story so far. The impact effect is a move from *A* to a position like *B*. There has been a rise in the price level and an increase in unemployment associated with a decline in domestic output. The disagreement is about the next step in the argument.

The Keynesians do not have a next step. The economy has settled into a depression at *B* so expansionary fiscal policies are required. Raising aggregate demand will move the economy to *C*, thereby eliminating unemployment. The problem with this analysis, however, is that even *C* is not a full equilibrium. This is because AS_{s1} was drawn for an *expected* price level somewhere between that at *A* and that at *B*. As these price level expectations are revised upwards, the short-run *AS* curve will shift up further. If policy-makers raise aggregate demand still further to avoid unemployment, this upward spiral will continue, as they found to their cost.

The Monetarist analysis points to the fact that *B* is not a point of full equilibrium. If the monetary and fiscal pressures which are due to the authorities remain unchanged, the economy will eventually return to a

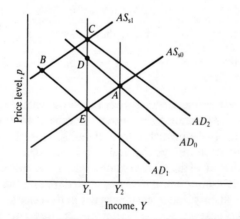

Figure 12.2 The oil price rise with supply effects.

point somewhere in the region of *D*. This is because excess supply in some markets will cause some prices to fall, so eventually short-run AS will shift back down. Also there will be some north-eastward shift of AD due to a change in the pattern of expenditures following the increase in import prices. The ultimate effect of the oil price rise on the import bill will, *ceteris paribus*, be less in the long run than in the short run because expenditure patterns take time to adjust. At *D* the price level may be slightly higher or lower than at *A*, but it will not be substantially different.

The problem with this Monetarist analysis is that we have no information as to how long it will be before the economy returns from *B* to *D*. The problem with the Keynesian policy prescription is that it necessarily leads to a higher price level and, therefore, to faster inflation in the interim. The key difference in analysis of the problem is that Monetarists see the economy as self-stabilising within a reasonable time period. Keynesians recommended policies to counter the impact effects on the assumption that the economy would not be self-stabilising with any rapidity and the unemployment target should be given high priority.

North Sea oil

If the oil price rise caused so much trouble when we were an importer, the emergence of a self-sufficiency in oil production should have been of unambiguous benefit. For example, consider the economy to have been initially at *D* in Figure 12.2, on AD_0 and with long-run supply at Y_1. A once-and-for-all increase in oil supply might be considered to shift aggregate supply to Y_2. The economy would then go to *A* with higher output and lower prices. How, then, could North Sea oil production be associated with rising unemployment as was argued in Chapter 7?

The answer is that the above analysis is not correct. What we have just analysed is something like an autonomous productivity rise in the single homogeneous sector that constitutes our macroeconomy. What we need to analyse is change in production in one sector only. The effects are complex because they involve intersectoral resource shifts, intersectoral demand shifts, and changes in the composition of foreign trade and capital flows as well as the aggregate expenditure and output effects which are the traditional domain of macroeconomics. Such structural changes have more commonly been treated within the domain of international trade theory.

A comprehensive analysis from a trade theoretical perspective is available in Corden and Neary (1982). Their model contains two traded goods – oil and manufactures – and one non-traded good services. What happens, they ask, when there is a production boom in one of the traded goods (oil)?[1] A central conclusion of their analysis is as follows:

In the simplest of the models considered, which assumed that only labour was mobile between sectors, de-industrialisation (a decline in the non-booming part of the traded goods sector, assumed here to be manufacturing) was shown to follow in most of the usual senses of the term, including a fall in manufacturing output and employment, a worsening of the balance of trade in manufacturing and a fall in the real return to factors specific to the manufacturing sector. . . . (p. 841)

This means that it should not be surprising that a decline in manufacturing output has accompanied the growth in oil production. Deindustrialisation – a shift away from industrial production and towards services – is called for if we wish to reap the full benefits of oil. Their analysis is, however, an equilibrium analysis in the sense that there is continuous full employment and a continuous trade balance. What we do not know is how big this adjustment has to be. How much of the fall in manufacturing output and rise in unemployment was actually due to exchange rate overshooting in response to tight monetary policy, as has been emphasised by Buiter and Miller (1981a,b)?[2]. This is hard to say, though it is clear that the combination of tight monetary policy and North Sea oil was fatal for a significant number of manufacturers.

The policy choices posed by this problem have been analysed by Corden (1981) under the title of 'exchange rate protection'. The presence of a booming sector, like oil, will appreciate the domestic currency, and there seems little doubt that this was a significant part of the 1979–81 episode. The appreciation had a profound effect on manufacturing competitiveness. Should the government have let this appreciation occur, thereby taking the benefits of oil in a terms of trade gain but at the cost of some disruption to manufacturing? Or should it, rather, have held down the exchange rate either by intervention directly (buying dollars) or by expansionary monetary policy? There was probably not much the government could (or should) have done about the equilibrium adjustment. However, there surely was (and is) a case for policies which offset any tendency for overshooting. There was also a case for policies which recognise the changing employment patterns towards an expansion of services (including some of those provided by the public sector, unpalatable as this latter point may be for Conservative administrations).

The preceding arguments are essentially in favour of allowing the exchange rate to rise after the advent of North Sea oil. However, there is one major caveat, which is that North Sea oil is a finite resource. What difference does it make that the oil will one day run out?

With regard to deindustrialisation, if it were possible to move resources costlessly around the economy, then the analysis would be essentially unchanged. As oil production falls, the exchange rate should depreciate, inducing a shift back into manufacturing production. However, in practice resource shifts are very difficult. Not least of the costs is the lost human capital involved in individuals leaving jobs and industries in which they have spent a lifetime accumulating specific skills. *Physical* capital is also not easily exported to other industries. Considerable scrapping of the manufacturing capital stock seems to have taken place in the early 1980s. Estimates of the growth in the capital stock between 1979 and 1982 vary from the widely disbelieved 3.3 per cent recorded by the Central Statistics Office (CSO) to − 14.0 per cent (Robinson and Wade, 1985). A central estimate, based on CBI survey data and the Kalman filter, is − 5.4 per cent (Minford, Wall and Wren-Lewis, 1988; see also Wadhwani and Wall, 1986). Changes of this magnitude are to some extent irreversible − we are left with a permanently smaller manufacturing sector. So there is a case for temporarily protecting manufacturing from the full, short-run effects.

The other policy issue relates to the distribution of North Sea benefits over time. The point is that the income is temporary. Basic economic theory tells us that the optimal response to such a transitory windfall is to smooth out the effects to give a permanent boost to consumption. This is, of course, the major insight that the permanent income/life-cycle hypothesis yields. Although the theory is usually applied to individuals, it should also hold in aggregate. There are two ways in which the aggregate economy can expedite this 'consumption smoothing' process. The first is to allow the government to use its exceptional tax revenues from oil production not to raise government spending or lower taxes, but to repay the national debt. This is indeed what has happened in the United Kingdom. Alone among the industrialised countries, the United Kingdom reduced the proportion of national debt to GDP, from 51.5 per cent in 1978 to 43.2 per cent in 1987. This has the effect of reducing the tax burden on future generations. Oil revenues financed lower taxes in the future, and thereby enabled higher future consumption. The other method was to run large current account surpluses on the balance of payments, accumulating foreign assets. Nationally, these assets deliver a future stream of income which can finance future consumption from the rest of the world.

The Thatcher miracle

We now turn to the medium term, and to growth. During the 1980s, considerable attention was paid to manufacturing productivity (output per head). The government was not slow to publicise the figures, but other commentators also recognised that something peculiar seemed to be happening. Figure 12.3 tells an interesting story. The chart shows how productivity has risen since 1959, for the manufacturing sector and the whole economy. It also shows the estimated trends.

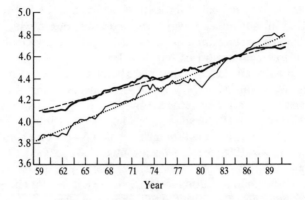

Figure 12.3 Productivity for manufacturing and the whole economy (log scale): ———— whole economy, ——— manufacturing, ················ manufacturing trend, – – – – whole economy trend.

The figures for the whole economy show no evidence for a productivity miracle. Indeed, the period from 1979 to 1991 is scarcely better than the post-oil shock period, despite the substantial contribution to GDP from oil production.

So the case for a miracle rests in manufacturing. The chart is drawn with a log scale, which lets us see immediately the *rate of growth* of productivity, which is the slope of the line.[3] The chart, like UK economic history, can be divided into three periods. The first is from 1959 to the 1973 oil crisis, the second from 1973 to 1979, and the last from 1979 onwards. The latter period can be thought of as the Thatcher decade. Table 12.1 gives the key figures. They should not be taken too literally, as productivity growth (like output) is sensitive to the cycle, but they do give a broad picture.

The basic picture for manufacturing is of moderately high growth in the 1960s and 1980s, and a moribund period in the 1970s. The figure shows that there was a period of exceptional productivity growth in the 1980s; between the last quarters of 1980 and 1986 productivity grew at an annualised rate of 6.1 per cent. However, as Figure 12.4 reveals, this surge was coincident with

Table 12.1 Productivity growth rates (annualised percentages).

| | Percentage growth rates | |
Period	Whole economy	Manufacturing
1960Q1–1991Q3	1.9	2.9
1960Q1–1973Q1	2.5	3.4
1973Q2–1979Q2	1.2	1.0
1979Q2–1991Q3	1.4	3.3

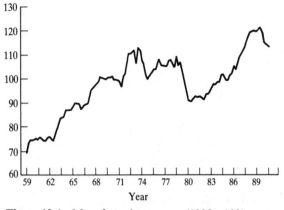

Figure 12.4   Manufacturing output (1985 = 100).

what turned out to be an unsustainably rapid recovery in manufacturing output from the very severe slump in 1980.[4]

So why did the growth rate of manufacturing productivity rise? There are a number of potential explanations.

The most profound is technical progress. This can encompass progress in management and organisation, as well as the invention of new processes. We relegate discussion of the broader determinants of this to the next section; but disregarding the causes, the empirical question of whether this actually occurred in the period in question is really the issue we seek to resolve here.

Second, and more mundanely, any apparent effect may be a purely statistical artefact, due to measurement problems, or the relative decline of low productivity sectors as unproductive firms go out of business (which will tend to raise average productivity). While this argument is plausible and had many adherents among anti-government commentators in the 1980s, this was not in fact the case in the United Kingdom: see Layard and Nickell (1989). Third, productivity will rise if the capital stock grows. While there has been positive net investment in the manufacturing sector since 1979, it is manifestly not the case that there has been an unusual rise. Indeed, as we saw above there is plenty of evidence that the capital stock fell in the early 1980s, although this is not picked up by the official CSO measure.

A more subtle explanation is that the *capital to labour ratio* has increased. Figure 12.5 shows the quantities of capital and labour required to produce a fixed level of output Q_0. The optimal point on any isoquant is determined by the relative price of capital and labour. From basic theory, as the relative price of labour rises, the firm will slide along the isoquant while the optimal supply of output will fall (from Q_0 to Q_1). Thus (in this

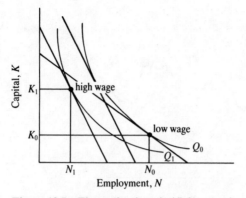

Figure 12.5 The optimal capital/labour ratio.

case) the response to a rise in wages is to raise the capital stock only slightly but to raise the capital to labour ratio much more dramatically. The effect comes not from a rise in the capital stock but a *fall* in employment. This explanation is rather plausible for the United Kingdom. Figure 12.6 shows how real wages and manufacturing employment moved from the late 1970s. The rise in real wages and the fall in employment after 1979 are both equally marked, although there are clearly other factors involved. The remarkable phenomenon is that the unprecedented fall in demand around 1980 had apparently no effect on real wages. As we have seen, output fell because the real exchange rate rose, choking off the demand for exports and reducing the demand for domestic production as imports became relatively cheaper. This contraction in demand necessitated a fall in real wages in order to maintain competitiveness, but this did not occur. As output slumped, productivity fell, pushing up real unit labour costs. The rise in unit labour

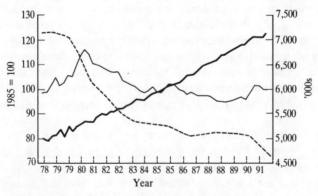

Figure 12.6 Manufacturing employment and real wages:
───── real earnings, ─ ─ ─ employment, ──────real unit labour costs.

costs mirrors a fall in profitability: firms responded by shedding labour, increasing productivity so that real unit labour costs fell again. As the exchange rate fell, output was able to rise again in the mid-1980s and the fall in employment returned to its long-run trend. However, the substantial rise in the level of real wages left a permanent residue in the form of a higher capital to labour ratio. Of course, this begs the question of why real wages were so stubbornly immune to the effects of recession: this issue was discussed in Chapters 5 and 7.

The explanation offered here seems to explain the bulk of the productivity rise; the econometric evidence is quite consistent with this story, as research at the National Institute reveals (*Financial Times*, 25 October, 1989). However, many people close to the industrial ground fervently believe that there has been a shake-up in industrial relations and management practice in the United Kingdom.

The anecdotal evidence for this hypothesis is very convincing. Many studies report that work practices now make for more flexibility, and therefore efficiency, than ever before – see Cross (1988a), for example. Industrial relations have clearly improved in quantifiable respects – the level of strikes in 1991 was the lowest for a century on some measures. It is quite likely that without this shift in attitudes and practice the move to a higher capital intensity could never have taken place on the scale that was needed; but this shift may well prove to have been a one-off boost to productivity, rather than a source of *continuing* productivity increases.

Nevertheless, it is worth considering why this organisational change came about. Essentially, there are two candidates for the explanation: first, the reduction in union power engendered by Mrs Thatcher's union reforms, and secondly the massive shock to industry in the early 1980s. The anti-union legislation weakened the capacity of unions to resist changes in their work practices, while the latter effect provided a stick of unprecedented size with which to encourage management to push through change and unions to accept it. A popular argument for the poor long-run performance of the United Kingdom economy is that the UK has been spared the major shake-ups that have struck most other, faster growing countries. The 1980–81 recession provided just such a shake-up. Layard and Nickell (1989) quote the chairman of a large manufacturing company as saying: 'Both management and workers looked over the edge of the pit and stepped back'.

Long-run growth

The last section examined whether an increase in the trend growth rate of productivity occurred in the 1980s: the conclusion was, probably not. The reason why this issue has such potency is because the growth rate of the UK economy has been the subject of intense study and interest for decades. In a sense, growth is *the* major macroeconomic issue; in the long run, it dominates everything else. In the end, most economic shortcomings will be forgiven if growth is high; certainly inflation, and probably also unemployment – and this matters. In 1870 Britain had a GDP *per capita* that was about 25 per cent greater than the United States and five times that of Japan (Feinstein, 1988). By 1984, after 114 years of relatively low growth, the United Kingdom was only 70 per cent as productive as the United States and 90 per cent of Japan. In one sense this is the single most important topic that observers of the British economy should be examining.

In the light of this discussion, it may appear remarkable that one of the major engines of growth has largely been ignored by the economics profession. Robert Solow (1957) showed how growth can be 'accounted' for by the sum of three factors: growth in the labour force (which is more or less exogenous), growth in the capital stock via investment, and finally technical progress. Estimates vary, but it soon became clear that a substantial component of economic growth must be ascribed to the latter effect; Solow thought about 90 per cent for the United States, although later estimates put this nearer 50 per cent (Kendricks, 1973).[5] However, the response of the economics profession was in large part literally to ignore the effect; technological progress was measured as the 'Solow Residual' – the bit of output growth left over when growth in capital and labour had been stripped out. This does not mean that growth was ignored. Considerable effort has been put into determining the rate of capital accumulation. This process began at least a hundred years ago; Marx's opus was entitled 'Capital', after all. In the neoclassical tradition the basic framework was established in the 1950s by Solow (1956) and Swan (1956).

Gradually, this asymmetric approach to growth theory began to seem more and more unsatisfactory. Quite apart from the intellectual problem, there was an apparent empirical problem with the standard neoclassical model. If the state of technological progress is simply an exogenous lump available to all, to be gathered out of thin air as it were, then poor countries differ from rich ones only by virtue of having less capital. By diminishing returns, this implies that the return on investment is higher in poor countries, and the theory predicts that their growth should be correspondingly higher. So poor countries should 'catch up' the rich; there should be convergence in international income levels. The problem for the theory is that while there is some evidence of convergence among industrial countries, there are really very few signs of convergence where one would most expect it – between developing and developed countries. Indeed, the world seems to be categorisable into 'growth clubs', within which convergence occurs, but not between; see Dowrick and Gemmell (1991) for some evidence on these issues. The decline of Britain is another piece of evidence. What should have happened is that the rest of the world caught up with us – not, as actually happened, overtook.

There are two main stories of endogenous growth,[6] both of which revolve round the notion that knowledge is crucial to the production process. The first of these was introduced by the Nobel prize-winning theorist Kenneth Arrow in 1962, but his idea lay largely moribund until Romer revived it in 1986. Arrow's insight was that agents learn by doing. This notion, well established in nitty-gritty studies of industrial organisation, holds that the more you do something, the more efficient you become; productivity is positively related to experience. Moreover, this productivity bonus is to some extent a shared resource; how to do things becomes common knowledge. The significance of this is that there are *external benefits* to growth, as the pool of experience is available to all. As usual, the existence of an externality leads to inefficiency. Competitive economies will grow too slowly in these circumstances. Note that with constant returns to physical factors, the additional intangible factor of production (knowledge) implies there is increasing returns to scale. Normally, this would be inconsistent with perfect competition (as the size of firms is unbounded), but as the returns operate through an externality, each firm alone acts as if there are constant returns. Romer's variant on this basic model was to allow knowledge to exhibit increasing marginal productivity, although the *production* of knowledge – via investment expenditures on research and development – possesses conventional diminishing returns. The significance of increasing returns to knowledge is that it allows us to step away from Arrow's model which possesses a unique steady state, albeit inefficient, to a multiplicity of endogenous growth paths. The intriguing possibility emerges of capital flows from poor to rich countries, seeking the higher rates of return.

The second story puts the emphasis on knowledge embodied in people. A human capital intensive research sector of the economy produces ideas, which enhance productivity. These ideas are embodied in the production process, and also add to the stock of existing knowledge, thus increasing the productivity of the research sector. These ideas can be traced back to Uzawa (1965), but it was Robert Lucas (1988) who reintroduced them in a modern context. As in the Romer model, there is an important externality, which could provide a strong argument for public subsidy in education and research.

The policy implications of these theories are fairly clear. In the learning-by-doing case, growth feeds on growth; there should be a kind of multiplier effect following from growth. Fast-growing economies will tend to maintain growth, or indeed accelerate. The human capital tale justifies subsidies to education, training and research as a response to the knowledge externality.[7] So far as Britain is concerned, the explanation of our low growth could lie in the vicious learning-by-doing cycle whereby low growth perpetuates itself, or in our education and research sector. Although the share of research in relation to GDP in the United Kingdom is of a comparable order to other countries, it is skewed towards defence, a relatively unproductive area. For example, in 1960 the air industry export market was one quarter the size of the chemicals market, but 35 per cent of *all* research and development expenditure was in aerospace. By contrast, Germany devoted 33 per cent of expenditures to the chemical industry. It is also well established that although the United Kingdom has an elite educational system second to none in the world, it fails to educate the average citizen as well as in other industrialised countries. It is obviously difficult to make formal comparisons in some subjects, but in mathematics standard attainment tests are easily available. Sig Prais at the National Institute of Economic and Social Research (NIESR) has made many studies of comparative attainment in different countries. The most recent review of his and others' findings is given in Green and Steedman (1993). One of his findings is that the average UK schoolchild in secondary education lagged no less than *18 months* behind their German counterpart; the average German $12\frac{1}{2}$-year-old performed as well as the average British 14-year-old. In France, 66 per cent of 16-year-olds have qualifications equivalent to GCSE grade A–C mathematics; in Germany, the figure is 62 per cent, but in England it is a mere 27 per cent. In the field of vocational training, France and Germany awarded 98,000 and 134,000 mechanical and engineering qualifications in 1987; in Britain, the figure was 30,000. The typical British worker is poorly educated and badly qualified.

Plausible as the policy prescriptions of the new theories are, as yet it is unclear to what extent they hold. Testing the models is, in their very nature, very difficult. We need to identify a specific factor – for example, the human capital knowledge base – *and* find a measure of it. The example makes it obvious how difficult this is likely to be. As yet, convincing evidence for the new theories is yet to arrive. Unfortunately, given the profundity of the implications if the models are true, this does not mean we can ignore the problem.

Summary

Supply shocks and the determinants of long-run growth are difficult to analyse in the framework of traditional macroeconomic models. There was some confusion about the appropriate response to the 1973 oil price rise. There was also a tendency among all shades of opinion to discuss the 'solution' to the difficulties of the early 1980s without recognising that it was not an old-style 'macroeconomic' problem. That is, a major influence on the recent evolution of the UK economy has been North Sea oil. Without recognising this as a structural problem there is a serious danger that 'solutions' will be ill-conceived. More recently, the increase in manufacturing productivity was mistaken by many, including influential and powerful policy-makers, for an exogenous shift rather than, as seems likely, an endogenous response to high real wages and a one-off shake-up in organisational practices. However, this experience may have helped us to appreciate the importance of addressing the most fundamental macro-economic problem – how to structure the economy to first raise, and then maintain, economic growth.

Notes

1. Chatterji and Price (1988) examine a similar model where there is a unionised sector.
2. See Chapter 6.
3. This follows as $d(\ln x) = dx/x$, which is the proportional rate of growth.
4. These figures should be approached cautiously. It is likely the data to 1991 *understate* the productivity rise, for cyclical reasons.
5. Solow's original approach, although widely followed, is certainly flawed. In particular, the breakdown he proposes is crucially dependent on the assumptions of perfect competition and constant returns to scale. However, refinements are available which relax these restrictions, as in Hall (1991).
6. Our discussion here is not meant to be comprehensive, and excludes any mention of several issues. In particular, the analysis of the relationship between government capital expenditure and growth in Chapter 10 is also relevant. A good, wide-ranging treatment may be found in the collection of articles on the new approaches to economic growth in the *Oxford Review of Economic Policy*, Vol. 8, no. 4, especially the introductory article by A. Boltho and G. Holtham, 'The Assessment' (pp. 1–14). There is also an excellent non-technical article in the 4th January 1992 issue of *The Economist*. Scott (1989) has also been very influential, emphasising the role of technical progress embodied in the capital stock.
7. See Chapter 10.

13

Macroeconomics in the 1990s:
Plus ça change?

Macroeconomic policy in the United Kingdom seems to get worse and worse. The subject promised to provide an end to the business cycle, high levels of employment and stable low inflation growth. Instead the business cycle is alive and well, unemployment is at a post-war high and government policy, if anything, seems to exacerbate cycles rather than stabilise them. It is tempting to conclude that policy-makers have learnt nothing from over fifty years of macroeconomics.

Such a conclusion would be unnecessarily pessimistic. Macroeconomic policies are not always bad. There have been good episodes as well as not so good. Some countries have better policies than others. The purpose of studying macroeconomics is exactly to learn from the evidence what works and what does not. Of course, there are plenty of disagreements, but this is a healthy sign. Active debate is how a subject moves forward. Controversy is not a sign of failure, it is a testament to the importance of the issues involved.

Economic policy failure cannot all be blamed on economists. Policy choice and implementation is the responsibility of elected politicians. Politicians in power must take responsibility for their own actions. The electorate has a regular opportunity to dismiss governments which deliver incompetent economic management.

Getting economic policy right, however, is no easy matter. The environment in which policy has to be made has changed considerably over the last few decades and it may change even more by the end of the century. This means that policies must be adapted to the changing conditions. Simple policy rules cannot just be reapplied blindly. Judging the nature and significance of change is difficult. It is worth reviewing the main changes in the macroeconomic environment in the recent past before discussing some of the issues which are likely to be high on the agenda in the 1990s.

Keynesians to Monetarists and back?

In the 1950s and 1960s there was consistently low unemployment, low inflation and minimal cycles. There was also steady growth, low by the international standards of the time, but up to the average long-term growth rate for the UK economy. Many believed (and some still do) that this Golden Age for the British Economy was the result of the successful application of Keynesian economic policies.

However, there was very little room for policy manoeuvre at this time. The pegged exchange rate regime established by the Bretton Woods Agreement imposed a powerful external discipline on policy. Any attempt at demand-induced expansion quickly led to reserve losses and forced a policy reversal. The world economy had stable prices and steady growth, with the United States following conservative monetary and fiscal policies – at least until the early 1960s. Monetary policy in the United Kingdom was dominated by the exchange rate constraint – as we saw in Chapter 6, independent monetary policy is not possible under fixed exchange rates. Indeed, while interest rates were adjusted to maintain reserves when balance of payments crises threatened, control of the monetary system was achieved partly by direct controls on bank lending and by a draconian battery of exchange controls.

The annual spring Budget in which tax rates were set became the key exercise in economic control (expenditure plans were laid out in the Autumn Statement). The theory said that if the economy needed stimulation taxes should be lowered. Overheating called for higher taxes. In practice, the scale of budgetary changes was very small throughout the 1950s and 1960s. Budget deficits and surpluses were always less than 1 per cent of GDP. Hence there was no significant fiscal leverage over the economy at this time. Even so, J.C.R. Dow (1965) concluded that fiscal policy, even at this time, was on balance destabilising. This was because the policy lags were such that, when governments did try to stimulate the economy, the impact occurred in relative boom times and vice versa for deflation. This means that fiscal policy was not actually the key stabilising influence in this period, on the contrary. Reasons for stability must accordingly be sought in the exchange rate regime and the stability of the world environment.

It is a surviving myth in British Keynesian circles that the high employment/low-cycle character of the British economy was a testament to the successful application of Keynesian principles – notably the use of discretionary fiscal policy. The reality was that the room for discretion was severely limited and so it was the external convertibility constraint which prevented the fiscal authorities from being more adventurous (and possibly more damaging).

The external environment started to change in the second half of the 1960s. The United States embarked upon expansionist fiscal policies – partly associated with the domestic 'War on Poverty' and partly associated with the Vietnam War.

Inflation in the United Kingdom was boosted by the devaluation of November 1967, but there then followed three years of very tight fiscal and monetary policies designed to reduce domestic 'absorption' and correct the balance of payments current account deficit. So successful was this policy (attributable to the Labour Chancellor Roy Jenkins) that by 1970 the United Kingdom had a balance of payments surplus, a budget surplus and falling inflation. The bad news was that there was rising unemployment. When unemployment reached a then post-war high of one million in 1971, the Tory Government of Edward Heath embarked upon the most incompetent and damaging episode of economic management seen since the Second World War (with the possible exception of the recent 1988–92 period).

There was a widely held belief at the time that Britain's economic growth would have been faster in the 1950s and 1960s had it not been held back by the exchange rate constraint. Keynesian aggregate demand stimulus could be used to create a 'dash for growth'. This became possible after August 1971, when the Americans floated the dollar and effectively brought the Bretton Woods pegged exchange rate era to an end. Monetary policy was relaxed in September 1971 (see Chapter 7) and there was a give-away budget in March 1972. The result was a short sharp boom in output and a fall in unemployment but also a substantial rise in inflation (which took the best part of a decade to eliminate) and a build-up of the government budget deficit to a figure well in excess of 10 per cent of GDP.

The boom of 1972–73 did nothing to increase long-term growth, indeed the 1970s proved to be one of the worst-ever decades for economic growth in Britain. Investment hardly responded at all to the Barber Boom (named after Anthony, now Lord, Barber, the Tory Chancellor from 1971–74). Unemployment resumed its upward trend as soon as the short boom had bust and policy had been reversed. Of course, the 1973 oil crisis enabled the politicians to try to shift the blame onto external conditions beyond their control, but there is no doubt that the mistakes in policy of this time put the British economy at a severe disadvantage for the rest of the decade, at least.

An inflation rate of over 25 per cent in 1975 which followed the monetary growth rates of 25–30 per cent (in £M3) in 1972–73 convinced even the most casual observer that 'money causes inflation'. In this respect, it was Mr Barber who did more to convert the UK establishment from Keynesian economics to Monetarism than anyone. Mr Barber lost his job in February 1974. The Labour Government under Prime Minister Harold Wilson (and from 1976 James Callaghan) initially resisted the case for deflation on the grounds that the oil price rise was already deflationary (see Chapter 12).

However, the growing budget deficit, rising inflation and deteriorating balance of payments forced a series of crisis measures. Cash limits were imposed on public spending in 1975 (previously public expenditure plans had been in real terms) and explicit monetary targets were introduced in 1976.

In the autumn of 1976 an application was made to the IMF for a loan to enable the authorities to support sterling which had become very weak in foreign exchange markets. The IMF negotiated tough conditions, requiring further cuts in public spending and targets for the rate of growth of domestic credit. This episode marks the end of a major growth period in public services in the United Kingdom – notably, health, education and public housing. Health and education expenditure continued to grow on an upward trend to date but never at the rate achieved in the 1960s and early 1970s.

Some believe that the Labour Government was forced to change course by the IMF. The alternative hypothesis is that they knew what had to be done but were happy to shift the blame onto an external organisation. In any event, the IMF loan marks a turning point in the external position of the UK economy. The sterling exchange rate appreciated consistently from 1976 until 1981 (see Figures 6.5 and 6.6). In so doing it produced a completely new set of problems.

The economy recovered slowly but surely after the 1974–75 recession, though there was growing industrial unrest especially in the public sector as a result of a succession of pay freezes (or pay limits). The appreciating exchange rate was a cause of concern as early as 1977 when Labour Chancellor Denis Healey intervened in the foreign exchange markets to stop the pound rising. In 1978 he was forced to give up this attempt by conflicts between exchange market intervention and domestic monetary control.

The Tory Government of Margaret Thatcher, elected in May 1979, explicitly planned to eliminate inflation by use of monetary targets, and hence earned the label 'Monetarist'. However, their targets were little tighter than those inherited from the previous Labour Government. Neither did they tighten fiscal policy immediately. They planned a 'Medium Term Financial Strategy' which would reduce the budget deficit over time, but this was blown off course by significant public sector pay rises which were the outcome of the Glegg Commission recommendations. (This had been set up by the previous Labour Government to look into public sector pay.)

There was indeed a major recession in 1980, which hit manufacturing especially hard. It is one of the enduring myths in Britain that this was caused entirely by the Monetarist policies of Mrs Thatcher; this is hardly credible (see Chrystal 1984). The proximate cause of the collapse of UK manufacturing was undoubtedly the high UK real exchange rate. However, this had been appreciating since 1976. At least as significant has to be the fact that Britain started producing oil in 1976. By 1980 it was a net exporter and in 1979 the price of oil doubled. Certainly, the high interest rates of late 1979 (see Figure 8.3) influenced the timing of the recession, but these rates were not abnormal by international standards at the time so they cannot explain the high pound.

Exchange controls were abolished in October 1979 and monetary policy was relaxed by June 1980 (at least by M3 standards). Fiscal policy was not tightened until the 1981 budget. The economy grew steadily for the next eight years (though admittedly from a low base of activity).

The significance of the policy of the first Thatcher Government was not that it introduced Monetarism in the sense of having a rigid monetary growth rule which they stuck to. On the contrary, from 1980 on, monetary targets were perpetually exceeded and generally ignored. Mrs Thatcher even rejected monetary base control in favour of judgemental methods which were to prove disastrous later in the decade. Indeed, monetary targets themselves were not especially controversial. Once exchange rate pegging was abandoned, there had to be some guiding principles of monetary policy. Targets for money growth were introduced by a Labour and not a Conservative government. The Labour government, on the whole, met its targets, the Tories never did. The real policy innovation under Thatcher was the targeting of fiscal policy on the budget deficit rather than on the business cycle. Raising taxes in recession was the big shock. No Keynesian could ever recommend this.

On the monetary policy side, a so-called Monetarist government had lost all faith in monetary targeting as early as 1984 (Lawson, 1992). Targets for broad money were officially abandoned in 1986 and an implicit exchange rate target of DM3 per pound was adopted by Chancellor Nigel Lawson. This was implicit because it was never officially announced, and would not have been approved by Mrs Thatcher, who accepted the line that 'you cannot buck the market' – notwithstanding the obvious fact that Britain had had an external convertibility constraint for well over 90 per cent of the time in the previous 300 years!

The counter-Keynesian fiscal philosophy continued. In 1987 there was a major tax-cutting budget at a time when the economy was close to the peak of a boom. This combined with the continued laxity of monetary policy fuelled a house price explosion and eventually an upturn in retail price inflation (see Chapter 8).

Monetary policy was tightened sharply from the autumn of 1988. The housing market was affected immediately, but the momentum in the rest of the economy was such that recession only started to be obvious in 1990.

Indeed, the impact of already tight monetary policy was reinforced by entering the EC Exchange Rate Mechanism in October 1990 at what is now regarded as a high real exchange rate. This was a particularly unfortunate time to join, as unification costs in Germany were forcing high interest rates there. This prevented interest rates from being lowered in the United Kingdom until long after the depth of recession demanded such a policy. It was only after sterling was forced to leave the ERM in September 1992, by speculative pressure, that interest rates were allowed to fall sharply.

The relaxation of monetary policy after September 1992 was uncontroversial from a Keynesian perspective. The controversy surrounded the previous policy of maintaining the ERM band irrespective of the damage inflicted on the economy. The credibility of those responsible for this massive policy U-turn seems impossible to re-establish. Again the controversy is more serious about what to do with fiscal policy. Projections in early 1993 are of a budget deficit of over £50 billion which is well in excess of 5 per cent of GDP. Some recommend raising taxes, though the Keynesian instinct continues to be that this would knock the economy back just as it is coming out of a long recession.

While there are many question marks surrounding monetary policy, it seems that fiscal policy continues to be the main source of controversy – at least in the old-fashioned issue of domestic economic management. The context of monetary policy may eventually change and it is to this that we now turn.

ERM, EMU, ECB, ECU and all that

The Maastricht Treaty between members of the European Community calls for the adoption of a single currency administered by a European Central Bank (ECB) by 1999 at the latest. Nobody can say, at the present time, whether this will happen on time, or even if it will happen at all. Indeed, Britain preserved a right to opt out of the single currency provision. However, it is unlikely that Britain would stay out if all other countries in the European Community were to proceed.

Once a single currency is established, clearly there would simply be one European monetary policy, one European inflation rate and one European exchange rate. At that time we could no longer talk about the monetary policy of Britain, any more than we talk about the monetary policy of Essex. However, there is a long way to go before we get to that stage. The problem for the foreseeable future is going to be the transition. How do we get from here to there with the minimum cost in terms of shocks to the real economy?

The Treaty is fairly clear about what are referred to as 'Convergence Criteria'. On the monetary side, member states must have been members of the Exchange Rate Mechanism (ERM) with narrow bands for at least two years prior to adoption of the single currency. They must also have long-term interest rates not more than 1.5 per cent above the average of the three lowest, and they must have inflation rates not more than 2 per cent above the average of the three lowest. Fiscal policy is proscribed by the criteria of keeping budget deficits at no more than 3 per cent of GDP and total public debt at no more than 60 per cent of GDP.

If taken seriously, these criteria are going to impose major constraints on the range of options available to policy-makers well in advance of the implementation of the single currency. Indeed, no country would currently meet all of these criteria. Those countries which already have accumulated debt in excess of 100 per cent of GDP such as Italy and Belgium would appear unable to do anything drastic enough to reverse significantly this position.

It may be that 'special cases' will be admitted at the end of the day. In the meantime all governments will be under pressure to keep a tight rein on both monetary and fiscal policies. From a British perspective, it also means that there is a presumption that at some stage we must rejoin the ERM. As the events of September 1992 demonstrated, this transition arrangement (the ERM) is much harder to maintain than will be the single currency. There may be more efficient transition mechanisms, such as a float towards a currency conversion (which would be announced irrevocably in advance – as happened with the conversion of the Ostmark into DM). However, the ERM route seems to be the accepted one.

Another problem would be posed if some countries are ready for the single currency while others are not. The core ERM countries – Germany, France, Belgium, Luxembourg and Holland – could well be ready to go it alone before others feel it is appropriate. Indeed, the Dutch currency has been pegged almost exactly to the DM for some time and these five members of the ERM narrow bands have not had a realignment for many years (at the time of writing).[1] It is also for them that the benefits of a single currency are likely to be greatest – given their geographical proximity.

If these five countries do decide to go ahead with the single currency, or its equivalent – the rigid pegging of exchange rates at round numbers – there would be a great deal of pressure on other governments to join in. In Britain, the City would be very reluctant to see the rest of the European Community develop a monetary system in which it did not have a key role. All of this is uncertain, but what is certain is the greater significance of the European Community for UK macroeconomic policy in the 1990s.

Policy coordination

Worldwide cycles combined with significant imbalances between nations are likely to continue the recurrent pressure for international policy coordination. Whether a systematic method for coordinating policy between the major nations can be established is far from clear. Inevitably, however, there will be calls from deficit countries to surplus countries to 'take their share of adjustment'. Japan is especially vulnerable in this respect in the light of its semi-permanent balance of payments surplus.

Politicians are often tempted to try to shift the blame for their own economic mismanagement onto other countries. However, the evidence based upon attempts at coordinated intervention in the 1980s suggests that this could do more harm than good. Some economists take the view that if each country keeps its own economic management under competent control then there would be need for international coordination. However, there is some case for believing otherwise sound, but non-coordinated, policy may be positively damaging.

In practice, the trend seems to be towards regional groupings of countries which create trade blocs (such as the European Community and the North American Free Trade Association) and also within which there is a high degree of macro policy coordination (or at least a leader–follower relationship). The prospects for any macro policy coordination between these blocs still seem quite remote.

Unemployment

Whatever the international environment may dictate, there can be little doubt that the overwhelming macroeconomic policy problem of the 1990s will be the same as that which created the subject in the first place – unemployment. Each successive cycle in the last thirty years has taken unemployment to new peaks. At the time of writing this pattern shows no signs of reversing.

The downward trend of employment in manufacturing has been evident since the 1960s, notwithstanding the upward trend in output. New features of the early 1990s include the trimming of staff in the privatised utilities and substantial layoffs in financial services (especially banks), both of which were subject to heightened commercial pressures in the 1980s. Financial services were significant net employers of labour in the 1980s, but this has now reversed. With the Civil Service and military also laying off people it is hard to see where greater employment opportunities are going to come from in the foreseeable future.

Growth in output is likely to return to trend in the mid-1990s but the long-run average real growth of 2 per cent will do little to dent the high unemployment figures. Productivity growth is such that British industry can produce this growth in output with continued declining employment roles. Only a substantial growth in numbers involved in full-time education offers the potential for significantly cutting unemployment – especially among the young. Given the fiscal implications of such an expansion, it does not seem likely to happen.

The long-run pressures on the social security system which are predicted to arise from the ageing of the population implies that pressure on the government budget is going to be very great in any event. High unemployment makes this even worse. The reality is that, whatever government is in power, they are going to find it very hard indeed to finance the conflicting array of demands on the public purse at politically acceptable rates of taxation.

The biggest uncertainty in the fiscal policy area remains the extent to which governments will find it expedient to return to using fiscal policy as a countercyclical stabilisation tool. The moving of the Budget from the spring to November in 1993, where it will become a combined exercise in spending plans and tax setting, may change the emphasis away from using taxes as a control device. What should be obvious, however, is that, as monetary policy gets more closely tied into that of EMS partners, fiscal policy will be the only tool left for influencing the course of the economy. Whether that also comes to be determined at the European level remains to be seen.

Conclusion

Macroeconomic policy in Britain in the post-war period, up to 1971, was heavily constrained by the Bretton Woods exchange rate system. In the 1970s and 1980s, the degree of monetary and fiscal policy discretion was great. It would be hard to make a case for the view that the UK authorities did a good job. In twenty years or so Britain suffered cumulative inflation of nearly 600 per cent, had three major recessions and saw an upward trend in unemployment. Perhaps, fortunately, the 1990s seem likely to be characterised by increasing external constraints on policy actions. Even if the European currency arrangements fall apart, there must be some hope that macro policy will be better in future than it has been in the recent past. After all, it is hard to believe that it could be much worse!

Note

1. Notwithstanding the 'temporary' shift to a 15 per cent band.

References

Akerlof, G. A. (1982) 'Labor contracts as partial gift exchange', *Quarterly Journal of Economics*, Vol. 97, pp. 543–89.

Akerlof, G. and Yellen, J. (1985) 'A near-rational model of the business cycle with wage and price inertia', *Quarterly Journal of Economics*, Vol. 100, pp. 823–38.

Alesina, A. (1987) 'Macroeconomic policy in a two-party system as a repeated game', *Quarterly Journal of Economics*, Vol. 102, pp. 651–78.

Alesina, A. (1989) 'Politics and business cycles in industrial democracies', *Economic Policy*, Vol. 8, pp. 55–87.

Alexander, S. S. (1952) 'Effects of a devaluation on a trade balance', IMF Staff Papers, Vol. II, April, IMF, Washington, pp. 263–78.

Alogoskoufis, G., Manning, A. and Philippopoulos, A. (1992) 'Wage inflation, electoral uncertainty and the exchange rate regime: theory and UK evidence', *Economic Journal*, Vol. 102, pp.1370–94.

Alt, J. and Chrystal, K. A. (1983) *Political Economics*, University of California Press, Berkeley, CA.

Andersen, L. C. and Jordan, J. L. (1968) 'Monetary and fiscal actions: a test of their relative importance in economic stabilization', *Federal Reserve Bank of St Louis Monthly Review*, Vol. 50, November, pp. 29–44.

Arrow, K. (1962) 'The economic implications of learning by doing', *Review of Economic Studies*, Vol. 29, pp. 155–73.

Artis, M. J. and Lewis, M. K. (1976) 'The demand for money in the UK 1963–1973', *Manchester School*, Vol. 44, pp. 147–81.

Artis, Michael and Ostry, Sylvia (1986) 'International Economic Policy Coordination', Chatham House Papers, No. 30, Royal Institute of International Affairs, Routledge and Kegan Paul, London.

Attfield, C. L. F., Demery, D. and Duck, N. W. (1981) 'A quarterly model of unanticipated monetary growth, output and the price level in the UK 1963–78', *Journal of Monetary Economics*, Vol. 8, November, pp. 331–50.

Azariadis, C. (1975) 'Implicit contracts and under-employment equilibria', *Journal of Political Economy*, Vol. 83, December, pp. 1183–202.

Backus, D. and Driffil, J. (1985) 'Inflation and reputation', *American Economic Review*, Vol. 75, June, pp. 530–8.

Bacon, R. and Eltis, W. (1976) *Britain's Economic Problem: Too Few Producers*,

Macmillan, London.

Baily, M. N. (1974) 'Wages and employment under uncertain demand', *Review of Economic Studies*, Vol. 41, p. 37–50.

Ball, L. and Romer, D. (1990) 'Real rigidities and the non-neutrality of money', *Review of Economic Studies*, Vol. 57, pp. 183–203.

Barnett, W. A. (1980) 'Economic monetary aggregates: An application of aggregation and index number theory', *Journal of Econometrics*, Vol. 14, September, pp. 11–48.

Barnett, W. A. (1982) 'The optimal level of monetary aggregation', *Journal of Money Credit and Banking*, Part 2, Vol. 14, November, pp. 687–710.

Barnett, W. A., Fisher, D. and Serletis, A. (1992) 'Consumer theory and the demand for money', *Journal of Economic Literature*, Vol. 30, December, pp. 2086–119.

Barro, R. J. (1977) 'Unanticipated money growth and unemployment in the US', *American Economic Review*, Vol. 67, March, pp. 101–15.

Barro, R. J. (1978) 'Unanticipated money, output and the price level in the US', *Journal of Political Economy*, Vol. 86, August, pp. 549–80.

Barro, R. (1983) 'Rules, discretion and reputation in a model of monetary policy', *Journal of Monetary Economics*, Vol. 12, pp. 101–22.

Barro, R. (1987) 'Ricardo and Budget Deficits', Henry Thornton Lecture, City University Business School, London.

Barro, R. J. (1990) 'Government spending in a simple model of endogenous growth', *Journal of Political Economy*, Vol. 98, pp. S103–25.

Barro, R. J. and Grossman, H. (1976) *Money, Employment and Inflation*, Cambridge University Press, Cambridge.

Batchelor, R. and Sheriff, T. D. (1980) 'Unemployment and unanticipated inflation in post-war Britain', *Economica*, Vol. 47, May, pp. 179–92.

Batten, D. S. and Hafer, R. W. (1983) 'The relative impact of monetary and fiscal actions on economic activity: a cross country comparison', *Federal Reserve Bank of St Louis Review*, Vol. 65, No. 1, January, pp. 5–12.

Begg, D. K. H. (1982) *The Rational Expectations Revolution in Macroeconomics*, Philip Allan, Oxford.

Belongia, M. T. and Chrystal K. A. (1991) 'An admissable monetary aggregate for the UK', *Review of Economics and Statistics*, Vol. 73, No. 3, August, pp. 497–503.

Bernheim, B. D. (1987) 'Ricardian equivalence: An evaluation of theory and evidence', *NBER Macroeconomics Annual*, Vol. 2, NBER, Cambridge, MA, pp. 263–303.

Blanchard, O. and Summers, L. (1986) 'Hysteresis and the European unemployment problem', *NBER Macroeconomics Annual*, Vol. 1, NBER, Cambridge, MA, pp. 15–77.

Blinder, A. and Solow, R. (1973) 'Does fiscal policy matter?', *Journal of Public Economics*, Vol. 2, pp. 319–37.

Branson, W. H. and Buiter, W. H. (1983) 'Monetary and fiscal policy with flexible exchange rates', in J. S. Bhandari and B. H. Putnam (eds), *Economic Interdependence and Flexible Exchange Rates*, MIT Press, Cambridge, MA, pp. 251–65.

Brunner, K. (1968) 'The role of money and monetary policy', *Federal Reserve Bank of St Louis Review*, Vol. 50, No. 7, July, pp. 9–24.

Brunner, K. and Meltzer, A. H. (1976) 'Government, the private sector and "crowding out"', *The Banker*, Vol. 126, July, pp. 765–9.

Buiter, W. (1987) 'Budget deficits', in R. Dornbusch and R. Layard (eds), *The Performance of the UK Economy*, Clarendon Press, Oxford.

Buiter, W. and Miller, M. (1981a) 'The Thatcher experiment: the first two years',

Brooking Papers on Economic Activity, Part 2, pp. 315–67.

Buiter, W. and Miller, M. (1981b) 'Monetary policy and international competitiveness: the problems of adjustment', *Oxford Economic Papers*, Vol. 33, pp. 143–75.

Buiter, W. and Miller, M. (1983) 'Changing the rules: Economic consequences of the Thatcher regime', *Brookings Papers on Economic Activity*, Part 2, pp. 305–65.

Caplin, A. S. and Spulber, D. F. (1987) 'Menu costs and the neutrality of money', *Quarterly Journal of Economics*, Vol. 102, pp. 703–25.

Carlson, K. M. and Spencer, R. W. (1975) 'Crowding out and its critics', *Federal Reserve Bank of St Louis Monthly Review*, Vol. 57, December, pp. 2–17.

Carlton, D. (1986) 'The rigidity of prices', *American Economic Review*, Vol. 76, pp. 637–58.

Carraro, C. and Giavazzi, F. (1991) 'Can international policy coordination really be counterproductive?' in C. Carraro, D. Laussel, M. Salmon and A. Soubeyran (eds), *International Economic Policy Coordination*, Blackwell, Oxford, pp. 184–98.

Chatterji, M. C. and Price, S. (1988) 'Unions, Dutch disease and unemployment', *Oxford Economic Papers*, Vol. 41, pp. 302–21.

Chrystal, K. A. (1984) 'Dutch disease or Monetarist medicine?: The British Economy under Mrs Thatcher', *Federal Reserve Bank of St Louis Review*, Vol. 66, No. 5, May, pp. 27–37.

Chrystal, K. A. (1989) 'Overshooting models of the exchange rate', in D. Greenaway (ed.), *Current Issues in Macroeconomics*, Macmillan, London, pp. 214–30.

Chrystal, K. A. (1992) 'The fall and rise of saving', *National Westminster Bank Quarterly Review*, February, pp. 24–40.

Chrystal, K. A. and Alt, J. (1979) 'Endogenous government behaviour: Wagner's Law or Gotterdamerung?', in P. M. Jackson and S. T. Cook (eds), *Current Issues in Fiscal Policy*, Martin Robertson, Oxford, pp. 123–40.

Chrystal, K. A. and Alt, J. (1981) 'Public sector behaviour: the status of the political business cycle', in D. Currie, R. Nobay and D. Peel (eds), *Macroeconomic Analysis Essays in Macroeconomics and Econometrics*, Croom Helm, London, pp. 353–82.

Chrystal K. A. and MacDonald, R. (1993) 'Exchange Rates and Financial Innovation: The Sterling/Dollar Rate 1972–1990', Discussion Paper, January, City University Business School, London.

Chrystal, K. A. and Wood, G. E. (1988) 'Are trade deficits a problem', *Federal Reserve Bank of St Louis Review*, Vol. 70, January/February, pp. 3–11.

Church, R. and Whitley, R. (1991) *Comparative properties of UK models*, Warwick Macroeconomic Forecasting Bureau, Warwick, mimeo.

Clower, R. (1965) 'The Keynesian counter-revolution: a theoretical appraisal', in F. H. Hahn and F. P. R. Brechling (eds), *The Theory of Interest Rates*, Macmillan, London, pp. 103–25.

Cooper, R. and John, A. (1988) 'Coordinating coordination failures in Keynesian models', *Quarterly Journal of Economics*, Vol. 103, pp. 441–63.

Corden, W. M. (1981) 'Exchange rate protection', in R. N. Cooper, P. B. Kenen, J. B. De Macedo and J. Van Ypersele (eds), *The International Monetary System Under Flexible Exchange Rates: Global, Regional and National*, Ballinger, Cambridge, MA, pp. 17–34.

Corden, W. M. and Neary, J. P. (1982) 'Booming sector and deindustrialization in a small open economy', *Economic Journal*, Vol. 92, December, pp. 825–48.

Cross, M. (1988a) 'Changes in working practices in UK manufacturing industry

1981–88', *Industrial Relations Review and Report*, No. 415, pp. 2–10.

Cross, R. (ed.) (1988b) *Unemployment, Hysteresis and the Natural Rate Hypothesis*, Basil Blackwell, Oxford.

Currie, David, Levine, Paul and Vidalis, Nic (1987) 'International cooperation and reputation in an empirical two-bloc model', in Ralph C. Bryant and Richard Portes (eds), *Global Macroeconomics: Policy Conflict and Cooperation*, St Martins Press (for CEPR and the IEA), London, pp. 73–121.

Cuthbertson, K. (1985) *The Supply and Demand for Money*, Blackwell, Oxford.

Cuthbertson, K. (1991) 'Money demand analysis: an outline', in M. P. Taylor (ed.), *Money and Financial Markets*, Blackwell, Oxford, pp. 15–63.

Cuthbertson, K., Hall, S. G. and Taylor, M. P. (1992) *Applied Econometric Techniques*, Philip Allan, Oxford.

Deaton, A. (1992) *Understanding Consumption*, Oxford University Press, Oxford.

Dornbusch, R. (1976a) 'The theory of flexible exchange rate regimes and macroeconomic policy', *Scandinavian Journal of Economics*, Vol. 78, No. 2, pp. 255–75.

Dornbusch, R. (1976b) 'Expectations and exchange rate dynamics', *Journal of Political Economy*, Vol. 84, No. 6, pp. 1161–76.

Dow, J. C. R. (1965) *The Management of the British Economy*, Cambridge University Press, Cambridge.

Dowrick, S. and Gemmell, N. (1991) 'Industrialisation, catching-up and economic growth: a comparative study across the world's capitalist economies', *Economic Journal*, Vol. 101, pp. 263–75.

Drake, L. and Chrystal, K. A. (1994) 'Company sector money demand: new evidence on the existence of a stable long run relationship for the UK', *Journal of Money Credit and Banking*, in press.

The Economist, 4 January 1992, pp. 25–30.

Eltis, W. and Sinclair, P. J. N. (eds) (1981) *The Money Supply and the Exchange Rate*, Oxford University Press, Oxford.

Feinstein, C. (1988) 'Economic growth since 1870: Britain's performance in international perspective', *Oxford Review of Economic Policy*, Vol. 4, pp. 1–13.

Fischer, S. (1977) 'Long-term contracts, rational expectations, and the optimal money supply rule', *Journal of Political Economy*, Vol. 85, February, pp. 191–205.

Fisher, I. (1973) 'A statistical relation between unemployment and price changes'. Reprinted in *Journal of Political Economy*, Vol. 81, March/April, pp. 596–602.

Fisher, P., Hudson S. and Pradhan, M. (1993) 'Divisia Indices for Money: An Appraisal of Theory and Practice', Bank of England Working Paper No. 9, April, Bank of England, London.

Frankel, J. A. (1979) 'On the Mark: a theory of floating exchange rates based on real interest differentials', *American Economic Review*, Vol. 69, September, pp. 610–22.

Frankel, J.A. and Rockett, Katherine (1988) 'International macroeconomic policy coordination when policy makers do not agree on the true model', *American Economic Review*, Vol. 78, June, pp. 318–40.

Frenkel, J. A. and Johnson, H. G. (eds) (1976) *The Monetary Approach to the Balance of Payments*, George Allen and Unwin, London.

Frenkel, J. A. and Johnson, H. G. (eds) (1978) *The Economics of Exchange Rates*, Addison-Wesley, London.

Frey, B. (1978) *Modern Political Economy*, Martin Robertson, Oxford.

Frey, B. and Schneider, F. (1978) 'A politico-economic model of the UK', *Economic*

Journal, Vol. 88, June, pp. 243–53.

Friedman, Milton (1953) 'The case for flexible exchange rates', in *Essays in Positive Economics*, University of Chicago Press, Chicago, pp. 157–203.

Friedman, Milton (1959) Testimony in Hearings before the Joint Economic Committee, Washington, p. 609.

Friedman, Milton (1960) *A Program for Monetary Stability*, Fordham University Press, New York.

Friedman, Milton (1968) 'The role of monetary policy', *American Economic Review*, Vol. 58, March, pp. 1–17.

Friedman, Milton and Schwartz, A. J. (1963a) 'Money and business cycles', *Review of Economics and Statistics*, Supplement, Vol. 45, pp. 32–64.

Friedman, Milton and Schwartz, A. J. (1963b) *A Monetary History of the US 1867–1960*, NBER, New York.

Friedman, Milton and Schwartz, A. J. (1982) *Monetary Trends in the US and UK*, University of Chicago Press, Chicago.

Ghosh, Atish R. and Masson, Paul R. (1988) 'International Policy Coordination in a World with Model Uncertainty', *IMF Staff Papers*, No. 35, June, IMF, Washington, pp. 230–58.

Giavazzi, F. and Pagano, M. (1988) 'The advantage of tying one's hands', *European Economic Review*, Vol. 32, pp. 1055–82.

Goldfeld, S. and Blinder, A. (1972) 'Some implications of endogenous stabilisation policy', *Brooking Papers on Economic Activity*, Part 3, pp. 585–640.

Gordon, D. (1974) 'A neoclassical theory of underemployment', *Economic Inquiry*, Vol. 12, pp. 43–59.

Gordon, R. A. (1961) *Business Fluctuations*, 2nd edn, Harper and Bros, New York.

Gordon, R. J. (1978) *Macroeconomics*, Little Brown, Boston.

Gray, J. A. (1976) 'Wage indexation: a macroeconomic approach', *Journal of Monetary Economics*, Vol. 3, pp. 221–35.

Green, A. and Steedman, H. (1993) *Educational provision, educational attainment and the needs of industry: a review of research for Germany, France, Japan and Britain*, NIESR, London.

Grossman, J. and Hart, O. D. (1981) 'Implicit contracts, moral hazard and unemployment', *American Economic Review*, AEA Papers and Proceedings, Vol. 71, May, pp. 301–7.

Hall, M. (1983) *Monetary Policy Since 1971: Conduct and Performance*, Macmillan, London.

Hall, R. (1991) 'Invariance properties of Solow's productivity residual', in P. Diamond (ed.), *Growth/Productivity/Unemployment: Essays in Honour of Robert Solow's 65th Birthday*, MIT Press, Cambridge, MA, pp. 71–112.

Hall, S. G., Henry, S. G. B. and Wilcox, J. B. (1989) 'The Long Run Determinants of the UK Monetary Aggregates', Bank of England Discussion Paper, August, Bank of England, London.

Hamada, Koichi (1976) 'A strategic analysis of monetary interdependence', *Journal of Political Economy*, Vol. 84, August, pp. 677–700.

Hansen, A. (1953) *A Guide to Keynes*, McGraw-Hill, New York.

Harrod, R. F. (1936) *The Trade Cycle: An Essay*, Oxford University Press, Oxford.

Hendry, D. F. (1988) 'The encompassing implications of feedback versus feedforward mechanisms in econometrics', *Oxford Economic Papers*, Vol. 40, pp. 132–9.

Hendry, D. F. and Ericsson, N. R. (1991) 'Modeling the demand for narrow money in the UK and the US', *European Economic Review*, Vol. 35, pp. 833–86.

Hendry, D. F. and Mizon, G. E. (1978) 'Serial correlation as a convenient simplification, not a nuisance', *Economic Journal*, Vol. 88, September, pp. 549–63.

Henry, S. G. B. and Ormerod, P. A. (1978) 'Incomes policy and wage inflation: empirical evidence for the UK 1961–1977', *NIESR Economic Review*, Vol. 98, August, pp. 31–9.

Hibbs, D. (1987) *The Political Economy of Industrial Economies*, Harvard University Press, Cambridge, MA.

Hicks, J. R. (1937) 'Mr Keynes and the Classics, a suggested interpretation', *Econometrica*, Vol. 5, April, pp. 147–59.

Hicks, J. R. (1950) *A Contribution to the Theory of the Trade Cycle*, Oxford University Press, Oxford.

Hicks, J. R. (1974) *The Crisis in Keynesian Economics*, Basil Blackwell, Oxford.

Holtham, Gerald and Hughes Hallett, Andrew (1987) 'International policy cooperation and model uncertainty', in Ralph C. Bryant and Richard Portes (eds), *Global Macroeconomics: Policy Conflict and Cooperation*, St Martins Press (for CEPR and the IEA), London, pp. 128–84.

Jackman, R. and Layard, R. (1982) 'An inflation tax', *Fiscal Studies*, Vol. 3, pp. 47–59.

Jackman, R. and Layard, R. (1986) 'Is TIP administratively feasible?', in D. C. Colander (ed.), *Incentive-Based Incomes Policy*, Ballinger, Cambridge, MA, pp. 95–109.

Jackman, R. and Layard, R. (1990) 'The real effects of tax based incomes policy', *Scandinavian Journal of Economics*, Vol. 92, pp. 309–42.

Jackson, P. M. and Cook, S. T. (eds) (1979) *Current Issues in Fiscal Policy*, Martin Robertson, Oxford.

Johnson, H. G. (1976) 'The monetary approach to balance of payments theory', in J. A. Frenkel and H. G. Johnson (eds), *The Monetary Approach to the Balance of Payments*, George Allen and Unwin, London, pp. 147–67.

Jonson, P. (1976) 'A model of the UK balance of payments', *Journal of Political Economy*, Vol. 84, No. 5, p. 979–1012.

Kendricks, J. (1973) *Post-War Productivity Trends in the United States 1948–1969*, NBER, New York.

Kenen, Peter B. (1989) *Exchange Rates and Policy Coordination*, University of Michigan Press, Ann Arbor, MI.

Keynes, J. M. (1936) *The General Theory of Employment, Interest and Money*, Macmillan, London.

Kydland, F. and Prescott, E. (1977) 'Rules rather than discretion: The inconsistency of optimal plans', *Journal of Political Economy*, Vol. 85, pp. 473–91.

Kydland, F. and Prescott, E. (1982) 'Time to build and aggregate fluctuations', *Econometrica*, Vol. 50, pp. 1345–70.

Laidler, D. E. W. (1974) Public expenditure, inflation and the balance of payments, 9th Report for the Expenditure Committee, HC–328, session 1974–75, HMSO, London.

Laidler, D. E. W. (1976) 'Inflation in Britain: a Monetarist perspective', *American Economic Review*, Vol. 66, September, pp. 485–500.

Laidler, D. E. W. (1978) 'Money and money income: an essay on the transmission mechanism', *Journal of Monetary Economics*, Vol. 4, April, pp. 151–91.

Laidler, D. E. W. (1980) 'The demand for money in the US – yet again', in K. Brunner and A. H. Meltzer (eds), Vol. 12, Carnegie–Rochester Conference Series on Public Policy, Spring, North Holland, Amsterdam, pp. 219–72.

Laidler, D. E. W. (1982) *Monetarist Perspectives*, Philip Allan, Oxford.

Lawson, Nigel (1992) *The View from No 11: Memoirs of a Tory Radical*, Bantam Press, London.

Layard, R. (1982) 'Is incomes policy the answer to unemployment?', *Economica*, Vol. 49, August, pp. 219–39.

Layard, R. and Nickell, S.J. (1989) 'The Thatcher Miracle?', CEPR Discussion Paper No. 315, LSE, London; shorter version in *American Economic Review*, Vol. 79, pp. 215–19.

Layard, R. and Nickell, S. J. (1990) 'Is unemployment lower if unions bargain over employment?', *Quarterly Journal of Economics*, Vol. 105, pp. 773–87.

Layard, R., Nickell, S. J. and Jackman, R. (1991) *Unemployment*, Oxford University Press, Oxford.

Leijonhufvud, A. (1968) *On Keynesian Economics and the Economics of Keynes*, Oxford University Press, Oxford.

Leontief, W. (1946) 'The pure theory of the guaranteed annual wage contract', *Journal of Political Economy*, Vol. 54, pp. 76–9.

Levich, R. M. (1989) 'Is the foreign exchange market efficient?', *Oxford Review of Economic Policy*, Vol. 5, No. 3, Autumn, pp. 40–60.

Lipsey, R. G. (1960) 'The relationship between unemployment and the rate of change of money wage rates in the UK 1862–1957: a further analysis', *Economica*, Vol. 27, pp. 1–31.

Lucas, R. E. (1972) 'Expectations and the neutrality of money', *Journal of Economic Theory*, Vol. 4, pp. 103–24.

Lucas, R. E. (1973) 'Some international evidence on output–inflation trade-offs', *American Economic Review*, Vol. 63, pp. 326–34.

Lucas, R. E. (1975) 'An equilibrium model of the business cycle', *Journal of Political Economy*, Vol. 83, December, pp. 1113–44.

Lucas, R. E. (1976) 'Econometric policy evaluation: a critique', in K. Brunner and A. H. Meltzer (eds), *The Phillips Curve and Labour Markets*, Vol. 1, Carnegie-Rochester Conference Series on Public Policy, North Holland, Amsterdam, pp. 19–46.

Lucas, R. E. (1977) 'Understanding business cycles', in K. Brunner and A. H. Meltzer (eds), *Stabilization of the Domestic and International Economy*, Vol. 5, Carnegie-Rochester Conference Series, North Holland, Amsterdam, pp. 7–29.

Lucas, R. E. (1981) *Studies in Business Cycle Theory*, Basil Blackwell, Oxford.

Lucas, R. E. (1988) 'On the mechanics of economic development', *Journal of Monetary Economics*, Vol. 22, pp. 3–42.

Lucas, R. E. and Rapping, L. (1969) 'Real wages, employment and inflation', *Journal of Political Economy*, Vol. 77, pp. 721–54.

Lucas, R. E. and Sargent, Thomas J. (1981a) 'After Keynesian macroeconomics', in R. E. Lucas and T. J. Sargent (eds), *Rational Expectations and Econometric Practice*, George Allen and Unwin, London, Chapter 16.

Lucas, R. E. and Sargent, Thomas J. (eds) (1981b) *Rational Expectations and Econometric Practice*, George Allen and Unwin, London.

Lynde, C. and Richmond, J. R. (1993) 'Public capital and long run costs in UK manufacturing', *Economic Journal*, Vol. 103, pp. 880–93.

MacDonald, R. (1988) *Floating Exchange Rates: Theories and Evidence*, Unwin Hyman, London.

McDonald, I. and Solow, R. (1981) 'Wage bargaining and employment', *American Economic Review*, Vol. 71, pp. 896–908.

McKinnon, Ronald I. (1963) 'Optimum currency areas', *American Economic Review*, Vol. 53, September, pp. 717–25.

McKinnon, Ronald I. (1984) *An International Standard for Monetary Stabilization*, Institute for International Economics, Washington.

Macrae, E. (1977) 'A political model of the business cycle', *Journal of Political Economy*, Vol. 85, No. 2, pp. 239–63.

Malinvaud, E. (1977) *The Theory of Unemployment Reconsidered*, Basil Blackwell, Oxford.

Mankiw, Gregory and Romer, David (1991) *New Keynesian Economics*, Vols 1 and 2, MIT Press, Cambridge, MA.

Matthews, R.C.O. (1959) *The Trade Cycle*, Nisbet and Cambridge University Press, Cambridge.

Meade, J.E. and Andrews, P.W.S. (1951) 'Summary of replies to questions on the effects of interest rates', in T. Wilson and P.W.S. Andrews (eds), *Oxford Studies in the Price Mechanism*, Oxford University Press, Oxford, pp. 27–30.

Meese, R.A. and Rogoff, K. (1983) 'Empirical exchange rate models of the Seventies: Do they fit out of sample?', *Journal of International Economics*, Vol. 14, pp. 3–24.

Miller, M.H. (1976) 'Can a rise in import prices be inflationary and deflationary', *American Economic Review*, Vol. 66, September, pp. 501–19.

Miller, M.H. (1985) 'Measuring the stance of fiscal policy', *Oxford Review of Economic Policy*, Vol. 1, No. 1, pp. 44–57.

Minford, M., Wall, M. and Wren-Lewis, S. (1988) 'Manufacturing Capacity', National Institute Discussion Paper No. 146, NIESR, London.

Minford, P. (1991) *Rational Expectations and the New Macroeconomics*, Martin Robertson, Oxford.

Mitchell, W.C. (1941) *Business Cycles and Their Causes*, University of California Press, Berkeley, CA.

Modigliani, F. (1944) 'Liquidity preference and the theory of interest and money', *Econometrica*, Vol. 12, January, pp. 45–88.

Modigliani, F. (1977) 'The Monetarist controversy or should we forsake stabilization policy?', *American Economic Review*, Vol. 67, March, pp. 1–19.

Muellbauer, J. and Murphy, A. (1989) *Why Has UK Personal Saving Collapsed?*, July, Credit Suisse First Boston, London.

Mundell, R.A. (1961) 'A theory of optimum currency areas', *American Economic Review*, Vol. 51, November, pp. 657–64.

Mundell, R.A. (1968) *International Economics*, Macmillan, London.

Muth, J.F. (1961) 'Rational expectations and the theory of price movements', *Econometrica*, Vol. 29, July, pp. 315–35.

Nelson, C.R. and Plosser, C.I. (1982) 'Trends and random walks in macroeconomic time series', *Journal of Monetary Economics*, Vol. 10, pp. 139–62.

Niehans, J. (1981) 'The Appreciation of Sterling – Causes, Effects and Policies', Money Study Group Discussion Paper, London.

Nordhaus, W. (1975) 'The political business cycle', *Review of Economic Studies*, Vol. 42, pp. 169–90.

Okun, A.M. (1981) *Prices and Quantities: A Macroeconomic Analysis*, Basil Blackwell, Oxford.

Oswald, A. (1987) 'Efficient Contracts are on the Labour Demand Curve: Theory and Facts', LSE Centre for Labour Economics Discussion Paper No. 284, London School of Economics, London.

Oudiz, Gilles and Sachs, Jeffrey D. (1984) 'Macroeconomic policy coordination among the industrial economies', *Brookings Papers on Economic Activity*, Part 1, pp. 1–75.

Oxford Review of Economic Policy, Vol. 8, No. 8.

Parkin, M. and Bade, R. (1982) *Modern Macroeconomics*, Philip Allan, Oxford.

Parkin, M. and Sumner, M.T. (eds) (1972) *Incomes Policy and Inflation*, Manchester University Press, Manchester.

Parkin, M., Sumner, M.T. and Jones, R.A. (1972) 'A survey of the econometric evidence of the effects of incomes policy on the rate of inflation', in M. Parkin and M.T. Sumner (eds), *Incomes Policy and Inflation*, Manchester University Press, Manchester, pp. 1–29.

Patinkin, D. (1956) *Money Interest and Prices*, Row, Peterson and Co., Evanston, IL.

Pepper, G. (1990) *Money Credit and Inflation*, Institute of Economic Affairs, London.

Pesaran, H. (1982) 'A critique of the proposed tests of the natural rate-rational expectations hypothesis', *Economic Journal*, Vol. 92, pp. 529–54.

Pesaran, H. (1987) *The Limits to Rational Expectations*, Basil Blackwell, Oxford.

Phelps, E.S. (1968) 'Money-wage dynamics and labour market equilibrium', *Journal of Political Economy*, Vol. 76, July/August, pp. 678–711.

Phillips, A.W.H. (1958) 'The relation between unemployment and the rate of change of money-wage rates in the UK, 1861–1957', *Economica*, Vol. 25, November, pp. 283–99.

Pissarides, C. (1990) *Equilibrium Unemployment Theory*, Basil Blackwell, Oxford.

Prescott, E. (1986) 'Theory ahead of business cycle measurement', *Federal Reserve Bank of Minneapolis Quarterly Review*, Fall issue, pp. 9–27.

Price, S. (1988) 'Human capital, unemployment and hysteresis', in R. Cross (ed.), *Unemployment, Hysteresis and the Natural Rate Hypothesis*, Basil Blackwell, Oxford, pp. 158–79.

Price, S. (1991) 'Costs, prices and profitability in UK manufacturing', *Applied Economics*, Vol. 23, pp. 839–49.

Price, S. (1992a) 'Forward looking price setting in UK manufacturing', *Economic Journal*, Vol. 102, pp. 497–505.

Price, S. (1992b) 'Human capital, hysteresis and unemployment among workers with finite lives', *Scottish Journal of Political Economy*, Vol. 39, pp. 201–12.

Price, S. and Sanders, D. (1992) 'Government Popularity', Essex Discussion Papers, No. 370, Essex University, Colchester.

Price, S. and Sanders, D. (1993) 'Modelling government popularity in post-war Britain', *American Journal of Political Science*, Vol. 37, pp. 317–34.

Robinson, B. and Wade, K. (1985) 'Unemployment, scrapping and factor prices', *LBS Economic Outlook*, Vol. 9, No. 10, pp. 1–4.

Rogoff, Kenneth (1985) 'Can international monetary policy cooperation be counterproductive?', *Journal of International Economics*, Vol. 18, May, pp. 199–217.

Rogoff, Kenneth and Sibert, A. (1988) 'Elections and macroeconomic policy cycles', *Review of Economic Studies*, Vol. 55, pp. 1–16.

Romer, P. (1986) 'Increasing returns and long-run economic growth', *Journal of Political Economy*, Vol. 94, pp. 1002–37.

Rotemberg, J.J. (1991) 'Monetary aggregates and their uses', in M.T. Belongia (ed.), *Monetary Policy on the 75th Anniversary of the Federal Reserve System: Proceedings of the Fourteenth Annual Economic Policy Conference of the Federal Reserve Bank of St Louis*, Kluwer Academic Publishers, Boston, MA, pp. 223–31.

Rotemberg, J.J. and Saloner, G. (1986) 'A supergame theoretic model of price wars during booms', *American Economic Review*, Vol. 76, pp. 390–407.

Samuelson, P. (1939) 'Interactions between the multiplier analysis and the principle of acceleration', *Review of Economics and Statistics*, Vol. 21, pp. 75–8.

Sargent, T. (1976) 'The observational equivalence of natural and unnatural rate theories of macroeconomics', *Journal of Political Economy*, Vol. 84, No. 3, pp. 631–40.

Sargent, T. J. and Wallace, N. (1975) 'Rational expectations, the optimal monetary instrument and the optimal money supply rule', *Journal of Political Economy*, Vol. 83, April, pp. 241–54.

Savage, D. (1978) 'The channels of monetary influence: a survey of the empirical evidence', *NIESR Economic Review*, No. 83, February, pp. 73–89.

Schumpeter, J. (1939) *Business Cycles: a Theoretical, Historical and Statistical Analysis of the Capitalist Process*, McGraw-Hill, New York.

Scott, M. (1989) *A New View of Economic Growth*, Clarendon Press, Oxford.

Shapiro, C. and Stiglitz, J. (1984) 'Equilibrium unemployment as a worker discipline device', *American Economic Review*, Vol. 74, pp 433–44.

Smith, Adam (1937) *Wealth of Nations*, Clarendon, Oxford.

Solow, R. (1956) 'A contribution to the theory of economic growth', *Quarterly Journal of Economics*, Vol. 70, pp. 65–94.

Solow, R. (1957) 'Technical change and the aggregate production function', *Review of Economics and Statistics*, Vol. 39, pp. 312–20.

Spencer, R. W. and Yohe, W. P. (1970) 'The crowding out of private expenditures by fiscal policy actions', *Federal Reserve Bank of St Louis Monthly Review*, Vol. 52, October.

Stiglitz, J. (1979) 'Equilibrium in product markets with imperfect information', *American Economic Review*, Vol. 69, p. 89–107.

Summers, L. (1988) 'Should Keynesian economics dispense with the Phillips curve?', in R. Cross (ed.), *Unemployment, Hysteresis and the Natural Rate Hypothesis*, Basil Blackwell, Oxford, pp. 11–25.

Sumner, M. T. (1978) 'Wage determination', in M. Parkin and M. T. Sumner (eds), *Inflation in the UK*, Manchester University Press, Manchester, pp. 75–91.

Swan, T. W. (1956) 'Economic growth and capital accumulation', *Economic Record*, Vol. 32, pp. 343–61.

Sweezy, P. M. (1939) 'Demand under conditions of oligopoly', *Journal of Political Economy*, Vol. 47, pp. 568–73.

Taylor, J. B. (1979) 'Staggered wage setting in a macroeconomic model', *American Economic Review, Papers and Proceedings*, Vol. 69, pp. 108–13.

Taylor, J. B. (1980) 'Aggregate dynamics and staggered contracts', *Journal of Political Economy*, Vol. 88, pp. 1–23.

Taylor, M. P. (1987) 'Financial innovation, inflation and the stability of the demand for broad money in the UK', *Bulletin of Economic Research*, Vol. 39, No. 3, pp. 225–33.

Townend, J. C. (1976) 'The personal saving ratio', *Bank of England Quarterly Bulletin*, Vol. 16, March, pp. 53–73.

Tufte, E. (1978) *The Political Control of the Economy*, Princeton University Press, Princeton, NJ.

Uzawa, H. (1965) 'Optimum technical change in an aggregative model of economic growth', *International Economic Review*, Vol. 6, pp. 18–31.

Wadhwani, S. and Wall, M. (1986) 'The UK capital stock', *Oxford Review of Economic Policy*, Vol. 2, pp. 44–55.

Weitzman, M. (1982) 'Increasing returns and the foundations of unemployment theory', *Economic Journal*, Vol. 92, pp. 787–804.

Williamson, John (1977) *The Failure of World Monetary Reform*, NYU Press, New York.

Williamson, John (1983) *The Exchange Rate System*, Institute for International Economics, Washington, DC.

Williamson, John and Miller, Marcus (1987) *Targets and Indicators: A Blueprint for the International Coordination of Economic Policy*, Institute for International Economics, September, Washington, DC.

Wilson, T. and Andrews, P. W. S. (1951) *Oxford Studies in the Price Mechanism*, Oxford University Press, Oxford.

Worswick, G. D. N. (1974) in Public Expenditure Committee, *Ninth Report*, Session 1974, HC328, HMSO, London.

Wren-Lewis, S. and Darby, J. (1989) 'UK Productivity: alas, the figures show no miracles', *Financial Times*, 25 October, 1989, p. 28.

Index